TRADITIONAL
Greek
COOKING

The Food and Wines of Greece

George Moudiotis

D0824528

Garnet
PUBLISHING

TRADITIONAL GREEK COOKING
THE FOOD AND WINES OF GREECE

Published by
Garnet Publishing Limited
8 Southern Court, South Street, Reading, RG1 4QS, UK

First Edition 1998

ISBN 1 85964 117 2

British Library Cataloguing-in-Publication Data
A catalogue record for this book is available from the British Library.

Copy-editor Wendy Hobson
House editor Jacqueline Baker
Production controller Nick Holroyd
Design David Rose
Additional design Robert Jones
Illustration Judy Stevens

Printed in Lebanon

Whilst every care has been taken in the preparation of this book, neither the
author nor publishers can accept any liability for any consequence arising
from the use of information contained herein.

TRADITIONAL

Greek

COOKING

Dedicated to my sons Christopher and Richard

CONTENTS

ACKNOWLEDGEMENTS

I would like to thank my publisher and editor, without whose skill and encouragement this book would not have been possible, my friend Miss Cassia Choules who spent days editing a number of chapters, and my family and friends, particularly my wife, Sigi, who patiently encouraged me and good-humouredly ate their way through so many of the recipes in this book.

AUTHOR'S NOTE

In romanizing Greek words, I have used a simple phonetic system, and have not marked accents. However, as an aid to pronunciation of the ingredients used in these recipes, I have added accents to the words listed in the glossary.

Introduction

Writers through the ages have extolled the virtues of Greece –
this small but extraordinary country which has given the world
a legacy of philosophy, art and architecture that is second to
none, the invention of politics and democracy that has been the
basis of every civilized country and a vision of the world that
goes beyond reality with her wonderful myths and legends.

An offspring of this civilization was the idea of 'good living' and 'good eating'. The Greek approach to food culture was
as scientific as the study of medicine, plants and animals: the
flavours of foods, methods of cooking, the selection of meals
for entertainment and special occasions, even the art of dining,
were all subjects of great interest. In the middle of the fifth
century BC – the time of Pericles, Aeschylus, Sophocles and
Euripides – when Athens was the centre of learning, there
were cookery schools and dining clubs, where cooks could
learn the science of cooking together with, for example, medicine and geometry, and discuss culinary matters along with
philosophy and politics.

The great library of Alexandria, established in the third
century BC, had over 700,000 scrolls (the equivalent of
140,000 modern books) in the year 641 AD, when the Caliph
Omar I ordered them to be burned. Among these were several
ancient Greek cookery books, none of which has survived.
References from other sources, however, tell us that Glaucus
of Locris wrote *The Art of Cooking*, Euthydemus of Athens
wrote *On Vegetables* in 150 BC and Parmenon of Rhodes wrote
Cookery Lessons. Archestratus, who in the fourth century BC
was considered the father of Greek writers on cooking, wrote
his only known work, *Life of Luxury*, giving detailed instructions, among other practical things, on where in Greece you
could buy fresh fish or which ovens in Athens made the best
bread. Great cooks were also highly respected for their cre-
ativity and ability to produce exquisite and unusual dishes.
When a cook invented special dishes, he was honoured in
public and rewarded with titles, money and land. Athenaeus –
the author of the *The Deipnosophists*, which is the main source
of information on the subject today – tells us that:

1

Agis of Rhodes was the only cook who could bake a fish to perfection, Nereus of Chios could boil a conger eel to suit the gods, Charides of Athens could make an egg mosaic with white sauce. Black broth began to exist with Lampias, Afthoneus cooked sausages, Euthynus lentil soup, Aristion gilt-head sea bream for dining clubs.

What was the Greek dinner table like in the classical period? In Athens there were well-baked oven breads, a variety of olives, garlic and pies steeped in aromatic honey. The best small fish came from the Saronic Gulf; mackerel came from Elefsina, west of Athens; eels from the Lake Copais; domestic fowl from Tanagra in central Greece; and dried figs and nuts were served for dessert. For great banquets, the Athenians would feast on meat dishes, which tended to be mixed stews of unusual ingredients, exotic game or offal of all sorts. In Thessaly, people liked to eat well and dress well: the rich farmlands produced beef, cereals, grain and corn, and there was plenty of cheese, meat and wine on the table. Even richer was the food of the Macedonians in the north, who were renowned for their great consumption of beef and game, to an extent that the jealous Athenians used to say that the Macedonians ate meat even for dessert. Large breads baked in bronze trays were characteristic of the Macedonian bakery, as they are today. Seafood and eels from the clean waters of the river Strymon and squid from the sacred river of Dium were also highly esteemed. Further east, the area of Thrace and the island of Samos were famous throughout Greece for their wine, red mullet, mussels and oregano. The diet of the south was simpler and some areas of the Peloponnese, notably Sparta, relied entirely on garden produce, goats' milk, cheese, small fish and, occasionally, game. Although the average Greek in the mainland was not what we could call a great gourmet, the diet favoured by the Spartans was shuddered at by the Athenians.

The dinner table of the islands, on the other hand, had a different character altogether: there great fish, local wines and cheeses and a variety of nuts completed the menu. Crete was famous for its great variety of aromatic vegetables and wild greens; Lesbos had pearl barley 'whiter than snow', so that the 'gods would send Hermes shopping for it'; Chios had a reputation for the best red mullet, snails, figs and mastic; Rhodes exported saffron, raisins and dried fruits, and the island of Cos became well known for its marjoram and quince perfumes.

Alexander the Great was the first to unite the multiple city states of Ancient Greece. His exploits in Egypt, Persia, Babylon and India have resulted in the spread of the Greek way of life in those countries. In return, Greek cooks became aware of the value of new spices, exotic fruits and the delicacies of the East. However, although the lavish dinners of the Persians were very impressive, there is evidence to suggest that the returning Greek soldiers in Alexander's army were only too glad to get back to home cooking. Through Alexander's conquests, trade with the East increased, Greek became the commercial language of the Middle East and food specialists travelled freely to all the major cities in the Mediterranean. From Caucasia came apricots; from the Middle East came the wild pear which was eaten both raw and cooked and later made into jelly and preserves. The pistachio tree was brought from northern India, grafted and then spread into all Mediterranean lands. From Babylon came the carob which was used as a chocolate substitute, while the citron fruit came from central Asia and was used for its aroma and as an antidote to poisons. Lastly, the Greek table was enriched by the Persian peaches which were eaten as hors d'oeuvres.

In 146 BC the Romans sacked Corinth and Rome began to exercise a suzerainty over Greece until 395 AD, when Greece became part of the Eastern Roman Empire, known subsequently as the Byzantine Empire. During this period, inventive Greek cooks travelled to Rome, most of the Roman bread was produced by Greek bakers, sophisticated Greek food became the diet of the rich and educated, and a variety of new food ingredients and spices were used to create the lavish Roman dishes. Greek wines were considered the best and grape varieties were transplanted to Italy.

Constantinople became the capital of the Byzantine Empire which, for a thousand years, expanded and contracted spasmodically under the invasions of Huns, Goths, Slavs, Bulgarians and Ottoman Turks. Venetians and Genoese established coastal cities on the Greek islands and, in time, the Franks occupied Rhodes and Cyprus, Venice possessed parts of Greece, including Crete, and for almost four hundred years, from 1453 to 1830, the rest of Greece was subjugated as part of the Ottoman Empire. After the Greek War of Independence in 1830, the population of free Greece was 800,000, while 2.5 million Greeks were still living under Turkish rule. The last part of Greece to become free was the Dodecanese islands, as late as 1947. In the twentieth century alone, Greece has suffered two World Wars, two Balkan wars, a German-Italian occupation, a civil war and many military coups. This history of subjugation and exploitation would have crushed any lesser nation but not the Greeks, who possess a characteristic vigour and a faith in their own tradition. The last 1900 years were years of survival and the struggle for freedom. This complex history has meant that the Ancient Greek cuisine has not survived unadulterated but has been influenced by the cuisine of the invaders, by the introduction of new products such as tomatoes, potatoes, aubergines, artichokes, sugar and lemons, by the development of mechanization and new agricultural methods and by the mass-production economy.

Although modern Greek food is obviously Mediterranean, certain dishes which have their origins in Ancient Greece are now cloaked in Turkish names. Commonplace delicacies mentioned by Athenaeus in 200 AD as 'entrées served in vine leaves' are known today as *dolmades* (from the Turkish *dolmasi*). The word *meze*, which may originate from the Genoese *mezzano* or the Arabic *al mezah*, describes all sorts of hors d'oeuvres which are an innovation of the Greek cuisine of the third century BC. Even the popular meatballs of Greece, *keftedes* (from the Turkish or Persian *köfte*), are mentioned by Athenaeus. The well-known Greek dish aubergine moussaka or *melitzanes mousaká* (from the Greek *melitzána* and the Arab word *mousakka*) has its origin in Byzantine times when aubergines were first introduced to Europe. On the other hand, the influence of the Byzantine cuisine (which was based on Ancient Greek and Roman cooking) on the Turkish cuisine would no doubt be a study of great interest.

Today every visitor to Greece notices that the Greeks love to eat out, their social affairs are often conducted in public, the kitchen in a restaurant is open to the clientèle and an invitation to inspect, discuss and choose any dish on display is more than welcomed. Although many Greeks know about the advantages of *haute cuisine*, their tradition tells them that food should be fresh and well cooked in a plain fashion so that the natural flavour, texture and taste of the ingredients are preserved. This means that fish must be morning-fresh, meat young and tender, vegetables always in season, salads crisp and fruits melting in the mouth. Because most dishes are seasonal, many visitors in the summer may find Greek salads, *mezedes* and taverna dishes rather monotonous. The cuisine of the brief autumn, when the olive harvest and the game season begin, is quite different. Winter dishes, especially in the rural areas, consist of stews, roasts, pulses and root vegetables; families and friends get around the table and traditional cooking is at its best. Spring is dominated by the period of Lent and the festivities of Easter; both are usually celebrated in the open air, and picnics in the countryside when flowers begin to bloom in May characterize what is probably the most joyous time of the year.

The best traditional cooking will be found in ordinary households in Greece, in villages and a few restaurants in major cities. I wish to share with you some of the recipes that gave me the most pleasure to prepare and to enjoy with my family and friends, and to give you a glimpse of how Greek food integrates the qualities of the land, its people, their history and culture. As a 'visitor-stranger' to Greece (*xénos* in Greek), whose time is usually limited, you may find much of the pleasure of Greek food in the atmosphere of a noisy taverna and the *kéfi* – the zest, the jolly mood and spirit – of your company. This emotional association could be unforgettable. If the food there is also good, then life can't be too bad.

Mezedes

MEZE

An assembly of hors d'oeuvres or, as we know it today, the *meze* table was an innovation of the Greeks in the third century BC. Athenaeus (c170-230 AD) gives an account of gastronomy in the ancient world in his book, *The Deipnosophists*, (a seven-volume collection of culinary hearsay, loosely translated as *The Wise Men at Dinner*). Appetizers (*orektika* in Greek – a collective name for existing desires – a suitable name for these delicious samplings) were very much part of that gastronomy. It appears, however, that the taste of most Greeks at that time had become too sophisticated for such titbits.

> *For the cook sets before you a large tray on which are five small plates. One of these holds garlic, another a pair of sea urchins, another a dainty morsel soaked in sweet wine, another ten cockles, the last a small piece of sturgeon. While I am eating this, another is eating that; and while he is eating that, I have made away with this. What I want is both the one and the other, but my wish is impossible. For I have neither five mouths nor five right hands. Such a layout as that seems to offer variety, but is nothing at all to satisfy the belly.*

The word *meze* (plural: *mezedes* or *mezedakia*) refers to all sorts of savoury preparations served as an accompaniment to alcoholic drinks, ouzo or wine. It is part of a tradition in all Mediterranean countries and the Middle East to nibble some food while drinking – a tradition which goes back to ancient times.

Drinking by itself on an empty stomach is neither good for the stomach nor for the mind – so old philosophers thought. Eating, drinking and the art of conversation were considered the most enjoyable human activities in life: a philosophy to which most modern Greeks still adhere. *Mezedes* always accompany a session of drinking, and the Greeks are certainly never at a loss for conversation. This chapter demonstrates that they have a genius for preparing both simple and elaborate *mezedes*, with much variety, taste and colour.

A *meze* may consist of anything from a few olives or roasted nuts to a whole range of appetizers, dips, salads, spiced meats, smoked fish and even sweets and fruits. There are *mezedes* which are pre-prepared, such as smoked fish (sardines, eels, mackerel and trout), salted nuts, a variety of cheeses and olives, and all sorts of vegetable and fish pickles. There are also a number of small vegetable-based dishes and salads which are very popular: cucumber and yoghurt salad, aubergine salad, fried peppers, stuffed vine leaves and boiled or fried artichokes.

In small tavernas by the sea, you may be served delicious fried whitebait, pieces of marinated octopus, fried baby squid, juicy giant mussels and possibly a couple of grilled red mullet. In restaurants, you may expect something more sophisticated, such as fried calves' liver, fried hard cheese with a dash of lemon juice, grilled quails or even a salad of delicious lambs' brains.

If you travel around Greece, sampling some of the outstanding regional *mezedes* can be the most interesting culinary experience: delicious pies from Epirus and Thessaly, pork sausages and smoked meats (*pastourma*) from Macedonia, smoked roe of grey mullet (*avgotaraho*) from Mesolóngion in central Greece, cheeses cured in oil from the Ionian islands, spicy sausages (*sheftalies*) from Cyprus, tiny cheese pasties from the island of Mytilini and air-cured pork sausages (*louzes*) from Mykonos.

The Greeks will nibble endlessly at all these dishes in the course of heated discussion on politics, money problems, sex and philosophy. Quite often, a range of *meze* dishes will constitute a family's main meal, and that is certainly the case at buffet parties, large gatherings and festivals.

Elies Meze
OLIVES AS A MEZE

Greek olives are regarded as a delicacy. A *meze* of olives is a real treat; a simple treat, but full of aroma, taste and colour. People often distinguish three types of olives: green, violet and fully ripe black. Some Greek olives are neither green nor black; they are brown, purple, lavender, rose and a whole range of hues from pale green to jet black. They are picked at various stages of maturity in October and November – the olive harvest time which the whole country celebrates with dancing, singing and feasting. The process of selecting, salting, curing and maturing or marinating olives takes about two months, and by early spring the markets display an amazing variety.

There are the ripe and sweet olives of Amfissa near Athens; the mild and mellow olives from the island of Corfu; the young, green olives with a nutty flavour from Nafplion in the Peloponnese; the shrivelled and strongly flavoured olives (*throubes*) from the island of Thassos in the northern Aegean Sea; the crushed green olives (*tsakistes*) of Crete; the large, rich olives of Chalkidiki in Macedonia; and the firm and meaty Kalamata olives (*xydates*) from the south Peloponnese, which are slit and cured in wine vinegar, thyme and lemon peel. Other parts of Greece produce a variety of excellent olives. The island of Chios produces some of the most distinctive table olives, called *hourmades* (dates), because they are large, brown, wrinkled, with a nutty flavour, and look like dates. The island of Samos also grows large greenish olives that are well loved in Greece. Back in the mainland, the region of Thessaly produces the round, brown olives of Volos and the large, green olives of the Pelion area.

Olives are eaten everywhere: they are nibbled as snacks, used in salads, accompany cooked meals, particularly lentils, and are invariably served as *mezedes*. They are an acquired taste, but a taste well worth acquiring. With such a variety of flavours, they complement aperitifs, ouzo, wines and beer better than any other food. Below are some suggestions for serving olives:

1. Mix Kalamata olives with cubes of feta cheese and sprinkle with a little virgin olive oil and black pepper.
2. Serve black and green olives with pieces of salami, cheese

and some crisp vegetables.

3. Thread black olives on to skewers and grill on a barbecue.
4. Mix 'cracked' green olives with crushed garlic, chopped fresh coriander, olive oil and lemon juice.
5. Mix olives, cream cheese and yoghurt and sprinkle with paprika.
6. Remove the stones from large black or green olives, then stuff with chopped capers, salted anchovies and almonds.

Tyria Mezedes
CHEESE APPETIZERS

Cubes or slices of feta cheese, with a sprinkle of fresh oregano or flatleaf parsley, freshly ground pepper and a dash of sweet olive oil, are probably the simplest and most popular of *mezedes*. Look at the chapter on Cheeses and Yoghurts (page 193) for more information on Greek cheeses. The following are some suggestions for serving cheeses:

1. Pieces of feta on slices of grilled peppers sprinkled with olive oil and wine vinegar.
2. Grated *kefalotyri* or Gruyère cheese placed on fried slices of courgette or aubergine.
3. Thin slices of *kefalotyri* or *halloumi* cheese garnished with radishes or chopped spring onions.
4. Cream cheese or feta slices topped with fried sardines and garnished with thin lemon wedges and chopped fresh parsley.
5. *Mizithra* or *anari* soft cheese topped with Greek honey and a pinch of cinnamon.

Tyri Saganaki
FRIED CHEESE

A wonderful *meze* of fried cheese, often served with a glass of ouzo or a strong red wine, *saganaki* is the name of the heavy two-handled pan or skillet in which the cheese is fried.

Halloumi Saganaki
FRIED HARD CHEESE

———

SERVES
4

Hard cheeses are normally used for the traditional saganaki. *The mild* kaseri *made from ewes' or cows' milk,* halloumi *from Cyprus made from goats' milk,* kefalograviera *from Crete, Swiss Gruyère or extra hard Cheddar are suitable.*

Cut the cheese into 1 cm (½ in) slices, allowing two slices per person. Season the flour with a little salt and pepper, then toss the cheese in the flour.

Heat the oil in a non-stick pan until it begins to smoke, then fry the cheese for 2–3 minutes on each side until golden brown. Drain on kitchen paper and place on a warm plate. Sprinkle with lemon juice and serve hot.

350 g (12 oz) hard cheese, as suggested
2 tablespoons plain flour
Salt and freshly ground pepper
4 tablespoons virgin olive oil
Juice of 1 lemon

Saltsa Moustardas
MUSTARD SAUCE

———

If you wish to serve fried hard cheese with a more pungent sauce, combine all the following ingredients in a bowl, mix well and then pour over the fried cheese.

1 tablespoon wholegrain mustard
1 garlic clove, finely chopped
Finely grated zest of ½ lemon
Juice of 1 lemon
1 tablespoon chopped fresh parsley
1 tablespoon white wine vinegar
2 tablespoons olive oil
Salt and freshly ground pepper
A few capers and olives

Feta Saganaki
FRIED SOFT CHEESE

SERVES
4

350 g (12 oz) feta cheese
2 eggs, beaten
2 tablespoons plain white flour
4 tablespoons virgin olive oil
Freshly ground pepper
2 tablespoons finely chopped
fresh parsley

Soft feta can also be fried without melting, provided it is well coated with egg and flour and fried briefly on a low heat.

Place the cheese in a bowl of cold water and leave to soak for 1 hour. Drain and dry the cheese well on a kitchen cloth, then cut into 1 cm (½ in) slices. Dip each slice first in the egg, then in the flour. Heat the oil in a non-stick pan over a low heat, then fry the cheese for 1–2 minutes on each side until it begins to brown. Using a slotted spoon, transfer the cheese to a warm plate and sprinkle with pepper and finely chopped parsley. Serve hot.

Tzatziki
YOGHURT AND CUCUMBER DIP

SERVES
5-6

1 large cucumber
1–2 garlic cloves, crushed
3–4 tablespoons extra virgin olive oil
½ tablespoon white wine vinegar
3 tablespoons chopped fresh dill
Salt and freshly ground pepper
500 g (1 lb 2 oz) Greek yoghurt
A few olives

A light and refreshing dip or salad for a hot day, this is a popular accompaniment to almost any dish. If you have Greek yoghurt, use it straight from the pot. Other yoghurts tend to be sour and watery. Strain them in a muslin-lined sieve for at least two hours, then add 2–3 tablespoons of double cream.

Peel the cucumber and trim the ends. Cut in half lengthways and scoop out the watery centre using a teaspoon. Chop the cucumber into 1 cm (½ in) squares, or grate and chop coarsely, then drain in a colander for 10 minutes to remove any excess water.

Mix the cucumber with the garlic, 3 tablespoons of oil, the wine vinegar, 2 tablespoons of dill and salt and pepper. Empty the yoghurt into the mixture and blend well. Spoon into a serving dish and chill for 1–2 hours.

Sprinkle the remaining olive oil on top and garnish with the remaining dill and the olives before serving.

Melitzanosalata
AUBERGINE PURÉE

A delicious meze that retains the scorched aroma of grilled aubergines, this very popular dip is one of my favourites. Traditionally, the aubergines are cooked by burying them in the hot ashes of a fireplace, but nowadays they are grilled slowly on a barbecue, on top of a gas ring or in a hot oven, until the skin turns black and the aubergines are creamy and moist.

2 large, firm aubergines
1 small onion, finely chopped
1–2 garlic cloves, crushed
1 teaspoon white wine vinegar or the juice of ½ lemon
1 tablespoon mayonnaise or strained Greek yoghurt
4–5 tablespoons virgin olive oil
Salt and freshly ground pepper
Chopped fresh parsley
A few olives

Pierce the whole, unpeeled aubergines with a fork in several places. Put them on top of the gas ring or under the grill and cook, turning frequently, until the skin is charred on all sides and the inside very soft. Use a long fork to handle them. This is a little messy but worth the trouble. Alternatively, bake the aubergines in a preheated oven at 200°C/400°F/gas mark 6 for 45 minutes.

When they are cool enough to handle, hold them by the stalk and, using a small knife, carefully peel off the black skin under running water. There should be no speck of black skin left on the aubergines. Place the aubergines on a wooden board and cut off the stalks. Chop the flesh so that all the extra juices run out. This gets rid of any bitterness they may have.

Put all the ingredients into a blender or food processor and blend at low speed for a few seconds. The purée should not be too smooth. Taste and, if necessary, adjust the amount of oil, salt and wine vinegar. Transfer to a serving dish and chill for about 1 hour.

If you have no blender, mash the aubergines with a fork and blend the other ingredients by hand, or use a wooden pestle and mortar, as most Greek housewives do. You will need a bit more oil with this method to bind the ingredients and the result will have more flavour. Mix the purée with a fork just before serving and garnish with chopped parsley and a few olives. Serve with hot pitta bread.

Melitzanes Tiganités
FRIED AUBERGINES

———

For this meze, *aubergines are fried until crisp and golden, then served with tomato and herbs or a yoghurt and garlic sauce.*

Top and tail the aubergines but do not peel them. Slice them lengthways about 1 cm (½ in) thick, sprinkle with plenty of salt and set aside for 30 minutes. Wash them well, then pat dry on kitchen paper. Coat them lightly with plain flour, then fry in hot olive oil on both sides until golden. As the aubergines absorb a lot of oil, you may have to add more oil occasionally, but keep this to a minimum. Remove from the pan using a slotted spoon and drain on kitchen paper. Serve hot or cold.

Spread a little tomato purée on each aubergine slice and garnish with chopped fresh dill or chives. Alternatively, pour over them a mixture of chilled Greek yoghurt and little crushed garlic.

Melitzanes Tiganítes
AUBERGINE FRITTERS

———

SERVES

4

150 ml (¼ pint) warm water
100 g (4 oz) plain flour
2 tablespoons olive oil
A pinch of salt
2 egg whites
4 medium-sized aubergines

If you wish to make crisp aubergine fritters, whisk all the ingredients except the egg whites to a smooth batter, then set aside for 1–2 hours. Whisk the egg whites until stiff, then fold into the mixture.

Slice and prepare the aubergines as described in the previous recipe. Dip each slice into the batter and fry in plenty of hot oil for 1–2 minutes. Remove from the pan using a slotted spoon and drain on kitchen paper. Serve hot.

Kolokithakia Tiganita
FRIED COURGETTES

Courgettes suitable for frying must be small (about 7–10 cm, 3–4 in), fresh and firm. Top and tail them, and cut in half lengthways but do not peel them. If they are larger, slice them lengthways about 1 cm (½ in) thick, or into 5 mm (¼ in) thick rounds. Coat them lightly in flour seasoned with salt and pepper and set aside for 1–2 hours before frying; they become crispier this way.

Heat a little olive oil in a frying pan until hot but not smoking. Fry the courgette slices for about 2 minutes on each side until they turn golden brown. Do not overcrowd the pan and watch constantly so they do not brown too much. Using a slotted spoon, remove them from the pan and drain on kitchen paper. Arrange on a warm dish, sprinkle with chopped fresh dill and serve with a garlic sauce (*Skordalia*, see page 151) or a yoghurt and cucumber dip (*Tzatziki*, see page 12).

Kolokithakia Tiganítes
COURGETTE FRITTERS

Top and tail the courgettes and cut them diagonally into thin rounds. Prepare a batter as for the Aubergine Fritters (see page 14). Dip each courgette slice into the batter, then drop it very carefully into hot corn oil or vegetable oil and fry for 2 minutes until golden. Remove from the pan using a slotted spoon and drain on kitchen paper. Place them on a platter, garnish with chopped fresh dill and serve warm or cold.

SERVES

4

450 g (1 lb) medium courgettes

Oil for frying

2 tablespoons grated onion

100 g (4 oz) feta cheese or grated
Parmesan cheese

2 eggs, lightly beaten

3 tablespoons breadcrumbs

2 tablespoons chopped fresh parsley
or dill

Salt and freshly ground pepper

3 tablespoons plain flour

Kolokithakia Keftedes
FRIED COURGETTE BALLS

A very popular meze, *this comes from Macedonia.*

Trim and grate the courgettes. Blanch in boiling water for 2 minutes, then drain well and mash with a fork.

Heat a little oil and fry the onion until soft. Drain and combine with the courgettes, cheese, eggs, breadcrumbs and herbs and season with salt and pepper. If the mixture is not stiff enough, add a few more breadcrumbs. Chill for about 1 hour.

Shape the mixture into walnut-sized balls. Season the flour with salt and pepper and coat the balls in flour. Heat a little oil until hot but not smoking and fry for 2–3 minutes until golden on all sides, then drain on kitchen paper. Serve hot with a garlic sauce (*Skordalia*, page 00).

Spanaki Kroketes
SPINACH CROQUETTES

The same method used for frying courgette balls can also be used to make unusual croquettes with spinach, aubergines (see next recipe), potatoes or fish.

Replace the courgettes in the recipe above with 900 g (2 lb) fresh spinach. Wash it well, remove the stalks, chop it roughly and sauté in 25 g (1 oz) unsalted butter over a low heat for about 5–7 minutes until the spinach softens. Combine with the rest of the ingredients and shape into small croquettes or rissoles. Coat with seasoned flour and fry the croquettes as above.

Melitzanokeftedes
FRIED AUBERGINE BALLS

———

Replace the courgettes in the recipe above with two large aubergines prepared as described on page 13. Put the flesh of the aubergines in a blender or food processor and process to a thick purée. Combine with the rest of the ingredients above and shape into small balls. Coat with breadcrumbs and fry in plenty of hot oil until golden brown. A beetroot salad (*Panzaria Salata*, see page 55) is an ideal side dish to serve with aubergine balls.

Kolokithakia me Paston
COURGETTES WITH
SMOKED BACON

———

This is a delicious recipe and quick to make. The strong flavour of smoked bacon, especially the Continental kind (the highly flavoured speck, for example), combines well with the sweet taste of the courgettes.

Heat the butter and oil in a pan over medium heat and fry the bacon until lightly browned.

Peel and cut off the ends of the courgettes. Cut them into 1 cm (in) thick slices. Put them into the pan and coat them with the butter and oil. Season with a pinch of salt and plenty of pepper and fry for 5–7 minutes until they begin to soften. Season with dill before serving.

SERVES
4

1 tablespoon butter
2 tablespoons olive oil
100 g (4 oz) smoked bacon,
finely chopped
450 g (1 lb) medium courgettes
Salt and freshly ground pepper
1 tablespoon chopped fresh dill

17

Gigantes Plaki

GIANT BEANS BAKED IN THE OVEN

SERVES

6

450 g (1 lb) dried butter beans or
lima beans

150 ml (¼ pint) olive oil

2 onions, finely chopped

3–4 garlic cloves, thinly sliced

900 g (2 lb) ripe tomatoes, skinned
and chopped, or 2 x 400 g (14 oz)
cans of chopped tomatoes

4 tablespoons chopped fresh parsley

1 teaspoon sugar

Salt and freshly ground pepper

½ tablespoon dried oregano

Florina, the picturesque town situated at the height of 670 metres near the northern border of Greece and founded by Philip II of Macedonia, is reputed to produce the best dried beans for this dish – they are large, strong and sweet, hence the name gigantes, *or giant. Quite often, they are just boiled and presented with a simple vinaigrette or lemon dressing. In terms of flavour, Greek beans can be compared to haricot and cannellini beans. However, because of their size, large butter beans or lima beans are a better substitute.*

Put the beans in a large bowl, cover with cold water and soak for no longer than 8 hours, or they may ferment. Drain, remove any grit and rinse well. Place in a pan, cover with fresh cold water, bring to the boil and boil for about 45–60 minutes until slightly tender but holding their shape. No salt should be added during cooking. Strain the beans. If you are using butter beans, strain them for 1 hour, as they tend to absorb water.

Preheat the oven to 180°C/350°F/gas mark 4.

Heat the oil in a deep pan, add the onions and garlic and sauté for 1–2 minutes. Add the tomatoes, parsley, sugar, salt and pepper and simmer for 2–3 minutes. Place the beans in a shallow ovenproof dish, pour over the sauce from the pan, add a little more oil, salt, pepper and the oregano and bake in the oven for about 1 hour, without stirring, until the sauce is thick and the beans crisp and dry. Serve the beans with the sauce either hot or cold.

Houmous
CHICKPEA AND TAHINI DIP

SERVES
5–6

Houmous is a popular meze dip in Cyprus and the Middle East, usually served with pitta bread and quite often with fish, meats, chicken, shellfish and raw vegetables. It is made with chickpeas enhanced with the flavours of tahini and lemon juice. Tahini is a thick, oily paste made from finely ground and roasted sesame seeds. It is light beige in colour and has a mild, nutty flavour. The best tahini comes from Thessaloniki and the town of Volos in Thessaly, and is the main ingredient of commercial halva (page 184). In this recipe the lemon juice should not be allowed to overpower the taste of the dip.

450 g (1 lb) dried chickpeas
3 garlic cloves, 1 crushed, 2 halved
100 g (4 oz) tahini
Juice of 1 lemon
90 ml (3 fl oz) virgin olive oil
1 teaspoon paprika
Salt
A little chopped fresh parsley
A few olives
A drizzle of olive oil

Soak the chickpeas overnight in cold water with 2 cloves of garlic. Wash them, discard the garlic, cover with fresh water and bring to the boil. The garlic helps the peas to cook better. Skim off any scum that rises to the top, cover, lower the heat and simmer for about 2 hours until the chickpeas are tender. Drain, reserving some of the liquid. If you use tinned chickpeas, simply drain them well.

Place the peas in a blender or food processor and blend them at high speed until they are reduced to a rough purée. Shake the tahini in its jar until the oil and paste are mixed well. While the blender is still running, stir in the tahini, the crushed garlic, half the lemon juice and the olive oil. Add paprika and salt and correct the seasoning by adding more lemon juice and olive oil to taste. Adjust the consistency to a thick paste by adding some of the reserved liquid, if necessary. Spread the houmous on a flat plate and garnish with chopped parsley, olives and a drizzle of olive oil.

Variation
Houmous without tahini is usually regarded as unthinkable, yet a chickpea dip prepared with double cream can be equally delicious. Use 450 g (1 lb) dried chickpeas, 1 garlic clove, 1 lemon, 90 ml (3 fl oz) of oil and 2 tablespoons of double cream. Cook and combine these ingredients in a blender or food processor as above.

Avgotaraho Salata
GREY MULLET ROE SALAD

The roe of grey mullet is highly esteemed for its rich pink colour and exquisite flavour; it is often referred to as red caviare. In Greece it is called *avgotaraho*, in France *boutargue* and in Italy *botargo*. It is a wonderful delicacy and a very expensive appetizer. The best *avgotaraho* comes from the roe of lake fish from the lagoons of Mesolóngion in the west of the Gulf of Corinth.

The female grey mullet spawns in August in inshore waters or complex estuaries which the Greeks devise to lure the fish. The roe is enclosed in two sacks from which it must be removed before being soaked in brine for a few hours, and finally dried in the sun. At this stage, the eggs are ready to eat, but *avgotaraho* is usually lightly smoked and preserved by covering it in a layer of beeswax.

Avgotaraho salad is simplicity itself: just cut a thin slice, remove the wax, sprinkle on some lemon juice and serve with a country salad (*Horiatiki Salata*, see page 50) and crusty bread.

Taramosalata
FISH ROE SALAD

SERVES

4

100 g (4 oz) *tarama* or smoked cod's roe, membrane removed, if any

4 thin slices day-old white bread, crust removed, soaked in little milk or water

1 small onion, finely grated (optional)

1 garlic clove, crushed

Juice of 1 lemon

120 ml (4 fl oz) olive oil

1 tablespoon chopped fresh dill (optional)

2 tablespoons Greek yoghurt or double cream (optional)

Possibly the most splendid and universally popular Greek dish, it is sometimes marred in restaurants, for the sake of economy, by poor quality ingredients, a fishy smell and a frightening bright pink appearance. Avoid it. It is easy to make it at home. Authentic taramosalata is made from avgotaraho – *the roe of grey mullet – or commercial* tarama, *which is the salted roe of grey mullet, tuna or carp. Greek cooks use small quantities of* tarama, *then stretch it by adding olive oil, lots of onions, potatoes or bread. Some of these ingredients should be added only in moderation. The next best substitute for* tarama *is smoked cod's roe, which is readily available.*

Wrap the *tarama* in a piece of muslin, place it in a bowl with cold water and set aside for 30 minutes to remove some of the salt. Drain.

Squeeze the bread dry and place in a blender or food processor with the *tarama*, onion, if using, garlic and half the lemon juice. Blend for a few seconds until the mixture is light and creamy. Add the oil a drop at a time, making sure it has been absorbed before you add more. Taste and adjust the lemon juice and oil to taste. If you feel the mixture is too strong, add some Greek yoghurt or cream. Stir in the dill, if using, pour on to a serving plate and chill.

Garnish with black olives, radishes and vegetable sticks and serve with hot pitta bread.

For the garnish
Olives
Radishes
Vegetables julienne

Calamarakia Tiganita
FRIED SQUID

Fresh squid has a fine, delicate flavour all its own and a texture that is very popular with all Mediterranean people. In restaurants they usually serve squid fried; at home, it is stuffed, stewed in wine or cooked in a sauce. Squid belong to the family of cephalopods, together with octopus and cuttlefish. The small squid has no ink sac and is the sweetest of the three. Expertly cooked, it tastes as good as lobster. Squid which are shorter than 10 cm (4 in) are too messy to clean. Longer squid should be prepared as follows:

To Prepare Squid
Hold the body and gently pull away the head and tentacles. Pull off and discard the skin and remove the fins. Cut off just the tentacles and arms below the eyes with a sharp knife. Dislodge the small beak with your fingers and pull out and discard the long bone. Turn the squid inside out and rinse well to remove any grit. Wash all the pieces well in running water, sprinkle with salt and then let them drain.

To Fry Squid
Slice the squid into 1 cm (½ in) rings and marinate in lemon juice for 30 minutes. Dry the squid rings thoroughly. Put them in a plastic bag containing a little flour seasoned with salt and pepper and shake until they are well coated. Alternatively, dip them into a mixture of equal quantities of beaten egg and milk

and then into flour.

Heat oil in a deep pan and fry the squid rings for about 1 minute until nicely browned, crisp outside and soft inside. Do not overcrowd the pan. Do not fry for too long, otherwise they will toughen. Remove them using a slotted spoon and drain on kitchen paper. Sprinkle with chopped fresh parsley and serve hot with lemon wedges; cold *calamari* is tasteless. Accompany the dish with a strong garlic sauce (*Skordalia*, see page 151), a green salad, or a yoghurt and cucumber dip (*Tzatziki*, see page 12).

Barbounia Tiganita
FRIED RED MULLET

Red mullet served as a *meze* should be small and very fresh. Carefully scrape off the scales, remove the gills and gut the fish. Do not remove the head. Wash the fish well, season with salt and pepper, sprinkle with the juice of a lemon, then leave to marinate for 10 minutes. Then put the fish in a plastic bag containing seasoned flour and shake the bag until the fish is well coated. Heat plenty of olive oil until very hot but not smoking and fry the fish for about 5–7 minutes on each side, depending on the size of the fish, until well done and crunchy. Place on a plate with plenty of lemon wedges, and serve with a Greek country salad (*Horiatiki Salata*, see page 50) and a dry white wine (see pages 213-14).

Barbounia tis Skaras
GRILLED RED MULLET

Clean the fish and marinate it as above. Heat the grill and brush with a little olive oil to prevent the fish from sticking to the grill. Brush the fish with olive oil and place under the grill, about 7–10 cm (3–4 in) away from the heat. Grill until golden brown, turning the fish over once. Prepare an oil and lemon dressing (*Ladolemono*, see page 154) and pour over the fish. Serve hot.

Marides e Sardeles Tiganités
FRIED PICAREL OR SARDINES

———

A number of small fish (whitebait) from the fisherman's catch, such as sardines (*sardeles*) and brown picarel (*marides*), can be fried or grilled very simply. The usual method is to dip the fish whole into a flour batter and fry in hot olive oil. If the fish are longer than 5–7 cm (2–3 in), scale and gut them, then rinse and remove any traces of blood. Dry on kitchen paper and coat lightly with seasoned flour. Smaller fish can be quickly fried whole.

Heat a little olive oil in a pan and briefly fry a garlic clove and a sprig of fresh oregano or thyme. Then remove the herbs from the pan and fry the fish in the aromatic oil for 2–3 minutes. Remove the fish and drain on kitchen paper. Arrange the fish on a platter, sprinkle with lemon juice and serve with lemon wedges. A bowl of light garlic sauce (*Skordalia*, see page 151), yoghurt and cucumber dip (*Tzatziki*, see page 12), a tomato salad and a glass of cool retsina are the ideal accompaniment.

Htapodi Xidato
PICKLED OCTOPUS

———

SERVES

6

If you are buying a whole octopus, let the fishmonger clean it for you. Wash it in cold water and tenderize it by beating it with a wooden mallet. Frozen octopus does not need to be tenderized. The Greeks say that an octopus is tender when its tentacles become curly.

Put the octopus in a pan with the wine vinegar and enough water to cover, bring to the boil, cover and simmer for about 1 hour on a low heat until tender. Drain off the water and peel off the dark skin. You may serve the octopus whole or slice it into thin pieces, including the tentacles.

Combine all the ingredients for the sauce in a bowl and pour over the octopus while it is still warm. Set aside to marinate in the fridge for 24 hours, stirring occasionally.

If the octopus is whole, place it on a flat serving dish and

1 kg (2¼ lb) octopus
4 tablespoons white wine vinegar

For the sauce
4 tablespoons olive oil
2 tablespoons white wine vinegar
1 garlic clove, crushed
6 peppercorns
A little salt and freshly ground pepper

For the garnish
Chopped fresh dill or parsley

spread out its tentacles. Strain the sauce and pour over the octopus, then sprinkle with a few fresh herbs before serving.

Htapodi sti Skara
GRILLED OCTOPUS

———

This is a delicious *meze* to go with a glass of ouzo. Prepare and boil the octopus as above. Drain the water and slice the octopus into 5 cm (2 in) pieces. Marinate the pieces in a mixture of 4 tablespoons of olive oil, the juice of a lemon and a tablespoon of dry oregano for 1–2 hours. Drain and reserve the marinade.

Season the octopus pieces with salt and pepper and place them about 7 cm (3 in) away from a hot grill. Grill for a few minutes on either side, brushing often with the marinade mixture. Transfer to a hot serving plate, sprinkle with a little virgin olive oil and serve with lemon slices.

Garides Tiganités
FRIED PRAWNS

———

SERVES

4–6

700 g (1½ lb) large, unshelled raw prawns
Juice of 1 lemon
Olive oil for frying

For the batter
75 g (3 oz) plain flour
1 teaspoon baking powder
2 eggs, separated
Salt and freshly ground pepper
A little milk or water (optional)
1 tablespoon olive oil

Prepare the prawns by pulling off the heads and tails. De-vein by making a cut on the back of the prawns and removing the black intestine. Wash them well, drain and pat dry, then put them in a bowl and sprinkle over the lemon juice.

Make a thick batter by whisking the flour, baking powder, egg yolks, salt and pepper. Thin the batter down if required, by adding a little water or milk so you have a smooth, creamy mixture. Mix in the oil and let the batter stand for 1 hour. Whisk the egg whites until stiff, then fold them into batter.

Heat the frying oil in a pan until it begins to smoke. Dip the prawns into the egg batter and fry for a few minutes until golden brown and crispy. Remove them using a slotted spoon and drain on kitchen paper. Serve hot with a mayonnaise sauce (*Mayonneza*, see page 153) and a fresh green salad.

Garides sti Skara
GRILLED PRAWNS

———

Prepare the prawns by pulling off the shells and heads, retaining the tails. De-vein by making a cut on the back of the prawns and removing the black intestine. Wash them well, then place them in a colander to drain. Mix all the other ingredients in a bowl, add the prawns and leave to marinate for at least 1 hour. Transfer them on to a baking tray and grill them under a hot grill for about 3 minutes on each side. Serve hot with a cos lettuce salad (*Marouli Salata*, see page 50) and a dry white wine.

SERVES
4–6

700 g (1½ lb) large, unshelled
raw prawns

3 tablespoons olive oil

Juice of ½ lemon

1 garlic clove, crushed

½ tablespoon Dijon or English mustard

1 tablespoon finely chopped fresh
parsley

Salt and freshly ground pepper

Midia Tiganita
FRIED MUSSELS

———

Mussels are plentiful in Greece. A fried mussel meze is very popular and served in all tavernas, usually accompanied by a strong garlic sauce.

To Prepare Mussels
If you buy shelled and frozen mussels, thaw them first and wash them well. If you buy fresh mussels in the shell, wash and scrub them with a wire brush under cold running water. *Discard any which are open.* If any mussel seems unusually heavy it may be full of mud or sand; prise it open and clean it. Put the mussels in a pan with a little water, cover, bring to the boil and boil for a few minutes until the mussels open. When cool enough to handle, lift the mussels out by hand, as there may still be some sand on the bottom of the pan. *Discard any mussels that remain closed.* Remove the mussels from the shells using a sharp knife and discard the dark part of the mussels.

To make the batter, sift the flour, salt and pepper in a bowl and make a well in the centre. Pour in the oil and beer or yeast and water and mix well by hand. If the batter is too thin, add a little more flour; it should be the consistency of thick cream. Leave to stand for 1 hour, otherwise it will not stick to the fish.

Whisk the egg whites until stiff, then fold into the batter.

SERVES
2

225 g (8 oz) frozen mussels or 900 g
(2 lb) mussels in the shell, prepared

Olive oil for frying

2 lemons cut into wedges

For the batter

75 g (3 oz) plain flour

Salt and freshly ground pepper

2 tablespoons olive oil

300 ml (½ pint) light beer or lager or
a pinch of yeast diluted in water

2 egg whites

Put all the clean mussels into the bowl with the batter. Heat the frying oil in a pan until very hot and drop in the mussels carefully one at a time, using a slotted spoon. Do not over-crowd the pan. Cook for a few minutes until browned and crispy. Remove and drain on kitchen paper. For an attractive presentation, replace the cooked mussels in their shells and serve with lots of lemon wedges.

Midia Saganaki
MUSSEL STEW MEZE

SERVES
2–3

225 g (8 oz) clean mussels or 900 g (2 lb) unshelled mussels

2 tablespoons water or mussel cooking liquid

4 tablespoons olive oil

3 tablespoons finely chopped fresh parsley

½ small chilli pepper, seeded and finely chopped

Salt and freshly ground pepper

Juice of 1 lemon

100 g (4 oz) feta cheese, cut into small cubes

Cooked mussels are often served with a sauce made from the cooking liquid, which is usually mopped up with crusty bread. The peppery sauce of this dish, which is very popular in Macedonia, has a flavour that is intensified by the addition of lemon juice and crumbled feta cheese. Quite often, herbs, mustard or more hot chilli are added, but these tend to overpower the sweet flavour of the mussels.

Prepare the mussels as described on page 25. Strain and reserve some of the liquid.

Heat the oil over medium heat, add the parsley, chopped chilli, salt and pepper and fry for 1 minute, then add the mussel liquid and mussels and simmer for 5 minutes only, as longer cooking will toughen the mussels. Remove from the heat, add lemon juice, the feta cheese and more chilli if you prefer, and serve immediately.

Palamida Marinati
MARINATED BONITO

**900 g (2 lb) bonito or tuna, cut into
2 cm (³⁄₄ in) steaks**

Bonito is a large silvery fish with a pointed snout which migrates from the Black Sea to the Mediterranean waters in the late autumn. Even though bonitos are fast swimmers, spending most of their time offshore, some species can be found in coastal waters; that makes them good for sport and fishing. They belong to the same family as tuna and mackerel but have a richer and more delicate flavour that is similar to chicken.

For the marinade
2 tablespoons olive oil
2 garlic cloves, crushed
Juice of 3 lemons
3 onions, sliced
¹⁄₂ teaspoon cayenne pepper
**2 tablespoons chopped fresh parsley
or coriander**
Salt

Steaks cut from a large bonito fish are marinated raw in brine, drained, washed and then dry-salted with about 30 per cent salt for three to four weeks. The salt draws out moisture from the fish and preserves it for a long time. Salted bonitos, known as lakerda, are a great delicacy in Greece. In a similar process of dry-salting or brining, other meaty fish such as tuna and mackerel are preserved and served as meze. A range of marinades is used with raw fish, most of which are made with lemon juice, chilli or paprika, herbs and olive oil. Some marinades use pickled vegetables or unripe, green tomatoes.

For the garnish
Virgin olive oil
1 lemon, cut into wedges
Capers

Here is a traditional recipe for marinated bonito that makes an excellent meze for a party. It is served with a dash of virgin olive oil and a few lemon wedges.

Combine all the ingredients for the marinade in a glass bowl. Place the fish in the marinade and ensure that it is well coated. Cover the bowl and leave in the fridge for 20–30 hours, turning the fish over once or twice. Next, wash the fish well and pat dry on kitchen paper. Serve with a sprinkle of virgin olive oil, lemon wedges and capers.

Xifias Souvlaki
SWORDFISH KEBAB

SERVES
6

900 g (2 lb) swordfish steaks, filleted

2 onions, quartered

2 large peppers, seeded and cut into 2.5 cm (1 in) squares

4–5 tomatoes, quartered

For the marinade

4 tablespoons olive oil

Juice of 2 lemons

½ tablespoon dried oregano

1 small chilli pepper, seeded and chopped (optional)

Salt and freshly ground pepper

Fish souvlaki *is one of the most delectable* meze. *Swordfish steaks are marinated in a simple mixture of oil and lemon juice, then grilled until they begin to flake. Swordfish has a pink, firm, meaty flesh that turns white when grilled. Fish kebabs are also made with tuna, bonito or large prawns.*

Remove any skin from the fish. If the fish is frozen, remove any black pieces around the bones. Cut the steaks into 2–3 cm (1 in) cubes.

Mix all the marinade ingredients in a glass bowl and add the fish cubes. Cover the bowl and marinate for 1 hour at least. The salt will draw out the moisture and make the fish drier.

Remove the fish and reserve the marinade. Thread the fish cubes on to metal skewers, alternating with pieces of tomato, pepper and onion. Grill on the grill rack or use a cast-iron griddle. Heat the grill and cook the kebabs on all sides for 6–8 minutes only, or until the fish turns white and opaque, basting frequently with the marinade.

Souvlakia
GREEK KEBABS

SERVES
6

900 g (2 lb) lean lamb, steak, pork or chicken

6 bay leaves

2 green peppers, seeded and diced (optional)

2 onions, quartered (optional)

2 tomatoes, quartered and seeded (optional)

For the marinade

4 tablespoons olive oil

4 tablespoons lemon juice

1 garlic clove, finely chopped

Souvlakia is the Greek word for all types of meat that are spiced, threaded on skewers and grilled over charcoal. Lamb, veal, pork, beef, chicken, fish, even vegetables, are barbecued in this way. Almost every region in Greece has its own marinade using a blend of local herbs and spices, berries, honey and yoghurt. The Greeks consume souvlakia *the way the British consume hamburgers and the Americans hot dogs.*

There are many types of souvlakia. *Lamb* (arni) *is cut from the rump into long strips or cubes and any fat or sinew is trimmed off. Beef* (moshari) *and pork pieces are cut from the loin or leg. Fillets of veal are cut finely and threaded with slices of kidneys. Swordfish* (xifias), *cut in chunks or steaks and marinated in lemon, olive oil and thyme, is probably the most popular fish* souvlakia *you will find in fish tavernas.* Souvlakia *are easy to make and enjoy as a* meze *or main course. They may be served with saffron rice, a green salad and pitta bread,* tzatziki *or fresh vegetables. The Greeks love to drink beer or* retsina *with* souvlakia.

2 bay leaves, crumbled
1 tablespoon dried oregano
1 tablespoon chopped fresh thyme
Salt and freshly ground pepper

Trim the meat of excess fat or rough sinews and cut into bite-sized cubes. The Greeks are rather particular about cutting the meat into precise cubes.

Combine all the ingredients for the marinade in a glass bowl and add the meat. Cover and marinate for 2 hours or longer, turning the meat round now and again.

Pass the marinade through a sieve and reserve. Thread the meat cubes on to wooden or metal skewers, occasionally alternating the meat pieces with a bay leaf, pepper, onion and tomato slices. Do not overload the skewers. Brush the grill with oil and barbecue the *souvlakia* over hot coals for 3–4 minutes on each side, basting them with the marinade. Alternatively, bake in a preheated oven at 200°C/400°F/gas mark 6 for 15–20 minutes. In either case, the meat should be browned and crusty on the outside, pink and juicy – possibly slightly underdone – on the inside for lamb and beef. Pork *souvlakia* should be cooked through.

Serve the *souvlakia* with a Greek salad and chips, or simply with plenty of crusty bread. In restaurants, they are often served with plain boiled rice.

Variations
1. Boil the marinade until the quantity is reduced by half. Add a knob of butter and whisk until melted. Serve the sauce with the *souvlakia*.
2. There are many variations of the marinade used for *souvlakia*. One that originates from Constantinople (now Istanbul) is particularly delicious. Pound a garlic clove and combine with 225 g (8 oz) Greek yoghurt, salt, pepper and dried oregano. Mix in the meat cubes and leave in the fridge overnight. Thread the meat on to skewers and grill as before.
3. Greeks quite often do not marinate *souvlakia*. Instead, they sprinkle with pepper, plenty of oregano and a little oil and grill them briefly. Salt is avoided as it tends to dry the meat. These *souvlakia* are served on a warm platter with plenty of chopped fresh parsley and freshly squeezed lemon juice.

Souzoukakia

GRILLED MEAT RISSOLES

SERVES
6

700 g (1½ lb) minced lean lamb or
beef

1 onion, finely chopped

2 garlic cloves, crushed

1 teaspoon dried oregano

1 egg, lightly beaten

1 tablespoon white wine vinegar

50 g (2 oz) breadcrumbs

4 tablespoons water

Salt and freshly ground pepper

*You will find these excellent rissoles served fried or grilled in
most tavernas.*

Combine all the ingredients in a bowl and mix with your hands
until well blended. Shape the mixture into rissoles about 2 cm
(1 in) thick and 7 cm (3 in) long. Brush with olive oil and grill
them on all sides until well browned. Drain on kitchen paper
and serve with a pungent sauce (*Skordalia*, see page 151) or a
yoghurt and cucumber dip (*Tzatziki*, see page 12).

Souzoukakia Smyrneika

SMYRNA MEAT RISSOLES

SERVES
6

700 g (1½ lb) minced lean lamb
or beef

1 onion, finely chopped

3 garlic cloves, crushed

1 tablespoon white wine vinegar

4 tablespoons water

50 g (2 oz) breadcrumbs

1 egg, lightly beaten

1 teaspoon ground cumin

Salt and freshly ground pepper

Olive oil for frying

For the sauce

450 g (1 lb) tomatoes, skinned and
chopped

1 tablespoon tomato purée

½ teaspoon sugar

3 tablespoons dry red wine

1 tablespoon plain flour

A pinch of chilli powder or 1 teaspoon
paprika

*Smyrna (now Izmir in Turkey) was the home of some 600,000
Greeks before 1920. By the end of 1922, Smyrna was virtually
burned to the ground and over a million destitute Greeks from
all over Turkey arrived in Greece, in the biggest disaster in
Greek history. They brought their own culture and entrepre-
neurial skills and were soon assimilated into the fabric of
Greek society. Their customs and traditions have been
preserved, and their taste for Eastern spices – cumin, nutmeg
and cinnamon – and aromatic, nut-filled pastries, has
enriched the Greek cooking tradition. The following is one of
many variations of meat rissoles. It is served with rice pilaf,
pasta or boiled potatoes.*

Mix all the ingredients for the rissoles, except the oil, and
knead the mixture for 5 minutes. Chill in the fridge for 1 hour.

Wet your hands and shape mixture into rissoles about 3
cm (1 in) thick and 7 cm (3 in) long. Do not coat them with
flour. Fry them in plenty of hot oil for about 5 minutes until
well browned. Remove them using a slotted spoon and drain
on kitchen paper.

Put 3–4 tablespoons of the oil used for frying into a
flameproof casserole and add all the other ingredients for the

sauce. Simmer over low heat for about 15–20 minutes, stirring continuously, until the sauce thickens. Add the rissoles, adjust the seasoning and simmer, uncovered, for a further 2–3 minutes. Transfer the contents of the casserole to a warm serving dish and garnish with the parsley.

Variation

Add 1 bay leaf, 1 teaspoon of chopped fresh basil and ½ teaspoon ground cinnamon to the ingredients for the sauce. Before you are ready to serve, remove the bay leaf.

Keftedakia
LAMB OR BEEF MEATBALLS WITH HERBS

SERVES
4

A very popular meze for every occasion, keftedakia *are ideally served hot with a glass of ouzo. I have added a little ouzo to the meatballs themselves, just to keep them moist!*

Sprinkle the onion with a little salt and rub it in with your hands. Pour boiling water over the onion and strain. Soak the bread in water for 5 minutes, then squeeze it dry. Mince the meat twice, or ask the butcher to do this for you.

Combine all the ingredients in a bowl and mix well with your hands for 1–2 minutes. Cover and place in the fridge for 1 hour.

Shape into walnut-size balls, large cigar shapes or flattened balls and roll in plenty of flour. Fry in hot, but not smoking, olive oil for 3–4 minutes on each side until the meatballs are golden brown. Remove from the pan and drain on kitchen paper. The meatballs should be crisp outside and soft inside. Sprinkle with a little chopped parsley and some lemon juice and serve hot.

For the garnish
2 tablespoons chopped fresh parsley

1 onion, finely chopped
3 slices day-old white bread, crusts removed
450 g (1 lb) lean minced lamb or beef or a mixture
2 eggs, lightly beaten
2 garlic cloves, crushed
½ tablespoon white wine vinegar
½ tablespoon olive oil
2 tablespoons chopped fresh parsley
1 tablespoon dried oregano or thyme
1 teaspoon dried mint
½ teaspoon ground cumin
1 tablespoon ouzo (optional) or lemon juice
Salt and freshly ground pepper

For frying
Plain flour
Olive oil or sunflower oil or butter

For the garnish
1 tablespoon chopped fresh parsley
1 tablespoon lemon juice

Keftedakia sti Skara
GRILLED MEATBALLS

Substitute the wine vinegar, ouzo and lemon juice with 3–4 tablespoons of dry red wine. Cook under the grill or barbecue for 3–5 minutes on each side.

Keftedakia Saltsa Domata
MEATBALLS IN TOMATO SAUCE

Pour the oil used for frying into a fine sieve and strain. Place 2 tablespoons of the strained oil into a clean pan together with 2 tablespoons of plain flour and mix well to form a smooth paste. Add 2 crushed garlic cloves, 1 tablespoon of white wine vinegar, 450 g (1 lb) of skinned and finely chopped tomatoes, 2 tablespoons of tomato purée, a pinch of sugar, salt and pepper. Cook the sauce for 8–10 minutes. Pour the sauce over the *keftedakia* and serve.

Sikotakia Riganata
LAMBS' LIVER WITH LEMON AND OREGANO

SERVES

4

450 g (1 lb) lambs' or calves' liver
2 tablespoons plain flour
Salt and freshly ground pepper
3–4 tablespoons olive oil
Juice of 1 lemon
1 teaspoon dried oregano
1 teaspoon virgin olive oil
Chopped fresh parsley

When in Greece, make sure you taste this classic dish of young lambs' liver fried briefly and then served with olive oil and mountain thyme. This recipe uses oregano which is less pungent. Calves' liver, which is equally delicious, may be used as a substitute.

Remove any membrane and cut the liver into thick strips, then into pieces about 3 cm (1 in) square. Season the flour with salt and pepper and lightly dust the liver. Heat 2–3 tablespoons of olive oil, adjust the heat to medium-low and fry the liver for about 2–3 minutes until brown and crusty on the outside but moist in the centre. Transfer to a warm plate, sprinkle with lemon juice, oregano, a little olive oil, salt, pepper and chopped parsley.

Sikotakia Krasata
LAMBS' LIVER IN WINE SAUCE

This is a variation of Sikotakia Riganata *and a main speciality of the islands of Rhodes and Corfu. It can be served either as a* meze *or a main course, in which case increase the quantities.*

Marinate the liver pieces in 2 tablespoons of wine for 1–2 hours. Drain and pat dry on kitchen paper.

Heat the oil and fry the livers for 2–3 minutes only. Add the remaining wine with the other ingredients, raise the heat and cook for a further 3–4 minutes, stirring continuously. Serve immediately with the sauce.

450 g (1 lb) lambs' or calves' liver, cut into 3 cm (1 in) squares

6 tablespoons dry red wine

3 tablespoons olive oil

1 tablespoon lemon juice

1 teaspoon mustard powder

½ teaspoon dried oregano

½ teaspoon sugar

Salt and freshly ground pepper

Myala
BRAINS

In his book *The Deipnosophists*, Athenaeus mentions a celebrated cook who boasted of one of the most sumptuous dishes he ever created: brains cooked with rose petals.

> *'I crush the most fragrant roses in a mortar, then lay on carefully boiled brains of fowls and pigs, from which the stringy fibres have been removed. I also add egg yolks followed by olive oil, pepper, wine and a sauce made of brine and small fish or caviare. All this I stir thoroughly and cook in a casserole over gentle and steady heat.' The dish had such a delicious smell that one of his companions remarked: 'If this dish were stirred in the bronze-floored mansions of Zeus, its fragrance would go forth even to earth and to heaven'.*

Lambs' brains are readily available in Greece and are very popular as a *meze*, a salad or even as baby food, since they are light and easily digestible. Expertly cooked, calves' or lambs' brains make a most delicate dish. **Warning**: in Britain, BSE (bovine spongiform encephalopathy), commonly known as 'mad cow disease', has not been eradicated. For this reason, calves' brains should not be used and lambs' brains should be used only if they are obtained from a reliable, independent butcher. It is essential that the lambs' brains are very fresh and that they are cooked the same day. If they are frozen, make sure they are completely frozen, then thaw them thoroughly before using them.

Most Greek recipes originate in Macedonia. Veal or lamb brains dipped in a light egg batter and then fried in hot butter taste delicious. Brains poached and then served cold in a lemon sauce with fresh dill and fennel leaves are excellent.

Soupes

SOUPS

Soups are usually served as a first course at lunchtime and occasionally, especially in the winter, as a full meal in the evening. In some parts of Greece, soups are eaten for breakfast, as the Greek breakfast is often very frugal.

Hearty soups such as bean soup *(fasoulada)* and wheat and soured cream soup *(trahana)* are traditional country dishes that are delicious and nourishing. Full-bodied soups which contain meat, fish, chicken or lots of vegetables constitute a meal in themselves; they are often garnished with cheese and olives and eaten with crusty bread.

A range of puréed soups made from vegetables, cereals and various pulses are boiled with herbs and spices and then passed through a sieve. Some have a delicate flavour, some are highly spiced, and they are usually garnished with fried croûtons, chopped parsley or whole pieces of cooked meat or shellfish. On the other hand, regional soups such as the fisherman's soups from Corfu *(bourtheto)* and the Cyclades islands *(kakavia)*, Easter soup *(mayiritsa)*, wheat and soured cream soup *(trahana)* from Epirus and tripe soup *(patsa)* from Macedonia are spectacular soups each with a unique texture and flavour.

At the other end of the spectrum, clear or consommé soups are rare. They are considered too time-consuming by busy housewives. Instead, there is a variety of delicious cream soups made with the simplest of ingredients: tomatoes, celery, asparagus or wild greens. These light soups are actually broths with added vegetables, rice or pastas; they have a pleasant smell and wholesome taste but offer minimum nourishment. They have the consistency of light custards with a binding of egg and lemon sauce, flour or yoghurt.

For one bad egg, the soup was ruined.

———

A proverb from Lesbos

Avgolemono Soupa
EGG AND LEMON SOUP

SERVES
6

For the chicken stock

1 boiling or roasting chicken or its
carcase and giblets

1 carrot

1 onion with skin

1 small celery stick

1 small leek

3 litres (5¼ pints) cold water

1 small glass of dry white wine

1 bunch of fresh parsley

Salt and freshly ground pepper

For the soup

40 g (1½ oz) or a good handful of
medium-grain rice

100 g (4 oz) cooked chicken, diced
(optional)

Salt and freshly ground pepper

2–3 eggs, separated

Juice of 1 lemon

A classic egg and lemon soup with a light, creamy texture, this is delightfully refreshing on a hot summer's day. It is usually made with chicken stock, but is equally good made with fish or vegetable stock. The chicken stock for this soup should be light and look like clear amber.

Clean the chicken and remove its skin and membranes and the fat from the giblets. Put the chicken in a large pan, breast downwards, with all the other ingredients. Bring to the boil, then lower the heat and skim off any scum that rises to the surface. Simmer gently for about 2 hours, covered or partly uncovered depending on how concentrated you wish the stock to be. Strain carefully through a fine sieve and spoon off the fat.

Bring the stock to the boil and add the rice. Return to the boil, lower the heat and simmer gently for 10 minutes. Add the chicken and simmer for a further 5 minutes until the rice is tender. Season with salt and pepper and keep warm over a low heat.

Whisk the egg whites until slightly stiff. Beat the yolks in a separate bowl and pour into the egg whites. Add half the lemon juice and mix lightly.

Remove the soup from the heat. Add a ladleful of hot liquid into the egg mixture and mix well. Continue adding the liquid, a ladleful at a time, then pour the egg-lemon mixture back into the soup, stirring constantly. Adjust the seasoning and add more lemon juice, if you wish. Let the soup stand for 3 minutes before serving with toasted bread or hot pitta bread. If you wish to reheat the soup, do so over very low heat, stirring continuously, and do not allow to boil.

Psarosoupa me Avgolemono
FISH SOUP WITH EGG AND LEMON SAUCE

———

This variation of the egg and lemon soup theme is worth making just to find out how delicious an avgolemono *fish soup can be. It is a luxurious soup and costs only a drachma to make! Ask the fishmonger to give you pieces left over from filleting and any fish bones.*

Put all the ingredients for the fish stock in a pan, bring to the boil, then simmer over moderate heat for 1 hour. Strain through a fine or muslin-lined sieve and return the clear stock to the pan. Continue simmering, but never bring to the boil, until the stock is reduced to about 900 ml (1½ pints). Season to taste with salt and pepper, add the rice and simmer for 15 minutes until it is cooked.

Whisk together the eggs and half the lemon juice. Whisk a ladleful of stock into the egg mixture. Pour the egg mixture back into the stock and mix well. Taste and add more lemon juice, if required. Sprinkle with parsley and serve. To reheat the soup, use a very low heat and do not allow it to boil.

Variations

1. If you wish to make a substantial soup which includes a whole fish, proceed by making the stock as above, then add any of the following suitable fish, either whole or cut into pieces: fresh cod (*bakaliaros*), grey mullet (*kefalopoulo*), scorpion (*skorpina)*, dogfish or rock salmon (*petropsaro)*, sea bass (*lavraki*), grouper *(rofos)* or sea bream (*sinagrida)*.

2. When adding a whole fish to this soup, either omit the rice or use only a small quantity.

3. If you prefer a creamier soup, add a knob of butter at the end of cooking and reheat the soup gently before serving.

For the fish stock

900 g (2 lb) fish pieces and bones

2 onions, sliced

1 carrot, sliced

1 bay leaf

150 ml (¼ pint) dry white wine

5–6 black peppercorns

Juice of 1 lemon

1 teaspoon dried oregano

1 tablespoon chopped fresh parsley

1.2 litres (2 pints) water

Salt and freshly ground pepper

For the soup

50 g (2 oz) medium-grain rice

3 eggs

Juice of 1 lemon

Chopped fresh parsley

Bourtheto Soupa
FISHERMAN'S SOUP FROM CORFU

900 g (2 lb) assorted fish (red mullet, swordfish, eel, grey mullet, squid, cuttlefish, sea scorpion, flounder)

150 ml (¼ pint) olive oil

3 onions, coarsely chopped

4 garlic cloves, chopped

4 ripe tomatoes, skinned and finely chopped

2 tablespoons tomato purée

A pinch of sugar

150 ml (¼ pint) dry white wine

150 ml (¼ pint) water

Salt and freshly ground pepper

Plenty of chopped fresh parsley

There are many variations of this soup both in Italy, whence it originates, and in Corfu, even in each village and port of the island. The flavour varies with the type of fish and wine in season, so do not worry about achieving a genuine bourtheto – *it probably does not exist.*

Clean and gut the fish well and leave whole. Heat the oil in a large pan and fry the onions and garlic gently until softened. Add all the remaining ingredients except the fish and parsley. Simmer over a moderate heat, stirring, for 10–15 minutes. Taste and adjust the amount of salt and pepper, if required.

If you are using squid or cuttlefish, put these in the pan first and cook them for about 15 minutes. Next, add the larger fish and cook for 1–2 minutes, then add the smaller fish and shellfish. Cover the pan and cook over a low heat for 15–20 minutes until the fish is firm and the sauce thick. Transfer to a deep serving dish, sprinkle with chopped parsley and serve hot with crusty country bread.

Kakavia
FISHERMAN'S SOUP

Imagine you are a weather-beaten Greek fisherman in your caique *returning home from a long trip with the catch of the day. Lady Luck held your nets! You caught some red mullet* (barbounia), *some dark scorpion fish* (scorpines), *bream* (salpes) *or even an exotic John Dory* (christopsaro). *All you need now is a* kakavi – *a round metal pot which you stand on a tripod or hang over a fire – and you are in the business of cooking the classical dish* kakavia.

There are many stories about the origin of kakavia – *how to cook it, what to put in it, what fish to use, what is the best water to use – all told through the ages by the best storytellers in the world: the Greek fishermen. They will tell you that* kakavia *was the original* bouillabaisse, *known in ancient times when places like Marseilles and most coastal cities in the Mediterranean were Greek colonies.*

Today, you will find kakavia *cooked in the traditional way in most Greek tavernas. The cheaper version may use small, tasty fish, such as tiny squid* (calamaria)*, brown picarel* (marides)*, small yellow sea bream* (gopa)*, fresh anchovies* (gavros)*, sardines* (sardeles) *and prawns* (garides)*. A more expensive version may use larger fish such as lobster* (astakos)*, sea bream* (sinagrida)*, sea bass* (lavraki) *and common sea bream* (fangri)*.*

It is easy to make a rich and enjoyable kakavia *at home. Cooks can do their own thing, without pretending that they are making a classic, authentic soup. Two words of warning: use fresh fish only (remember that the freshest fish cannot be ruined, but a stale fish can ruin even the greatest recipe) and avoid oily fish such as herring, mackerel and salmon, as they have a strong flavour. Here are two suggested groups of fish from which to make your selection, the first being the more expensive. Select a mixture that includes bony, firm and soft-fleshed fish to give you a well-flavoured soup:*

1. *Grey mullet, gurnard, monkfish, halibut, sole, turbot, sea bream, bass, John Dory*
2. *Cod, whiting, skate, plaice, coley, swordfish, red snapper, flounder, prawns, squid.*

When you have made your selection, ask your fishmonger to let you have some of the trimmings, bones and heads that he would otherwise throw away.

Clean and gut the fish, remove and discard the gills. Discard the heads of small fish.

Arrange the onion slices, tomatoes, garlic, bay leaves and thyme in a deep flameproof casserole. Place the fish, except any delicate fish such as whiting or flatfish, on top. Add the olive oil, salt, pepper and finally the water or stock. Bring to the boil and then turn down the heat to very low, skimming off any scum that rises to the surface. Cover the casserole and simmer for about 3 hours. Add any delicate fish, cover and simmer for a further 1 hour.

Lift out the large fish and other fish that are still whole, excluding their heads, and place carefully in a deep serving dish. Adjust the seasoning of the broth and add lemon juice to

SERVES

8

2 kg (4½ lb) mixed fish and fish pieces

450 g (1 lb) onions, sliced

450 g (1 lb) tomatoes, chopped

2 garlic cloves, crushed

3–4 bay leaves

1 tablespoon chopped fresh or 1 teaspoon dried thyme

120 ml (4 fl oz) olive oil

Salt and freshly ground pepper

2 litres (3½ pints) hot water or fish stock

About 2 tablespoons lemon juice

2 tablespoons chopped fresh parsley

taste, then strain the liquid over the fish. Sprinkle with plenty of chopped parsley and serve hot.

Variation

If you wish to prepare a simple *kakavia* for four people, select one or two large fish, clean them and place them flat in a large pan. Add enough fish stock or salted water to cover the fish, bring to the boil and simmer for about 10 minutes. Strain the liquid and return to a clean pan. Slice the fish carefully and remove and discard the bones, head, fins and tails. Place the clean pieces of fish in the soup and cook with the rest of the ingredients over a low heat for 20–30 minutes. Adjust the seasoning with salt, lots of pepper and lemon juice, and serve hot.

Fakes Soupa
LENTIL SOUP

SERVES
4–6

450 g (1 lb) brown lentils

150 ml (¼ pint) olive oil

450 g (1 lb) ripe tomatoes, chopped, or 1 x 400 g (14 oz) can chopped tomatoes

1 tablespoon tomato purée

1 large onion, halved

5 garlic cloves

1.2 litres (2 pints) meat stock

1 teaspoon sugar

1 tablespoon white wine vinegar

2 bay leaves

Salt and freshly ground pepper

1 tablespoon chopped fresh oregano

This is a popular winter soup which can be served with cooked meat, chicken, fish or pickled vegetables. In this recipe, the vinegar is cooked together with the garlic in order to bring out the flavour of the garlic; some cooks, however, prefer to add the vinegar at the end of cooking.

Wash the lentils, discard those floating on the water and remove any stones or grit. Put the lentils in a pan with plenty of water, bring to the boil and cook for 10 minutes, then drain.

Heat the stock in a large pan and add the oil, tomatoes, tomato purée, onion, garlic, sugar, wine vinegar, bay leaves and salt. Bring to the boil and add the lentils. Lower the heat, cover the pan and simmer for 45 minutes (30 minutes if you use red lentils) or until the lentils are soft.

Remove from the heat and discard the onion halves, garlic and bay leaves. Taste the soup and adjust the seasoning with salt and wine vinegar. Add some freshly ground pepper and the oregano and serve hot or cold. Accompany the soup with feta cheese, smoked fish, boiled vegetables or croûtons.

Fakes me Lahanika
LENTIL AND VEGETABLE SOUP

SERVES
4–6

At the beginning of spring, spinach is young and tender and makes an ideal addition to lentils. Other vegetables such as leeks, cabbage, lettuce or carrots can be added to the dish and cooked with or without the spinach.

Wash the lentils well, put them in a pan with plenty of water and boil for 10 minutes, then drain.

Heat the stock or water in a large pan and add the oil, spring onions, garlic, tomato purée, wine vinegar, bay leaves and salt. Bring to the boil and add the lentils. Lower the heat and simmer for about 30 minutes or until the lentils are almost soft. Add the spinach and cook for a further 10 minutes or until the lentils are tender. Turn off the heat and discard the garlic and bay leaves. Taste the soup and adjust the seasoning with salt and wine vinegar. Add freshly ground pepper and oregano and serve hot or cold. Accompany the soup with pieces of cheese, smoked fish or croûtons.

450 g (1 lb) brown or red lentils
1.2 litres (2 pints) stock or water
150 ml (¼ pint) olive oil
2–3 spring onions, chopped
1–2 garlic cloves
1 tablespoon tomato purée
1 tablespoon white wine vinegar
225 g (8 oz) spinach, chopped
2 bay leaves
Salt and freshly ground pepper
1 tablespoon chopped fresh oregano

Fava Soupa
SPLIT YELLOW PEA SOUP

SERVES
4–6

This is a nourishing soup which can be served with fried cheese or cooked meats, preferably pork. Cooking times vary according to the age of the peas. If you wish, you may omit the oil and sprinkle a little virgin olive oil and chopped fresh parsley on each plate just before serving.

Wash the split peas well and discard any floating on the water or any discoloured ones. Soak overnight in water if the peas are very old. Drain. Put the peas in a large pan with the rest of the ingredients, except the oil and lemon juice. Bring slowly to the boil, cover and simmer gently for 1 hour until the peas are tender. Add more water if necessary and stir occasionally. (If you are using pieces of pork or other meats, add these to the pot at the same time as the peas.)

450 g (1 lb) split yellow peas
1.5 litres (2½ pints) water
1 large onion, finely chopped
2 carrots, diced
2–3 tablespoons chopped celery leaves
2–3 tablespoons chopped parsley
4 tablespoons olive oil
Salt
1 tablespoon lemon juice

Add the olive oil and simmer for a further 15–20 minutes, stirring vigorously to a soft purée. Season to taste with salt and lemon juice and serve hot or warm with crusty bread or croûtons.

Trahanosoupa
WHEAT AND SOURED CREAM SOUP

75 g (3 oz) *trahana*

1 litre (1¾ pints) chicken or meat stock

2 tablespoons unsalted butter

75 g (3 oz) hard feta, *halloumi* or Parmesan cheese, grated

Juice of ½ lemon

Salt and freshly ground pepper

Chopped fresh parsley

Trahana *is a pasta made from coarsely ground wheat mixed with eggs and soured goats' milk, cream or yoghurt. To make* trahana, *mix 900 g (2 lb) of plain flour, 1 egg, 250 ml (8 fl oz) of full fat milk, 250 ml (8 fl oz) of soured milk or yoghurt, ½ tablespoon of salt and enough water to mix to a stiff dough. Divide the dough into walnut-sized pieces and roll into balls. Spread them out on a clean surface and leave them to dry, preferably in the sun, for two or three days. When they are very dry, rub them with your hands or press them through a wide-holed sieve until they are the size of small granules. Dry them further, if necessary, then store in an airtight jar.* Trahana *will keep for several months. Alas, the art of making* trahana *at home is fast dying out, but commercial* trahana *is now available from continental shops in packets or in plastic bags, either in powder form or in small ball shapes; the powder form makes a smoother soup.*

Trahana *can be used in place of pasta or rice, or it can be made into a thick porridge. Sprinkled with cheese, it tastes like sour oatmeal. Greek peasants usually eat this delicious soup for breakfast before setting off to work.*

Bring the stock to the boil, add the butter and *trahana* and cook for 10 minutes, stirring occasionally so that it does not stick to the pan. Add the cheese, lemon juice and salt and pepper and simmer over a low heat for a further 10 minutes until the soup is thick. Serve hot with plenty of freshly ground pepper, chopped fresh parsley and more lemon juice.

Variations

1. In the Peloponnese, the soup is first cooked to a thick consistency, then a glass of red or white wine is added towards the end of cooking time.
2. The lemon juice is sometimes omitted and tomato purée or finely chopped tomatoes are added in instead.

Fasoulada
DRIED BEAN SOUP

SERVES
4

A hearty and nutritious soup, this is considered to be the national dish of Greece, the staple food of the army and every poor man's meal. It is usually made at home and at village festivals; do not expect to find it in many restaurants. It can become a substantial meal by adding pieces of pork, bacon or sausage.

Soak the beans in cold water overnight.

Drain the beans, place in a large pan and cover with fresh water. Bring to the boil, cook for 10 minutes, then drain. Cover again with cold water, bring to the boil once more, lower the heat, cover and simmer for 1–2 hours or until the beans are tender but intact. Add all the other ingredients, except the parsley, and simmer for a further 30 minutes. Add the parsley and salt and pepper to taste and simmer for 1–2 minutes. Serve with bread, olives and a dry white wine.

450 g (1 lb) dried haricot beans
150 ml (¼ pint) olive oil
400 g (14 oz) can of chopped tomatoes
1 tablespoon tomato purée
1 large onion, finely chopped
2 carrots, diced
2 celery sticks with their leaves, chopped
Salt and freshly ground pepper
2–3 tablespoons chopped fresh parsley

Revithia Soupa
CHICKPEA SOUP

SERVES
4

Chickpeas are a good source of protein and very nourishing. They are ideal for salads, stews, soups and dips. Unfortunately the tinned ones lose their nutty flavour and crisp texture so it is best to prepare them yourself.

This soup is a traditional favourite and often cooked in large quantities at religious festivals for the whole village. Chickpeas require soaking in water until they have more or less doubled their weight – this will be 12 hours for good quality peas

450 g (1 lb) chickpeas
150 ml (¼ pint) olive oil
2 onions, thinly sliced
Juice of 1 lemon
1–2 tablespoons chopped fresh parsley
Salt and freshly ground pepper

and 48 hours for older ones. If you leave them soaking longer, they start to ferment. The secret of a good revithia soup is slow cooking and the amount of olive oil used; the lemon juice is added to give it a lift.

Soak the chickpeas overnight or until they have doubled their weight. Drain and rinse. Place the peas in a pan and cover with fresh water. Do not add salt. Bring to the boil, skimming off any scum that rises to the surface. Lower the heat, cover and simmer for about 1 hour. Add the oil and onions and simmer for a further 1 hour or until the chickpeas are soft. Add the lemon juice, parsley, salt and lots of freshly ground pepper and simmer for a further 15 minutes.

Hortosoupa
VEGETABLE SOUP

SERVES

4–6

25 g (1 oz) butter

1 onion, finely chopped

1 leek, finely chopped

1.2 litres (2 pints) chicken stock

300 ml (½ pint) tomato juice or 2 tablespoons tomato purée diluted in water

2 carrots, diced

1 celery stick, chopped

1 pepper, seeded and diced

1 courgette, diced

75 g (3 oz) fresh peas

Salt and freshly ground pepper

1 large potato, peeled and diced

Juice of 1 lemon

A colourful country soup, this is made with all sorts of seasonal vegetables, traditionally straight from the garden. Quite often, such soups are based on a single vegetable: tomatoes (domatosoupa), cos lettuce (maroulosoupa), spinach (spanakosoupa) or leeks (prasosoupa); or sometimes on beetroot, onions, cabbage, fresh beans and potatoes.

Melt the butter in a large pan and fry the onion and leek until soft. Add the stock, tomato juice and all the vegetables, except the potatoes. Bring to the boil, lower the heat, cover and simmer until the vegetables are nearly but not completely tender. Add the potatoes, salt and pepper and simmer until all the vegetables are cooked. Add the lemon juice and serve piping hot with croûtons or garlic bread.

Variations

1. To make a vegetable broth, rub the soup through a fine sieve or mincer and return to the pan. Add a knob of butter, sprinkle with chopped fresh parsley and serve hot.
2. If you wish to add rice or pasta, prepare the soup and then rub it through a sieve. Add the rice or pasta. Cook for 15 minutes until tender. Add the lemon juice and serve hot.

Kremidosoupa Kritiki
ONION SOUP FROM CRETE

———

Melt the butter and fry the onions until pale golden. Add the flour, stir well and fry for a moment or so until golden brown. Add the stock, pepper and a little salt to taste and simmer over a moderate heat for 10 minutes. Gradually add the hot milk and water, stirring continuously, and simmer for a further 15 minutes.

Meanwhile, place the bread slices on a baking tray, sprinkle generously with most of the cheese and grill until golden brown. Pile two grilled toasts on each soup plate, pour the soup around the toasts and sprinkle with more cheese and freshly ground pepper.

75 g (3 oz) unsalted butter
4 onions, thinly sliced
2 tablespoons plain flour
150 ml (¼ pint) meat or chicken stock
Salt and freshly ground pepper
600 ml (1 pint) hot milk
150 ml (¼ pint) hot water
8 thin slices of bread
225 g (8 oz) hard cheese, grated or thinly sliced

Mayiritsa
EASTER SOUP

———

This traditional soup is eaten once a year on Holy Saturday night on returning from the church at midnight after the Easter mass. It is the first meal for the whole family after the austere period of Lent. With the exception of the kidneys, this soup is often made with the liver, heart, intestines, even the head, feet and tripe of the lamb which was prepared during the day for the next day's festivities. Plenty of herbs such as dill, mint and fennel are also added. It is a memorable dish that is served with plenty of cheese and wine. If you prefer, you can use simply lamb meat, liver, heart and shoulder.

Clean the lamb meat thoroughly, then chop into small pieces. Soak the halved lamb's head in water for a few hours, then tie the two halves together. Wash the heart and liver, sprinkle with lemon juice or vinegar and chop finely. Wash the intestines very well, turn inside out using a knitting needle or skewer, then rub with lemon juice and salt, rinse in water and chop into 5 cm (2 in) lengths. Plunge all these ingredients into boiling water for 1–2 minutes, then strain immediately.

All lamb's entrails (1 head split in two, 1 liver, 1 heart, 225 g (8 oz) intestines)
2 litres (3½ pints) clear meat stock or water
3 bunches of spring onions, finely chopped
A small bunch of fresh dill or fennel leaves, finely chopped
1 teaspoon chopped fresh mint
1 large cos lettuce, inner leaves only, finely chopped
50 g (2 oz) butter
75 g (3 oz) long-grain rice
Salt and freshly ground pepper

For the avgolemono *sauce*
3–4 eggs, separated
Juice of 2 lemons

Melt the butter in a frying pan and sauté the onions and lettuce for a few minutes. Place the lamb, stock or water, fried onions and lettuce, dill, mint, salt and pepper in a large pan, bring to the boil and cook over moderate heat for 45 minutes. If you are using a lamb's head, remove it from the pan and either discard or roast it separately. When all the meats are tender, add the rice and boil for a further 12 minutes. Remove from the heat and set aside for 5 minutes.

Beat the egg yolks well, then beat in the lemon juice. Add a ladleful of warm soup to the egg mixture and mix well. Return the egg mixture to the pan and stir well. Reheat if necessary over very low heat, stirring constantly, and do not allow the soup to boil or it will curdle. If you wish the soup to be light and creamy, beat the egg whites separately, then add them to the soup.

Variations

1. The soup makes a substantial meal on its own. If you want a lighter soup, add an extra 600 ml (1 pint) of water or stock and do not fry the onions and lettuce.
2. For an even lighter soup, omit the egg and lemon sauce and just squeeze a little lemon juice into the soup just before serving.

Arni Kefalaki Soupa
LAMB'S HEAD SOUP

SERVES

4

1 head of a spring lamb
1.2 litres (2 pints) water
1 onion
1 leek, chopped
1 carrot, chopped
1 celery stick, chopped
1 large tomato, chopped
1 garlic clove, chopped
2 bay leaves
2–3 tablespoons chopped fresh dill
1 tablespoon lemon juice
Salt and freshly ground pepper

A lot of offal is highly prized in many countries, including Greece, and forms the basic ingredients for some of the most delectable dishes invented. This dish is a light and nourishing vegetable soup, served with the brain and tongue of a spring lamb. If you cannot obtain a lamb's head, use lambs' tongues only.

Ask the butcher to split the head in half, then tie the two halves together so that the brain will not spread out. Soak in plenty of water, then clean off all traces of blood.

Place the head in a large pan with the water, vegetables, garlic and bay leaves and bring to the boil, skimming off any scum that rises to the surface. Cover and simmer gently for about 2 hours, until all the pieces of meat are very tender.

Remove the head from the pan and carefully take out the brain and tongue and separate any meat from the bones. Peel away the skin of the tongue. If you are using lambs' tongues only, cook them in the same way, then peel away the skin. Strain the broth through a sieve and add the dill, lemon juice, salt and pepper to taste and reheat if necessary. Serve the broth with a piece of brain and a slice of tongue in each plate. Accompany the soup with a light garlic sauce (*Skordalia*, see page 151) in a separate dish.

Patsa ke Skembe Soupa
LAMBS' FEET AND TRIPE SOUP

——

Pigs', lambs', sheep's or calves' feet (patsa) *and tripe* (skembe) *are used to make this nourishing soup. Specialist restaurants called* patsagidika, *which serve only this soup, can often be found in market places and sea ports, where workers would pop in at any time of the the day for a quick plate of* patsa *soup. It is a dish that is often served with a sauce of raw garlic and vinegar called* Skordostoumbi *(see below). If you cannot obtain these ingredients, use ox tripe, which is frequently available in major supermarkets, and cook it for 1–1½ hours.*

The feet should be plucked and cleaned or singed. Ask the butcher to do this for you. If mutton feet are used, they should be cut in 2–3 pieces. Open out and scrape tripe until thoroughly clean, then cut into small pieces. Put the feet and tripe into a large pan, cover with water, bring to the boil and boil for 2–3 minutes. Drain, then cover with fresh water. Add the carrots, onions, celery and salt and bring slowly to the boil. Lower the heat, skim off any scum that rises to the surface, cover and simmer for about 2 hours until all the meats are tender. Set aside to cool and skim off the fat.

Remove the tripe and feet, cut into even smaller pieces, discarding the bones, and reserve. Pass the stock through a sieve back into a clean pan, add the meat pieces and simmer gently until ready to serve. Make an egg and lemon sauce (*Avgolemono*, see page 150) and combine with the soup. Alternatively, make the following typical sauce.

SERVES
6–8

1 kg (2¼ lb) feet and tripe (from lamb, mutton, veal or ox)

2 carrots, sliced

2 onions, sliced

2 celery sticks, chopped

Salt

Skordostoumbi
GARLIC AND VINEGAR SAUCE

———

Peel 2–3 garlic cloves and pound them with a pinch of salt and 2 tablespoons of white wine vinegar. Add to the soup and stir well.

SERVES

4

1.2 litres (2 pints) clear veal or chicken stock

8 egg yolks

Juice of 4 lemons

Finely grated rind of 1 lemon

8 tablespoons soured cream or Greek yoghurt

4 tablespoons single cream

Salt and freshly ground pepper

2 tablespoons chopped fresh dill or parsley

Lemonosoupa
ICED LEMON SOUP

———

Whereas iced tea is very popular in Greece during the summer, cold soups are rare. However, here is one refreshing cold soup which is ideal for dinner on a really hot evening.

Simmer the stock over a low heat for 10 minutes. Meanwhile, beat the egg yolks and combine with the lemon juice, rind and soured cream or yoghurt. Place the stock over a very low heat or in a bowl over simmering water and gradually add the egg mixture, stirring all the time until the soup thickens to a thin custard. Remove from the heat and add the cream, then season to taste with salt and pepper. Cool, then chill in the fridge. Serve in chilled bowl garnished with dill or parsley.

SERVES

4

2 medium cucumbers, peeled and diced

700 g (1½ lb) thick plain yoghurt

2 garlic cloves

2–3 tablespoons virgin olive oil

2–3 teaspoons lemon juice or white wine vinegar

1 teaspoon chopped fresh mint

Salt and freshly ground pepper

600 ml (1 pint) water

2 tablespoons chopped fresh dill or mint

Tzatziki Soupa
ICED CUCUMBER AND YOGHURT SOUP

———

Another refreshing chilled soup, this is based on the yoghurt and cucumber dip (Tzatziki, see page 12).

Pound the garlic with a pinch of salt, then combine with the cucumbers, lemon juice or wine vinegar, oil, mint and yoghurt and stir vigorously. Gradually add the water until you have a thick soup. Season to taste with salt and pepper, spoon into individual bowls and garnish with dill. Chill in the fridge or serve over ice cubes.

Salates

SALADS

The Greeks are lucky to have available a great variety of vegetables that are suitable for colourful and appetizing salads: sun-ripened beef tomatoes, cucumbers, colourful peppers, radishes, sweet onions, crisp lettuces, small artichokes, dark green courgettes and delicious wild and cultivated greens. They refer to these as *salatika*, which means any salad vegetable. A salad without some sort of dressing is unthinkable; in most cases, a dressing consists of a generous amount of good olive oil, a little salt, a touch of wine vinegar or lemon juice and occasionally some chopped onions and a little garlic. Fresh herbs are invariably used: dill, fennel leaves and lots of flatleaf parsley. Dried mountain herbs, such as oregano, rosemary and thyme, are often sprinkled in moderation to add aroma and complement the flavours of the main ingredients. Nothing can surpass an authentic Greek salad. As if these ingredients are not enough, most popular salads are complemented by loads of feta cheese and a handful of olives.

Each region has its own preference for salad ingredients. In Macedonia and Thrace, you will find that mixed salads often include some sort of pickled vegetables, pickled slices of baby aubergines, rippled carrots, hot chilli peppers and celery stalks. In Corfu and Kefalonia, shredded cabbage and carrot salads are heavily seasoned with pounded garlic. In the Aegean islands and Crete, cooked vegetable salads often accompany grilled fish.

With the possible exception of fruits, rice and pasta, which the Greeks rarely use in salads, most raw or cooked foods are included: cooked dried beans, cooked broad beans, cooked or puréed chickpeas, cooked or raw vegetables, seafood, meat and chicken. Apart from a few classic salads, such as yoghurt and cucumber (*Tzatziki*, see page 12), fish roe (*Taramosalata*, see page 20) and aubergine purée (*Melitzanosalata*, see page 13), which are strictly speaking purées and usually served as a *meze*, all Greek salads are eaten during the main meal; they are not starters or appetizers. Their purpose is to be a simple and colourful accompaniment to more complex dishes of meat, fish and game.

Better humble greens in peace than a fine fish in discord.

———

Cretan proverb

SERVES

4

3 large ripe tomatoes, cut into wedges

1 cucumber, peeled and cut into 1 cm (½ in) thick slices

1 sweet onion, cut into thin rings

12 Kalamata olives

225 g (8 oz) feta cheese, crumbled into chunks

Optional extra ingredients

1 cos lettuce, leaves torn into pieces

1 green pepper, seeded, roasted, skinned and cut into rings

A few spring onions, some whole, some chopped

1 tablespoon capers, drained

A few salted anchovies, chopped

Chopped fresh parsley, dill or fennel

For the dressing

5–6 tablespoons fine olive oil

2 tablespoons white wine vinegar

1 teaspoon dried oregano

Salt and freshly ground pepper

Horiatiki Salata
COUNTRY SALAD

This salad alone makes you love Greece! It is served in all tavernas with every meal. It is light, fresh and unpretentious and contains chunks of tomatoes, cucumber and lettuce in the summer and shredded cabbage in the winter. In all seasons, crumbly feta cheese, black olives and aromatic wild oregano are added.

Place all vegetables in a large bowl and scatter over the olives and cheese. Mix together the dressing ingredients, pour over the salad and toss lightly.

SERVES

4

450 g (1 lb) cos lettuce

4 spring onions, finely chopped

2 tablespoons chopped fresh dill or chives

1 tablespoon white wine vinegar or 2 tablespoons lemon juice

4 tablespoons virgin olive oil

Salt and freshly ground pepper

A few radishes

Marouli Salata
COS LETTUCE SALAD

Said to be originally from the Dodecanese island of Kos, cos lettuce is best in the spring and early summer, so this salad is traditional in Greece during the Easter festivities, and made with fresh and crispy lettuce. Chill the lettuce for an hour or longer before making this salad.

Remove any damaged leaves from the lettuce, tear each leaf away from the core, wash well and dry thoroughly. Shred all but the tiny leaves finely with a sharp knife. Shredding makes the leaves more manageable and helps them soak up the flavour of the dressing. Reserve the tiny leaves for the garnish. Mix together the lettuce, spring onions and fresh herbs. Just before you are ready to serve, mix together the wine vinegar, oil, salt and pepper. Pour the dressing over the lettuce and toss lightly. Garnish with the tiny lettuce leaves and the radishes.

Variations

You can add a number of other ingredients to this classic salad, but ingredients to avoid are crushed garlic, mustards, mayonnaise and salad creams.

1. Wash and shred a handful of dandelion (*radiki*) leaves and add to the lettuce with 100 g (4 oz) of crumbled feta cheese and 1–2 fresh mint leaves.
2. Clean a bunch of small red radishes and add to the lettuce with 100 g (4 oz) of crumbled feta cheese and a little chopped fresh parsley or coriander.
3. Add Kalamata olives, feta cheese, ½ tablespoon chopped fresh oregano and a variety of other salad leaves such as chicory, curly endive, rocket, watercress or young spinach leaves.

Kolokithakia Salata
COURGETTE SALAD

Small courgettes, simply boiled and served with a lemon and oil dressing mixed with fresh dill, are surprisingly one of the most delicious salads.

Use small courgettes only, about 10 cm (3–4 in) long. Do not peel them, just trim off the ends. Boil in salted water for 4–7 minutes until tender but firm. Drain the courgettes and leave them whole or slice them into chunky slices if you prefer. Arrange them in a deep serving plate.

Mix 2 parts virgin olive oil to 1 part lemon juice and season with salt, freshly ground pepper and plenty of chopped fresh dill. Pour over the courgettes, mix gently and serve while still warm.

If you wish to serve the courgettes cold, as most Greeks

prefer, cook and drain them, then leave them to cool. Wrap in clingfilm and chill until they change colour and become slightly dull. When you wish to serve them, remove the clingfilm and pour over the dressing. Serve with grilled or fried fish, or on their own accompanied with a garlic sauce (*Skordalia*, see page 151).

Variation

This alternative recipe comes from Macedonia. Boil the courgettes in water until tender, then drain. Add 1–2 tablespoons of white wine vinegar, some freshly chopped mint, salt and pepper and boil for a further 2–3 minutes. Transfer to a serving dish and sprinkle over a little virgin olive oil.

Courgette Flowers

When fresh and young, courgette flowers are one of the most delicious vegetables to eat. Dip the flowers whole in a light egg batter, fry in plenty of hot olive oil for 1–2 minutes and serve with a dash of lemon juice.

SERVES

2–3

6 globe artichokes
1 small cos lettuce

For the dressing
4 tablespoons white wine vinegar
6 tablespoons virgin olive oil
1 tablespoon lemon juice
½ teaspoon sugar
1 pickled cucumber, chopped
1 small onion, finely chopped
1 green pepper, seeded and finely chopped
1 hard-boiled egg, chopped

Anginares Salata
ARTICHOKE SALAD

Artichokes in Greece are grown around Corinth, the Argos region in the Peloponnese and also on the island of Crete. They are available during the winter and spring when they are combined in a variety of ways with other vegetables to produce the most delicious dishes. Here we have a light salad of small artichokes and baby cos lettuces.

To prepare the artichokes, follow the instructions on page 67. After soaking the artichokes, cut them in half, if large, and place in a pan. Cover with salted water containing the juice and rind of ½ lemon, bring to the boil, cover and simmer for about 20 minutes until the artichokes are tender. Remove the artichokes and leave to cool. Make a bed of lettuce leaves on a serving dish and place the artichokes on top. Combine all the dressing ingredients, pour over the artichokes and serve.

The dressing above is suitable only for artichokes served

cold. For a salad served either cold or hot, a perfect accompaniment is a light garlic sauce (*Skordalia*, see page 151) or a chilled yoghurt sauce (*Tzatziki*, see page 12) or even a simple dressing of melted butter and lemon juice.

Horta Salata
WILD GREENS SALAD

900 g (2 lb) wild greens such as dandelions, rocket, endive or spinach

6 tablespoons extra virgin olive oil

4 tablespoons lemon juice

A pinch of salt

2 tomatoes, sliced

1 lemon, cut into wedges

100 g (4 oz) feta cheese, crumbled into chunks

Agria horta, or wild greens, is the general term for a variety of edible vegetables found in the rural areas, hills and mountains of Greece. There is a long tradition, both culinary and medicinal, of the value of wild plants and greens. Many of the green salads we eat today in the West, for example, originate from the Ancient Greeks: watercress, chicory, rocket, dandelion.

Gathering them in the mountains and then bringing them down to town markets is a traditional trade that is still carried on by village folk. As you travel through Greece, you often see old ladies in the countryside, among the olive groves, stooping over thorny bushes gathering dandelions. Farmers cultivate all sort of wild greens in their gardens, as they would normally cultivate fruits and nuts.

Wild greens are known by strange names which often vary from region to region.

Paparounes: a sweet type of wild lettuce

Kafkalides: a plant with wide and flat sweet leaves

Zoungi: a plant with large sweet leaves, ideal with fish

Vlastaria: a type of bitter spinach with yellow flowers

Vlita: a plant with sweet and slightly sour leaves

Lapatha: a plant with sweet and tender stalks, similar to sorrel

Ombries: a plant with very bitter leaves

The following is a list of wild greens you can find in supermarkets or continental shops.

Rokka

Rocket

With its peppery and slightly mustardy taste, rocket is a perfect addition to mixed salads, especially tomato ones. The Greeks love to add handfuls of young rocket leaves to tomato or potato salads, even to soups and stews.

Radiki

Dandelion

There are several varieties of dandelion that grow wild in the mountains. The leaves look like crimson spinach and taste pleasantly bitter. Some of the bitterness can be removed by blanching the leaves in boiling water for a minute, draining and then boiling a second time.

Antidia

Curly-leaf Endive

Yet another wild green with a mild bitter flavour, curly endive (called 'chicory' in the USA and France) should be used when young and fresh, as its flavour becomes unpleasantly bitter when old. The Greeks use endive to make a delicious lamb fricassee dish.

Vrouves

Mustard or Charlock

This grows in corn fields and is gathered before it sprouts its yellow flowers in early spring. The Greeks use the top tender part of the stalk, which is sweet and delicate.

Glistrida

Purslane

A versatile salad green with a crunchy, peppery flavour, this can be combined with other salads, added to potatoes, peas, broad beans or served on its own as a side dish to grilled fish, chicken or meat. It has a particular affinity with young and sweet beet-roots; it is often served with lemon juice and olive oil dressing.

You can make a wild greens salad with a single vegetable or a combinations of greens. If the vegetables are older and possibly bitter, boil them first for 1 minute and drain, then proceed with the recipe. The Greeks prefer a little more lemon in these salads than usual; you may adjust the amount of lemon as you please.

Clean and wash the greens very well and discard the stems. Bring a little water to the boil in a pan, add the greens and boil for 3–5 minutes, stirring often, until wilted but not too soft. Drain well and place on a serving dish. Beat the other ingredients and pour over the greens. Garnish with tomato slices, black olives, lemon wedges or feta cheese and serve cold or at room temperature.

Panzaria Salata
BEETROOT SALAD

This is an excellent winter salad served on its own or with grilled fish or chicken. In Greece, beetroots are always sold uncooked and complete with their leaves during their season from May to October. Roots and leaves are cooked separately and marinated in a strong oil and vinegar dressing.

Peel the beetroots and cut them into thin slices. Place them in a serving dish. Whisk together the oil and lemon juice, then add the garlic, salt and pepper and pour over the beetroots. Leave to stand in the fridge for a few hours or overnight.

When ready to serve, sprinkle on the chopped onions and purslane and accompany the salad with a garlic sauce (*Skordalia*, see page 151) or a yoghurt and cucumber dip (*Tzatziki*, see page 12) and chopped walnuts.

900 g (2 lb) pre-cooked medium beetroots

6 tablespoons virgin olive oil

Juice of 1 lemon

2 garlic cloves, crushed

Salt and freshly ground pepper

A handful of purslane leaves or watercress, rocket or dandelion

4 spring onions or 1 onion, finely chopped

Piperies Salata
PEPPER SALAD

If you were preparing this salad in Greece you would probably be using the famous red peppers from Florina, a prosperous town in the north of Macedonia.

Wash the peppers and pat them dry. Bake them whole in a preheated oven at 200°C/400°F/gas mark 6 or under a hot grill for about 20 minutes until their skins becomes charred and blistered. Turn them over during cooking so that they brown evenly. Cover the hot peppers with clingfilm and let them sweat for 10 minutes. When cool, peel off the skins and discard the core and seeds. Slice the peppers in half and place on a serving dish. Combine all the other ingredients in a bowl and pour over the peppers. Serve at room temperature. This salad can keep for a few days, if covered in oil.

900 g (2 lb) small peppers of any colour

2–3 garlic cloves, sliced

3–4 tablespoons chopped fresh parsley

4 tablespoons olive oil

2 tablespoons white wine vinegar

Salt and freshly ground pepper

Patatosalata me Yiaourti

POTATO SALAD WITH YOGHURT

450 g (1 lb) potatoes

2–3 tomatoes, sliced

½ cucumber, sliced

1 small lettuce or cos lettuce,
finely chopped

1 small onion, finely chopped

2 hard-boiled eggs, quartered

Salt

For the dressing

1 egg yolk

½ teaspoon sugar

½ teaspoon English mustard

4 tablespoons virgin olive oil

Salt and freshly ground pepper

450 g (1 lb) strained Greek yoghurt

For the garnish

Kalamata olives

Chopped fresh dill

Freshly ground pepper

Thick Greek yoghurt, now commercially available worldwide, is ideal for this summer salad.

Boil the potatoes in their skins in salted water until just tender but not overcooked. Wash them with cold water, drain and leave to cool. Peel and cut into cubes. In a large salad bowl, combine the potatoes with the rest of the ingredients, season with salt and mix lightly.

Prepare the dressing by beating the egg yolk, sugar, mustard, oil and salt and pepper. Combine with the yoghurt and mix well until the dressing is smooth. You may omit the egg yolk and reduce the amount of oil if you are watching your weight. Pour the dressing over the salad, garnish with olives, some dill or parsley and freshly ground pepper and chill for 30 minutes before serving.

Salata Rousiki
RUSSIAN SALAD

————

SERVES
4

In spite of its name, this salad has been very popular in Greece for many decades. It is a wonderful composition of potatoes, carrots, beetroots and beans.

Mix together the vegetables, except the beetroot, in a serving bowl. Add the chopped egg whites, half the capers, the pickles, parsley, half the mayonnaise, salt and pepper and toss thoroughly without breaking up the ingredients. Pour over the remaining mayonnaise to cover the salad, and garnish with the beetroot slices and the remaining capers. Sprinkle the crushed egg yolks over the salad and serve.

2 large boiled potatoes, peeled and sliced or roughly diced

100 g (4 oz) cooked haricot or black-eyed beans

225 g (8 oz) cooked string beans

225 g (8 oz) cooked garden peas

2 cooked carrots, diced

3 hard-boiled eggs, whites chopped, yolks crushed

1 tablespoon capers

1 large dill pickle or 4–5 gherkins, finely chopped

1 tablespoon chopped fresh parsley

250 ml (8 fl oz) mayonnaise

Salt and freshly ground pepper

2 cooked beetroot, peeled and thinly sliced

Garidosalata
PRAWN SALAD

————

SERVES
2–3

This is mainly an Athenian salad. Ideally, large or Dublin Bay prawns make an impressive salad. They are cooked with a little vinegar in order to deepen their colour.

Boil enough water just to cover the prawns. Add a little salt, the wine vinegar and the prawns, lower the heat and simmer for 5–7 minutes but no longer, just until the prawns turn pink. Strain and allow the prawns to cool. Peel off the shells, retaining the heads and tails. De-vein them by making a cut on the back of the prawns and removing the black intestine.

Arrange the lettuce leaves in a serving bowl and place the prawns, eggs and pepper in the centre. Mix together the mayonnaise, lemon juice, salt, pepper and a little chopped parsley or fennel leaves and pour over the salad.

700 g (1½ lb) medium-sized raw prawns

½ tablespoon white wine vinegar

1 cos lettuce

3 hard-boiled eggs, quartered

1 pepper, seeded and finely shredded

120 ml (4 fl oz) mayonnaise

Juice of ½ lemon

Salt and freshly ground pepper

1 tablespoon chopped fresh parsley or fennel leaves

Lahanika

VEGETABLES

The Greek and, in general, the Mediterranean diet is based on vegetables, olive oil, grains and wine in moderation, and reputed to be the healthiest in Europe. A balanced diet including a high proportion of fresh vegetables contributes to a reduction in the risk of heart disease, and people believe that a vegetarian or almost vegetarian diet promotes longevity and better health. This is particularly observed in some remote villages in Crete, where the diet is almost entirely vegetarian.

The Greeks consume a third of their calories in the form of olive oil, which is high in mono-unsaturated fatty acids. The small farmer, the fisherman, the town trader all lead a relatively active life and they usually walk to work every day. Their mid-day meal is mostly vegetarian, with meat, chicken or fish served once or twice a week. Salads and bread feature in every meal.

As healthful as those traditional habits may be, vegetable eating is sadly on the decline in Greece; meat consumption and the use of refined cooking oils and margarine, frozen dinners and packaged snacks are steadily rising.

Greece produces a wide variety of vegetables which are grown with very few expensive fertilizers. Annual vegetable production is estimated to be around three million tons, most of which are cucumbers, tomatoes, aubergines, peppers and courgettes, representing the most dynamic export sector of the country. The quality of vegetables is excellent. Mild climatic conditions ensure an early start to the season.

Winter vegetables are available from September well into the spring, with globe artichokes and spinach in season until June, cabbage and cauliflower until February, leeks until April, spring onions until May. Then in the spring, there are cos lettuce, endives and peas from February to May. With the coming of the early lamb, these vegetables combine to produces a number of memorable dishes.

The summer vegetable season starts in May and lasts until November. Vegetables include tomatoes, courgettes, okra, cucumber, beetroot, aubergines and peppers. A variety of cultivated and wild greens begin to appear in the market after the autumn rains and last through the winter until early

She gathered vegetables all day in the meadow, she moulded the earth, she sifted the earth, she wove the earth till dawn.

——

George Hortatzis, Cretan poet (c. 1600)

59

summer. Potatoes, onions, carrots, celery and other root vegetables are available all the year round.

In the past, many vegetables were available only in a particular season and therefore many vegetable dishes were based on ingredients that were seasonal. In addition, certain dishes were modified to suit various religious dictates. Nowadays, many vegetables are grown in greenhouses and are readily available throughout the year, although they are usually more expensive and lack the flavour of the vegetables naturally grown in the open air. Thus, even now, using seasonal vegetables is usually the best option.

Dolmades
STUFFED VINE LEAVES

MAKES ABOUT
40

225 g (8oz) vine leaves (about 40)

Juice of 1 large lemon

¼ teaspoon sugar

90 ml (3 fl oz) olive oil

600 ml (1 pint) chicken stock or water

Salt and freshly ground pepper

2 eggs

For a meat stuffing

100 g (4 oz) medium-grain rice

225 g (8 oz) minced lamb or beef

2 small onions or 4–6 spring onions, finely chopped or grated

2 teaspoons chopped fresh dill

½ teaspoon chopped fresh mint

3 tablespoons chopped fresh parsley

For a vegetarian stuffing

150 g (5 oz) medium-grain rice

2 small onions or 4–6 spring onions, finely chopped or grated

2 teaspoons chopped fresh dill

½ teaspoon chopped fresh mint

3 tablespoons chopped fresh parsley

Dolmades, *or* dolmadakia *as they are called if they are small and compact, are little parcels of savoury rice with or without minced meat, wrapped in vine leaves. The leaves impart their own delicate flavour to the stuffing. Other edible leaves or vegetables may also be used, such as cabbage, spinach or cos lettuce, each imparting its own aroma.*

Dolmades *are best in the spring when the leaves are young and tender and about the size of the palm of your hand. Very young leaves are used straight from the tree; older leaves are blanched in boiling water. If you do not happen to have a vine tree, preserved leaves in brine are now widely available; these should be washed and soaked in cold water for 30 minutes before use. This recipe offers you a choice of a meat or a vegetarian stuffing.*

Wash and dry the vine leaves and spread them out shiny side down. Soak the rice in hot water for 5 minutes, rinse in cold water and then drain well.

In a large bowl, combine all the stuffing ingredients, including the rice, and mix well with your hands. Place a heaped teaspoon of stuffing near the stalk of each leaf. Fold the stem end and sides over and roll up loosely, allowing the rice room to expand during cooking. Line a heavy-based pan with a few leaves or broken ones and carefully place the little rolls close to each other in two or three layers. Cover the rolls with a flat heavy plate to prevent them from moving.

Mix half the lemon juice, the sugar, 4 tablespoons of olive oil, the chicken stock or water, salt and pepper, and pour gently over the *dolmades*; the liquid should come up to the brim of the covering plate. Cover the pan with a tightly fitting lid. Cook over a very low heat for about 1½–2 hours. Do not allow the rolls to dry out. When ready, the rice should be soft, all the liquid should have been absorbed and only the oil should remain in the pan.

To Serve the *Dolmades* Warm

Dolmades made with meat stuffing are delicious when served hot with a light egg and lemon sauce. They make an excellent light lunch. Transfer the *dolmades* very gently from the pan to a deep serving dish and keep warm. Make the sauce by beating the eggs and the remaining lemon juice until thick and smooth. Season with salt and pepper. Warm the sauce gently, then pour over the *dolmades*. Garnish with chopped fresh parsley and set aside for 10 minutes before serving.

To Serve the *Dolmades* with Yoghurt

Transfer the *dolmades* very gently from the pan to a serving dish and keep warm. Garnish the *dolmades* with a few drops of lemon juice and some chopped fresh parsley or dill. Serve with plain Greek yoghurt garnished with a few drops of olive oil. An excellent alternative is a bowl of yoghurt and cucumber dip (*Tzatziki*, see page 12).

To Serve the *Dolmades* Cold

Allow the *dolmades* to cool in the pan. Transfer them gently to a serving plate and chill, if you wish. Make a light dressing using a little oil, any juice remaining in the pan and a little more lemon juice, then pour over the *dolmades* just before serving. Garnish with lemon slices and olives and serve with a glass of ouzo.

Kolokithakia Gemista
STUFFED COURGETTES WITH
MINCE AND RICE

SERVES

4

1 kg (2¼ lb) or 6–8 medium
courgettes

50 g (2 oz) long-grain rice

5 tablespoons olive oil

1 onion, finely chopped

225 g (8 oz) lean minced beef, lamb
or veal

Salt and freshly ground pepper

Juice of 1½ lemons

3–4 tablespoons chopped fresh parsley

3–4 tablespoons chopped fresh dill

600 ml (1 pint) chicken or
vegetable stock

2 eggs

In this recipe, courgettes are stuffed with a mixture of minced meat and rice and served with a delicious avgolemono *sauce. This is one of many classic ways of cooking courgettes, so popular in Greek homes. The Greek housewife will prepare the dish in the morning and send it to the local bakery to be baked. When she collects it, it will be ready, hot and cooked to perfection; the baker knows how long it will take and how much extra water it will require during cooking, and will even add the right amount of seasoning.*

Use medium courgettes if you wish to serve the dish as a main course, otherwise use small courgettes for a first course or meze. You may omit the minced meat for a vegetarian dish. Cut the courgettes in half lengthways or use them whole as in this recipe.

Bring a pan of water to the boil, add the courgettes and blanch for 2 minutes, then drain. Cut off the stems and scoop out the centre of the courgettes using a long-handled teaspoon, a long knife or an apple corer. The courgettes should now resemble a tube of canelloni with one end closed. Collect the pulp, chop it finely and set aside.

Place the rice in a pan, cover with water and bring to the boil. Boil for 10 minutes, then rinse with cold water and drain. Heat a tablespoon of olive oil in a pan and fry the onion until golden brown. Add the minced meat, half the courgette pulp, the rice, salt, pepper and a squeeze of lemon juice. Simmer for 10 minutes, stirring frequently. Remove from the heat and add the chopped parsley and dill. Leave to cool.

Stuff the courgettes carefully with the meat and rice mixture, allowing space for the rice to expand. Lay the courgettes horizontally in a deep casserole. Pour in enough stock or water to come half way up courgettes, add 3–4 tablespoons of olive oil, a little more lemon juice, salt and pepper. Cover the casserole and simmer over a low heat for about 30–45 minutes until the courgettes are soft, basting occasionally. You may need to add a little more water. Remove from the heat.

Prepare the sauce by whisking the eggs in a large bowl

for 2 minutes, then adding the juice of half a lemon. Add a tablespoon of the liquid in the casserole to the egg mixture, whisking constantly. Repeat this five or six times, then pour the egg mixture into the casserole, shaking it to prevent the eggs from curdling. The heat of the courgettes should be enough to thicken the sauce. Serve hot with a green salad and a plate of feta cheese.

Variations
1. The combination of eggs and lemon produces a rich and creamy sauce. If you prefer a less rich sauce, leave out the eggs and add a little more lemon juice only.
2. You may also cook this dish in the oven with a tomato sauce. Prepare a tomato sauce separately (see page 148) and place the stuffed courgettes on top of the sauce in the casserole. Omit the stock and the *avgolemono* sauce.

Kolokithakia 'Papoutsakia'
STUFFED COURGETTES
'LITTLE SHOES'

SERVES

4

Courgettes or aubergines halved lengthways, with the centres scooped out ready for stuffing, resemble 'little shoes', hence the name papoutsakia. *When they are filled with a meat mixture and covered with a thick cheese sauce, they make an unusual and delightful dish which can be served as a first or main course.*

Bring a pan of salted water to the boil, add the courgettes and boil for 3 minutes. Drain and leave to cool. When cool enough to handle, cut them in half lengthways and, using a small spoon, remove some of the pulp. Chop half the pulp finely and reserve. If you are using aubergines cut them in half lengthways, including the stem end. Remove some of the pulp with a spoon, chop half the pulp finely and reserve. Sprinkle the aubergines with plenty of salt and leave for 30 minutes. Rinse and pat dry. Fry them gently in hot oil on both sides for a few minutes until lightly browned.

Next, prepare the stuffing. Heat the oil and fry the onions until soft. Add the minced meat, vegetable pulp and tomatoes

3 courgettes or aubergines, trimmed

6 tomato slices

25 g (1 oz) cheese, grated

For the stuffing

1–2 tablespoons olive oil

1 onion, finely chopped

450 g (1 lb) finely minced beef or lamb

225 g (8 oz) ripe tomatoes, skinned and chopped

A pinch of ground cinnamon

3–4 tablespoons chopped, fresh parsley

Salt and freshly ground pepper

For the cheese sauce

25 g (1 oz) unsalted butter

25 g (1 oz) plain flour

300 ml (½ pint) milk

2 eggs, beaten

A pinch of grated nutmeg

50 g (2 oz) Parmesan, hard Cheddar or *kefalotyri* cheese, grated

and season with salt, pepper and cinnamon. Cook for about 15 minutes, stirring occasionally, so that the stuffing is moist and well blended. Stir in the parsley and mix well.

Melt the butter in a small pan, stir in the flour and cook for 1 minute. Whisk in the milk, then stir over a low heat until thickened. Stir in the eggs, nutmeg and cheese. Whisk until the sauce is rather stiff.

Preheat the oven to 180°C/350°F/gas mark 4.

Place the vegetables on a well-oiled baking dish, split-side up, spoon over the meat mixture and cover the top with the cheese sauce. Garnish with the tomato slices and sprinkle with grated cheese and freshly ground pepper. Bake for about 1 hour until the top is nicely browned and the vegetables are soft. Serve hot.

SERVES

4

10 small courgettes

5 garlic cloves, thinly sliced (not crushed)

1 teaspoon paprika

2 teaspoons chopped fresh parsley

2 teaspoons chopped fresh dill

Salt and freshly ground pepper

450 g (1 lb) feta cheese, rinsed and cut into 10 slices

150 ml (¼ pint) olive oil

4 tablespoon breadcrumbs (optional)

Kolokithakia me Feta

COURGETTES WITH FETA CHEESE

This dish combines the sweetness of the courgettes and the salty taste of the feta cheese. Remember to rinse the feta well to reduce the excessive saltiness and serve as a meze with a glass of chilled ouzo.

Preheat the oven to 180°C/350°F/gas mark 4.

Trim the ends of the courgettes but do not peel them. Make a deep cut lengthways, like a pocket, avoiding cutting through to the end. Combine the garlic, paprika, herbs, salt and pepper and fill in the pockets of the courgettes carefully without slitting them. Insert a piece of cheese into each courgette. Place the courgettes in a shallow ovenproof dish, pour the olive oil over them, sprinkle with a few breadcrumbs and cover with foil. Bake in the oven for about 45 minutes, then remove the foil and bake for a further 15 minutes. Serve either hot or cold.

Piperies ke Domates Gemistes
STUFFED PEPPERS AND TOMATOES

This popular dish can be made with small or large peppers of any colour, large tomatoes or a mixture of both. You need to be aware that the peppers take twice as long to bake as the tomatoes.

Preheat the oven to 180°C/350°F/gas mark 4.

Cut off the tops of the peppers and set aside. Scoop out the core and seeds. If the peppers are tough, plunge them into boiling water for 1–2 minutes, then refresh under cold running water. This preparation gives them a more delicate flavour. Alternatively, prick each pepper with a fork in several places or cut them in half to form little boats.

Cut off the tops of the tomatoes and set aside. Using a teaspoon, scoop out the pulp and juice. Chop the pulp finely and use it for the stuffing. Season the tomatoes with salt and turn upside-down on a plate to drain.

Heat half the oil and fry the onion and garlic for 1–2 minutes. Add the minced meat and fry over a low heat until well browned. Add the rice, chopped tomatoes, tomato purée and half the tomato pulp, the dill, parsley, mint and finally the stock. Season generously with salt and pepper. Bring to the boil, then simmer, uncovered, for about 15 minutes, stirring once or twice, until all the liquid is absorbed. Set aside to cool.

Stuff the peppers and tomatoes up to the brim, leaving room for the rice to expand. Place the peppers upright, stuffing side up, on a shallow ovenproof dish and support them with a few potato wedges if necessary. Pour the remaining oil over them and top with the reserved pepper tops. Pour half a cup of water in the dish to keep the vegetables moist during cooking.

Bake in the oven for 15 minutes, then add the tomatoes to the pan and return to oven for a further 30 minutes until the vegetables are soft and browned on top. Baste occasionally during cooking with the liquid in the dish or with additional hot water. Serve hot with plain yoghurt or a yoghurt and cucumber dip (*Tzatziki*, see page 12).

4 large peppers

4 large firm tomatoes

150 ml (¼ pint) olive oil

A few potato wedges (optional)

For the stuffing

1 large onion, finely chopped

2 garlic cloves, crushed

225 g (8 oz) minced beef, lamb or pork

75 g (3 oz) long-grain rice

450 g (1 lb) tomatoes, finely chopped or 1 x 400 g (14 oz) can of chopped tomatoes

2 tablespoons tomato purée

2 tablespoons chopped fresh dill

2 tablespoons chopped fresh parsley

½ teaspoon chopped fresh mint

Salt and freshly ground pepper

150 ml (¼ pint) vegetable or chicken stock

Variations

There are as many variations and additions to this dish as there are Greek cooks!

1. Prepare a vegetarian stuffing by omitting the minced meat and increasing the quantity of rice. You may add chopped celery and fennel leaves for a more subtle taste. This is best when served cold.

2. Currants and pine nuts or cooked chickpeas can also be added to the stuffing.

3. A thick cheese sauce can be poured over the stuffed vegetables.

4. Crumbled feta cheese may be added to stuffing, but reduce the amount of salt.

5. Add a pinch of sugar to the stuffing, especially for tomatoes, and sprinkle the juice of a lemon over peppers prior to baking.

Kremidia Gemista
STUFFED ONIONS

SERVES

4

900 g (2 lb) large sweet onions

50 g (2 oz) butter, diced

For the stuffing

3 tablespoons olive oil

1 large onion, finely chopped

225 g (8 oz) minced beef

225 g (8 oz) minced pork

225 g (8 oz) tomatoes, skinned and finely chopped, or 1 x 200 g (7 oz) can of chopped tomatoes

1 tablespoon tomato purée

Salt and freshly ground pepper

150 ml (¼ pint) vegetable or chicken stock

50 g (2 oz) long-grain rice

3 tablespoons chopped fresh dill

This is a particularly delicious dish from the Attica region: large, sweet onions stuffed with a mixture of minced pork and beef and baked either alone or with stuffed cabbage and stuffed vine leaves (page 60). The combined dish is known as kelemia. *It is customary to serve the dish hot with a simple egg and lemon sauce (*Avgolemono, *see page 150).*

Preheat the oven to 200°C/400°F/gas mark 6.

Top and tail and carefully peel the onions. Using a sharp knife, make a cut on the side from top to bottom as deep as the core. Place the onions into a pan of boiling water and boil them for 10 minutes. Strain and cool, before separating the shells. Scoop out the centres and chop them finely.

Heat the oil and fry the extra onion with the chopped onion centres until softened. Add the minced pork and beef and fry for 10 minutes. Add the tomatoes, tomato purée, salt and pepper and fry for a further 10 minutes. Add the stock, rice and dill, mix well and cook for a further 5 minutes. Stuff the boiled onion shells with the mixture, then fold them to close. Place them on a shallow baking dish, pour the hot water around the onions and dot with the butter. Cover the dish with foil and bake in the oven for about 40 minutes until the onions are tender and golden brown. Remove from the oven. Whisk the egg yolks and lemon juice in a bowl, then pour over the dish. Garnish with grated cheese and serve hot.

For the sauce
3 egg yolks
Juice of ½ lemon
2 tablespoons grated Parmesan cheese

Anginares Gemistes
STUFFED ARTICHOKES

———

SERVES
6

Artichokes are very versatile vegetables, most recipes originating from the regions of Corinth-Argos in the Peloponnese and the island of Crete, where artichokes are mainly grown. Two popular recipes, Anginares me Koukia *and* Anginares à la Polita, *are given on pages 68 and 69. Another popular dish from Crete is artichoke moussaka, in which artichokes are stuffed with minced meat in the same way as aubergine moussaka (*Moussaka, *see page 90). Here is a vegetarian dish of stuffed artichokes with carrots, fresh peas and celery, and flavoured with dill. A little sugar is added to bring out the flavour of the vegetables and enrich the sauce.*

6 large or 12 small globe artichokes
150 ml (¼ pint) virgin olive oil
2 lemons
1 tablespoon chopped fresh dill
250 ml/8 fl oz/ 1 cup water
1 teaspoon sugar
Freshly ground pepper

For the stuffing
450 g (1 lb) peas in the shell
2 carrots, diced
1 celery stick, cut into 2.5 cm/1 in pieces
2–3 tablespoons chopped fresh dill
2–3 spring onions, thinly sliced, including the green part
1 teaspoon sugar
Salt and freshly ground pepper

To Prepare Artichokes

Work quickly when preparing artichokes as they discolour immediately they are cut. When you treat them with lemon juice, they should remain white with a soft shade of green. If you are using tinned artichoke hearts, drain and wash them well.

1. Wash the artichokes, drain and trim their stems. Pull off any coarse outer leaves. Cut one-third off the top of the artichoke.

2. Cut off the thorny tips of the remaining leaves with kitchen scissors. As you prepare each artichoke, rub with a cut lemon and then drop it at once into a bowl containing 1.2 litres (2 pints) of cold water and the juice of 1 lemon.

3. Remove the hairy choke using a spoon or the tip of a sharp knife, to form little cups.

4. Leave the prepared artichokes in the water for 1 or 2 hours to soak.

Shell the peas, wash and leave in a colander to drain. Unless the peas are very young, boil them in a cup of water for 15–20 minutes. If you use frozen peas, blanch them in boiling water for 1–2 minutes, then drain. Mix the peas with the remaining stuffing ingredients together with 2 tablespoons of the oil and the salt and pepper.

Drain the artichokes and divide the stuffing mixture between them. Place the artichokes in a round flameproof casserole and pour over the rest of the oil, the juice of ½ lemon, the dill, water, sugar and pepper. Cover the artichokes with a flat, heavy plate to keep them in place. Bring to the boil, then lower the heat to minimum, cover and simmer gently for 40–50 minutes until the artichokes are tender and the sauce has reduced. Set aside to marinate for 1–2 hours. Transfer to a serving dish, spoon the juices over all, sprinkle on some chopped dill, and serve with the remaining lemon, cut into wedges.

Anginares me Koukia
ARTICHOKES WITH BROAD BEANS

SERVES
4–6

6 medium globe artichokes

900 g (2 lb) small, fresh broad beans in the pod

3 tablespoons olive oil

5–6 spring onions, finely chopped

3 tablespoons fresh dill, finely chopped

Salt and freshly ground pepper

Juice of 2 lemons

Artichokes and broad beans are in season for four weeks in April only, when they are both small and tender. The combination of these vegetables produces one of the most exquisite dishes. When you buy artichokes, look for solid heads with tightly packed leaves and use them as soon as possible after buying. If you need to store them for a day or two, keep them in the fridge in a closed container. Artichoke hearts, either frozen or tinned, can be used in place of fresh artichokes, and you can use parsley instead of dill.

Prepare the artichokes as described on page 67.
If the broad beans are small and tender, cut around the pods to remove the strings and cut them in half, otherwise shell them, then wash and drain.

Heat the oil in a large pan and sauté the spring onions for 1–2 minutes only. Add the beans, artichokes and dill and enough hot water to cover the ingredients. Season with a little salt and pepper and bring to the boil, cover and simmer gently for 30–40 minutes until the vegetables are tender. Remove from the heat and stir in the juice of half a lemon. Transfer the artichokes to a serving dish, then spoon round the rest of the vegetables and some of the sauce. The dish may be served either hot or cold; in my opinion, it tastes better if served cold. A green salad, a plate of feta cheese and a dry white wine are all you need to accompany this delightful dish.

Anginares à la Polita
ARTICHOKES WITH POTATOES AND CARROTS

SERVES

6

A simple and exquisite vegetarian dish brought into the Greek cuisine by the Greeks who lived in Constantinople (now Istanbul). It is usually served on its own or as an accompaniment to roast lamb or beef. Virgin olive oil is best for this dish. Butter should be avoided.

12 small or 6 large globe artichokes

150 ml (¼ pint) olive oil

2 onions, thickly sliced

4–5 spring onions, chopped

3 carrots, sliced

6 small potatoes, peeled

2 tablespoons chopped fresh dill or parsley

Juice of 1 lemon

1 litre (1 ¾ pints) water or chicken stock

Salt and freshly ground pepper

1 tablespoon cornflour

2 egg yolks

Prepare the artichokes as described on page 67.

Heat the oil in a large pan and fry the onions for 2–3 minutes until soft and pale. Combine the spring onions and add the carrots and potatoes. Drain the artichokes and place them stem side up in the dish, then add the dill and the lemon juice. Add the water or stock to cover the vegetables and season to taste. Bring to the boil, cover and cook over a gentle heat for about 30–45 minutes until the artichokes are tender.

Carefully transfer the artichokes to a warm platter using a slotted spoon and arrange the rest of the vegetables around them. Dilute the cornflour with a tablespoon of cold water, mix with the egg yolks and add to the sauce in the pan. Bring to the boil and cook for 2–3 minutes, stirring, until the sauce is smooth with a light yellow colour. Pour the sauce over the vegetables, sprinkle on a little dill and serve at room temperature.

Variation
Frozen artichoke hearts are available all year round and are a good substitute to use in this dish. Thaw them before use, then add to the pan for the last 10 minutes of cooking. Tinned artichoke hearts are equally delicious.

Spanakorizo
RICE PILAF WITH SPINACH AND LEEKS

SERVES

4

900 g (2 lb) fresh spinach

2 large leeks

3 tablespoons olive oil

1 large onion, chopped

1 garlic clove, crushed

2–3 tablespoons chopped fresh parsley

Juice of ½ lemon

150 ml (¼ pint) hot water or clear chicken stock

Salt and freshly ground pepper

100 g (4 oz) long-grain or basmati rice

This is one of the many rice dishes in which the colour and flavour of seasonal vegetables are added to the rice. Here leeks are added to the traditional recipe of rice and spinach. It is superb as an accompaniment to meat meze, or as a main course with grilled chicken or fish. It can be served warm or cold, on its own, with lemon wedges and a sprinkling of grated cheese.

Trim the stalks from the spinach, wash several times to remove any grit and then cut into 1 cm (½ in) pieces. Wash the leeks well, trim off the root, discard any rough leaves and then slice them into 1 cm (½ in) slices, including the green part of the leaves. Blanch both vegetables in boiling water for 2–3 minutes, then remove with a slotted spoon to a colander to drain.

Heat the oil in a pan and fry the onion and garlic over a gentle heat until soft and pale gold in colour. Add the spinach and leeks and sauté for 2–3 minutes, stirring gently with a wooden spoon. Add the parsley, lemon juice and the hot water or stock and season with salt and pepper. Raise the heat and bring to the boil. Add the rice, cover, then lower the heat and simmer gently for 12–15 minutes until the rice is tender. Switch off the heat and leave to stand for 10 minutes, covered, before serving.

Prasorizo
PILAF RICE WITH LEEKS AND CELERY LEAVES

SERVES

4

900 g (2 lb) leeks

3 tablespoons olive oil

1 onion, finely chopped

450 g (1 lb) beef tomatoes, skinned and finely chopped

Salt and freshly ground pepper

2–3 tablespoons chopped fresh parsley

The addition of celery leaves in place of spinach gives a more aromatic flavour to this popular rice dish with vegetables. Serve with olives and crumbled feta cheese.

Wash the leeks well, trim off the root, discard any rough leaves and then slice them into 1 cm (½ in) slices, including the green part of the leaves. Blanch them in boiling water for

1–2 minutes, then remove them with a slotted spoon to a colander to drain.

Heat the oil in a pan and fry the onion over a gentle heat until soft and pale gold in colour. Add the tomatoes, leeks, salt and pepper and simmer for 2–3 minutes until the leeks are soft. Add the parsley, pepper, celery leaves, rice and hot water or stock, and bring to the boil. Cover, lower the heat and simmer gently for 12–15 minutes until the rice is tender. Remove from the heat, sprinkle over the lemon juice and leave to stand, covered, for 10 minutes before serving.

1 green pepper, seeded and finely chopped

450 g (1 lb) celery leaves, finely chopped

100 g (4 oz) long-grain or basmati rice

150 ml (¼ pint) hot water or clear chicken stock

Juice of ½ lemon

Lahanika sto Fourno
ROASTED VEGETABLES

————

SERVES

4

There is no better way to celebrate summer than this wonderful combination of summer vegetables roasted in the oven. A few vegetables have been selected here: tomatoes, courgettes, onions, celery and potatoes. You can always add baby carrots, chunks of aubergines, peppers, whole mushrooms, okra or fresh beans. It is a dish prepared in almost every region from Macedonia to Crete and is known by many names – briámi, tourloú, tavá, yiouvétsi – mainly referring to the type of dish in which the vegetables are baked.

Preheat the oven to 180°C/350°F/gas mark 4.

Select an ovenproof dish to contain all the vegetables. An earthenware dish is fine, a shallow metal baking dish is better. Brush the dish with a little oil and place a layer of half the tomato slices, then add the courgettes, onions, celery and potatoes. Cover with the remaining tomato slices. Sprinkle over the garlic and herbs, salt and pepper, and drizzle with the remaining olive oil. Bake uncovered in the oven for 1–1½ hours until the potatoes and other vegetables are slightly browned and tender, stirring gently once or twice. If they get dry, add a little hot water. Serve this dish straight from the oven, or, if you wish, sprinkle with the cheese and bake for a further 10 minutes. Serve hot or cold.

5 tablespoons olive oil

6–7 large tomatoes, thickly sliced

3–4 courgettes, cut into 7.5 cm (3 in) pieces

2 sweet red onions, roughly cut into wedges

2 celery sticks, cut into 7.5 cm (3 in) pieces

3–4 large potatoes, roughly cut into wedges

3 garlic cloves, finely chopped

3–4 tablespoons chopped fresh parsley

2 tablespoons chopped fresh dill or 2 teaspoons dried dill

½ teaspoon chopped fresh mint

Salt and freshly ground pepper

3 tablespoons grated Parmesan or *kefalotiri* cheese (optional)

Fasoulakia Yiahni
BRAISED FRESH BEANS

SERVES

4

900 g (2 lb) French or string beans or
700 g (1½ lb) frozen beans

150 ml (¼ pint) olive oil

1 onion, finely chopped

1 garlic clove, crushed

900 g (2 lb) ripe tomatoes, skinned
and chopped, or 2 x 400 g (14 oz)
cans of chopped tomatoes

1 tablespoon tomato purée

2 tablespoons chopped fresh parsley

½ teaspoon sugar

Salt and freshly ground pepper

For this dish, select young and small green beans and cook them whole or cut longer beans in half. Avoid runner beans or larger beans that need stringing. The choice of tomatoes is also important. Greek tomatoes have the taste of the sun in them and they are large and juicy. If you use tinned or greenhouse-grown tomatoes, it is advisable to add a tablespoon or two of concentrated tomato purée.

Wash the beans in cold water, top and tail and remove any strings if necessary. Heat the oil in a large pan and fry the onion and garlic until pale and soft. Add the tomatoes, tomato purée, parsley, sugar, salt and pepper and bring to the boil. Lower the heat and simmer gently for 10 minutes, uncovered. Add the beans and enough water to cover them, cover the pan and cook for 20–30 minutes until the beans are tender but still crisp and the sauce is reduced to half its original volume. Serve hot or cold as a main meal with a yoghurt and cucumber dip (*Tzatziki*, see page 12) or a beetroot salad (*Panzaria Salata*, see page 55).

Anginares Marinates
Marinated Artichokes

SERVES

4

2 x 400 g (14 oz) cans of artichoke
hearts

150 g (5 oz) pickling onions

4 tablespoons olive oil

1 teaspoon sugar

1 tablespoon white wine vinegar

2 garlic cloves, crushed

1 tablespoon tomato purée

1 teaspoon dried thyme or basil

Salt and freshly ground pepper

Lahanika Marinata
VEGETABLES COOKED
À LA GRECQUE

Cooking vegetables à la Grecque, *in the Greek manner, is an invention of the French cuisine. It simply consists of boiling the vegetables, then draining them well and dressing with a salad dressing made of olive oil, wine vinegar or wine and a little garlic. The dish is generally chilled before serving. Celery, cauliflower, mushrooms, carrots, onions, artichokes and even fish such as cod can may be prepared in this way.*

The Greeks prefer to marinate such vegetables and refer to these dishes as marinata. *They sometimes use strong marinades which can overpower the flavour of the vegetables, so here I use a lightly spiced marinade that is left overnight with the veget-*

ables and which gives the dish a much mellower taste. The range of vegetables can also be extended to include peppers, courgettes and aubergines.

Marinated Artichokes: Drain the artichoke hearts, rinse well in cold water and drain in a colander. Skin the onions and blanch them in boiling water for 5 minutes, then drain.

Heat 1 tablespoon of oil in a pan, add the sugar and fry the onions for 2–3 minutes.

Mix together the remaining oil, the vinegar, garlic, tomato purée, thyme or basil, salt and pepper and mix well. Add the contents of the pan and the artichokes, cover and place in a fridge. Leave to marinate for about 2 hours. Sprinkle with chopped parsley and serve chilled.

Marinated Mushrooms: Rub the mushrooms gently with a cloth. Do not peel them unless they are large. Heat the oil in a large pan and add 1 tablespoon of lemon juice, the wine, garlic, tomato purée, bay leaf, half the parsley, salt and pepper. Increase the heat and boil rapidly for a few minutes. Reduce the heat, add the mushrooms, cover and simmer gently for 7–10 minutes. Allow to cool and set aside for about 2 hours. Remove the bay leaf. Transfer to a serving dish, sprinkle on the rest of the lemon juice and garnish with the remaining parsley.

Marinated Peppers and Courgettes: Combine all the ingredients except the vegetables in a bowl. Pour the marinade into a pan, bring to the boil and cook for 2 minutes. Add the vegetables and simmer for 8–10 minutes until tender, adding a little water, if necessary. Transfer the vegetables with a slotted spoon on to a serving plate. Boil the marinade for a few minutes until reduced to half its original quantity. Pour over the vegetables and set aside for 1–2 hours before serving.

Manitaria Marinata

Marinated Mushrooms

SERVES

4

450 g (1 lb) firm button mushrooms

5 tablespoons virgin olive oil

Juice of ½ lemon

90 ml (3 fl oz) dry white wine

2 garlic cloves, crushed

1 tablespoon tomato purée

1 bay leaf

2 tablespoons chopped fresh parsley

Salt and freshly ground pepper

Piperies ke Kolokithakia Marinata

Marinated Peppers and Courgettes

SERVES

2

4 tablespoons olive oil

1 tablespoon white wine vinegar

2 garlic cloves, crushed

1 tablespoon tomato purée

½ teaspoons sugar

1 tablespoon chopped fresh parsley
or dill

Salt and freshly ground pepper

225 g (8 oz) peppers, sliced

225 g (8 oz) courgettes, cut into 2.5
cm (1 in) slices

Bizelia Ladera

FRESH PEAS COOKED IN OIL

SERVES

4

Peas (bizelia *or* arakas) *in springtime are sweet and crunchy and make a light side dish for chicken or fish. The pea pods are often included if they are very tender.*

1 kg (2¼ lb) fresh peas in their shells
or 450 g (1 lb) frozen garden peas or
petits pois

90 ml (3 fl oz) virgin olive oil

5–6 spring onions, chopped

3 tablespoons chopped fresh dill

½ teaspoon sugar

150 ml (¼ pint) chicken stock or
water

Salt and freshly ground pepper

1 teaspoon cornflour

Shell the peas and set aside. Heat the oil in a large pan, lower the heat and sauté the onions for 2–3 minutes. Add the rest of the ingredients, except the cornflour, cover the pan and cook at low heat for 15–20 minutes, stirring occasionally, until the peas are tender. Frozen garden peas need 5–10 minutes and less water, older peas may take a little longer. A little sauce should be left in the pan. Mix the cornflour with a little water, stir it into the sauce and heat until thickened. Serve the dish hot or at room temperature. A country salad (*Horiatiki Salata*, see page 50) is ideal with this dish.

Koukia Ladera

FRESH BROAD BEANS COOKED IN OIL

SERVES

4–6

1 kg (2¼ lb) fresh broad beans in
their shells

90 ml (3 fl oz) virgin olive oil

1 large onion or 1 bunch of spring
onions, chopped

1 garlic clove, crushed

450 g (1 lb) tomatoes, skinned and
finely chopped

½ teaspoon sugar

Salt and freshly ground pepper

300 ml (½ pint) vegetable or chicken
stock or water

Juice of ½ lemon

3 tablespoons chopped fresh dill,
fennel leaves or parsley

Fresh broad beans and peas which appear in the market early in the summer are also cooked in oil. Broad beans are delicious and sweet, and are often eaten raw in Greece. Here, broad beans are cooked as a simple stew; country folk cook them in garlic or in 1 or 2 tablespoons of prepared garlic sauce (Skordalia, see page 151). Broad beans are usually gathered and dried for the winter, after which they are soaked and cooked with dried chickpeas. It is an excellent dish to accompany roast chicken or grilled fish.

Shell the beans, string any small pods that are soft and tender and include these too. Heat the oil in a pan and gently fry the onion and garlic for 2 minutes. Add the beans, tomatoes and sugar, salt and pepper and fry gently for 3–4 minutes. Add the stock and fennel leaves if you are using them, and simmer on a low heat for about 20 minutes until the beans are tender and the stock has boiled away. Remove from the heat, add the lemon juice and dill or parsley, if using, and mix well. Leave to stand for 1 hour to amalgamate all the flavours. Serve cold or reheat and serve warm.

Melitzanes Yiahni
BRAISED AUBERGINES

A delicious summer lunch of sweet aubergines, peppers and garlic baked in the oven.

Preheat the oven to 180°C/350°F/gas mark 4.

Wash the aubergines and cut off the stems. Slice them lengthways into 1 cm (½ in) slices, sprinkle with lots of salt and leave to sweat for 1 hour. Rinse well and pat dry on kitchen paper. Heat a few tablespoons of oil and fry the aubergines until just brown on both sides. Transfer to kitchen paper to drain any excess oil. Heat a little more oil and fry the peppers until they begin to blister. Transfer to kitchen paper to drain.

Pour the remaining oil into a clean pan and heat until it begins to smoke. Lower the heat and fry the garlic for 1 minute. Add the tomatoes, tomato purée, oregano, salt and pepper, and simmer the sauce for 10–15 minutes.

Place the aubergines and peppers in an ovenproof dish and pour over the sauce. Cover with foil and bake in the oven for 45 minutes until the vegetables are soft and the sauce slightly reduced. Sprinkle with grated cheese and serve warm or cold.

4 medium aubergines

150 ml (¼ pint) olive oil

3–4 peppers, seeded and cut into chunks

4–5 garlic cloves, thinly sliced

900 g (2 lb) ripe tomatoes, skinned and finely chopped, or 2 x 400 g (14 oz) cans of chopped tomatoes

1 tablespoon tomato purée

½ teaspoon dried oregano

Salt and freshly ground pepper

***Kefalotiri* or Parmesan cheese, grated**

Revithia Yiahni
CHICKPEA STEW

Chickpeas are traditionally cooked on their own during Lent. In other times, pieces of pork or smoked sausage are added to chickpea stews and soups for a heartier meal. The amount of garlic used in stews should be moderate; a casserole dish rubbed with a cut clove of garlic provides enough flavour to the stew. If you have a pressure cooker, it is ideal for speeding up the cooking time.

Soak the chickpeas in cold water for at least 12 hours. Strain the peas, wrap them with a towel and rub them with your hands until the skins rub off. Put them into a bowl of water so that the skins will float and can easily be removed.

450 g (1 lb) chickpeas

3–4 tablespoons olive oil

2 onions, sliced

2 celery sticks, thinly sliced

1–2 garlic cloves, crushed

150 ml (¼ pint) tomato juice or 2 tablespoons of tomato purée diluted to the same quantity in water

1–2 tablespoons chopped fresh parsley or dill

Salt and freshly ground pepper

A squeeze of lemon juice

Put the chickpeas in a pan with plenty of water, bring to the boil, cover and simmer gently for about 2 hours or until they are completely tender, skimming off any froth which rises to the surface.

Heat the oil and fry the onions and garlic until golden. Add to the chickpeas together with the remaining ingredients except the lemon juice and cook over a medium heat for 20–30 minutes until the vegetables and chickpeas are tender and the liquid has reduced to a thick sauce. Season with salt and lemon juice.

Revithia me Melitzanes sto Fourno
BAKED CHICKPEAS AND AUBERGINES

SERVES

4–6

450 g (1 lb) chickpeas

150 ml (¼ pint) olive oil

1 onion, sliced

1 garlic clove, crushed

¼ teaspoon cayenne pepper

900 g (2 lb) aubergines

450 g (1 lb) ripe tomatoes, sliced

1–2 tablespoons chopped fresh parsley or dill

1 teaspoon dried oregano

Salt and freshly ground pepper

A delicious vegetarian dish from Macedonia.

Prepare and cook the chickpeas as described in the previous recipe, then drain, reserving the liquid. Heat 2 tablespoons of the oil and fry the onion and garlic until soft. Add to the chickpeas with the cayenne pepper and mix well. Remove from the heat. Prepare and fry the aubergines as described on page 75. Drain off any excess oil on kitchen paper.

Preheat the oven to 180°C/350°F/gas mark 4. Place half the chickpeas in an earthenware casserole, then add a layer of aubergines, followed by the rest of the chickpeas, topped by a layer of aubergines. Pour over about 120 ml (4 fl oz) of the reserved liquid, then arrange the tomato slices on top. Sprinkle with parsley or dill, oregano, salt and pepper and bake in the oven for 20–30 minutes until golden brown on top and moist inside.

Bamies Yiahni
OKRA STEW

Okra is a delicate vegetable which should be stewed with the minimum of liquid and disturbed as little as possible during cooking. Select small and bright green okra and preserve their colour by sprinkling them with lemon juice or vinegar. Rinse well before using.

Carefully peel the okra with a paring knife around the top so that the juices inside do not escape. Do not cut off the tips or slice the vegetables. Place in a glass bowl and sprinkle over the wine vinegar. Season with salt and pepper and set aside for 1 hour, preferably in the sun.

Heat the oil in a large pan and sauté the onion and garlic until pale and soft. Add the tomatoes, tomato purée, 3 tablespoons of parsley, the sugar, salt and pepper and bring to the boil. Lower the heat and simmer gently for 10 minutes, uncovered. Wash and drain the okra, then add to the pan and gently stir into the sauce.

Garnish with the tomato slices and season with a little salt and pepper. Cover and simmer gently for about 20–30 minutes until the okra is tender but not mushy. Shake the pan occasionally but never stir the vegetables, and add a little water to the sauce towards the end of cooking if it becomes dry. Sprinkle with the remaining parsley and serve warm.

450 g (1 lb) okra

2 tablespoons white wine vinegar

Salt and freshly ground pepper

150 ml (¼ pint) olive oil

1 onion, thinly sliced

1 garlic clove, crushed

450 g (1 lb) tomatoes, skinned and chopped, or 1 x 400 g (14 oz) can of chopped tomatoes

1 tablespoon tomato purée

3–4 tablespoons chopped fresh parsley

½ teaspoon sugar

1 large tomato, thinly sliced

Psimenes Bamies
BRAISED OKRA

The flavour of the okra is enhanced in this recipe as it is first fried in little olive oil until brown and crisp, then braised in a tomato and lemon sauce.

Prepare and peel the okra as described in the previous recipe. Rinse well and dry on kitchen paper. Heat the oil in a non-stick pan and fry the okra in batches until slightly brown and crisp on all sides. Transfer to a round pan using a slotted

450 g (1 lb) okra

2 tablespoons white wine vinegar

4–5 tablespoons olive oil

Juice of ½ lemon

1 onion, thinly sliced

1 garlic clove, crushed

450 g (1 lb) tomatoes, skinned and chopped, or 1 x 400 g (14 oz) can of chopped tomatoes

3–4 tablespoons chopped fresh parsley

½ teaspoon sugar

Salt and freshly ground pepper

spoon, arranging the okra pods like the spokes of a wheel. Sprinkle with lemon juice and arrange the onion, garlic, tomatoes and 3 tablespoons of parsley evenly over the okra. Sprinkle with sugar and season with salt and pepper and cover with a tightly fitting lid. Simmer over low heat for 30 minutes, shaking the pan occasionally. Transfer to a serving platter and sprinkle with the remaining parsley.

Kreata

MEAT

When some nomadic people from central and eastern Europe settled around the Aegean Sea in search of warmer climates some time before 1000 BC, they found that the soil of Greece was poor and shallow, and much of the land was mountainous. In those early days, the first Greeks were not agricultural people: because of their nomadic ancestry, they felt that cattle could be kept on the move and represented a greater value to them than fields of corn.

The nomads benefited from the olives and vines which flourished in the land. They based their diet on barley, which they decided to grow; they had meat, milk and cheese from cattle and goats, fish which they would grill or dry and use as a relish and, most important, corn which they imported from Sicily, Egypt and the Black Sea. All imports were paid for out of the profits of exporting wine and oil – Attic oil was then considered the finest in the world.

Grilling over an open fire, spit-roasting a whole animal and boiling meat with aromatic herbs became the traditional ways of preparing meat dishes in Ancient Greece. Today, little has changed from that tradition and, although most meat dishes are now cooked in modern ovens, the best and more succulent dishes are done on a spit with mountain herbs and marinades for unique flavour.

Lamb (*arni*) is now very popular. Lambing starts between December and April. The best lamb, milk-fed and less than four months old (*arnaki galactos*), is produced domestically. It is very expensive and in short supply. Older lamb is what most people buy at Easter time, when the whole countryside seems to be enveloped in the aroma of lamb roasting on the spit. During the summer, restaurants and tavernas occasionally roast a whole lamb for the evening – an event which attracts both tourists and the local clientèle. The demand for lamb in Greece is such that mature animals are now imported frozen from New Zealand, the Balkan countries and Eastern Europe.

The Ancient Greeks had a preference for mutton – and some Cretans still do today. Mutton, however, is not a

Swift Achilles, leaping up, killed a silver-white sheep, and his companions stripped off its skin and dressed it properly; then they cut it skilfully into small pieces, pierced them into spits, roasted them carefully, and pulled them all off the fire. Automenon distributed bread around the table in beautiful baskets, as Achilles gave out the meat.

———

Homer's *The Iliad*

favourite meat with most modern Greeks. They find its odour off-putting and its taste unpleasant; the Greeks simply do not know how to bring out the rich flavour of mutton.

Beef (*vodino*) is mainly imported from Europe because it is cheaper and leaner than the small, home-reared animals. Any animal up to three years of age is called *moshari*, which is often translated by restaurants as veal although it is really young beef and sometimes not very tender. Milk-fed veal or grass-fed calf meat is rare in Greece.

As well as lamb, Greeks love goat (*yida*) and young kid (*katsiki*). They breed their goats to have their kids in the spring when special festivals take place; kids are then roasted on a spit just like paschal lambs. Young kids feed on the new leaves of thyme bushes in the spring and that gives an exquisite aroma to their meat.

Pork (*hirino*) is available all the year round and is the cheapest meat in Greece. It is grilled and roasted or cooked with pulses in the winter and fresh vegetables in the summer.

To a visitor in Greece, animals appear to be chopped up in the most unfamiliar way; no two butchers divide an animal in the same way. Often, whole carcases are hung and displayed and the butcher can quite readily be persuaded to cut off any piece the customer wants.

This section contains traditional recipes which have been slightly adapted for the meat cuts, herbs and vegetables that are available in supermarkets or delicatessens.

Arni me Kolokithakia Avgolemono
LAMB WITH COURGETTES IN EGG AND LEMON SAUCE

SERVES
4

1 kg (2¼ lb) breast or shoulder of lamb

2 tablespoons olive oil

1 small onion, finely chopped

300 ml (½ pint) hot water or clear chicken stock

Salt and freshly ground pepper

The delicate flavour of lamb, the sweetness of courgettes and the pungency of the egg and lemon sauce (avgolemono) combine to produce this delicious dish.

Remove most of the fat from the meat. If you are using breast of lamb, do not remove the bones; if you are using a shoulder, remove the blade bone using a sharp knife. Cut the meat into serving portions and pat them dry.

Heat the oil in a deep flameproof casserole and sauté the onions and meat pieces for 2–3 minutes. Add the hot water or stock and bring to the boil, skimming off any scum that rises to the surface. Season with salt and pepper, cover and simmer over a low heat for about 1 hour until the meat is tender.

About 20 minutes before you are ready to serve, scrape the skin off the courgettes very lightly, cut off the stems, and cut them in half or leave whole if very small. Chop the white parts of the spring onions and add to the casserole with the courgettes. Simmer for a further 10–15 minutes until the courgettes are tender but firm. Remove from the heat and add the chopped dill.

Whisk the eggs and half the lemon juice in a bowl. Mix a spoonful of the meat sauce into the egg mixture, and continue mixing in this way, a spoonful at a time, until all the meat juices are well integrated. Pour the egg mixture over the meat and gently shake the casserole. Adjust the seasoning with salt, pepper and lemon juice to taste. Garnish with the chopped dill or parsley and leave to stand, covered, for 10 minutes for all the ingredients to blend. Serve hot. If you need to reheat the dish, do so on a very low heat, stirring occasionally. The sauce should be creamy and refreshing.

700 g (1½ lb) small or medium courgettes

A bunch of spring onions

1 tablespoon chopped fresh dill

2 eggs

Juice of 1 lemon

2 tablespoons chopped fresh dill or parsley

Arni Frikase
LAMB FRICASSEE WITH COS LETTUCE

SERVES
4

Fricassee is the general method of stewing meat in butter and then thickening the sauce with egg yolks or cream. This delightful dish, which is usually made during Easter, is probably the ultimate application of the method. Ideally, you would need baby lamb or kid, which are not easily obtainable, but fresh breast of lamb makes an excellent substitute.

Bone the meat, remove most of the fat, cut into serving portions and pat dry. Heat the butter or oil in a large pan and gently fry the onions until soft. Add the meat and sauté until it is evenly browned. Add the hot water or stock, season with salt and pepper and simmer over a low heat for 1 hour until the meat is tender.

1 kg (2¼ lb) breast or shoulder of lamb

25 g (1 oz) butter or 2 tablespoons olive oil

2 onions, finely chopped

600 ml (1 pint) hot water or clear meat or veal stock

Salt and freshly ground pepper

2 large cos lettuces

2–3 bunches of spring onions, finely chopped

2–3 teaspoons chopped fresh dill

1–2 teaspoons chopped fresh parsley
2 eggs
Juice of 1 lemon

Trim the stems from the lettuce, wash and dry the leaves and chop them into about 2 cm (1 in) pieces. Add the lettuce, spring onions, dill and parsley to the pan and simmer for a further 10–15 minutes, stirring occasionally. The lettuce should be slightly crisp.

Whisk the eggs and lemon juice in a bowl until frothy. Mix some of the meat sauce into the egg mixture and continue mixing, a spoonful at a time, until the meat juices are well integrated. Pour the sauce over the meat and gently shake the pan. Adjust the seasoning or the amount of lemon juice as required and serve immediately.

Variations

1. Although this recipe specifies whole eggs, you can use egg yolks only, or even omit the eggs and use lemon juice only.
2. The onions are often omitted. Plenty of chopped spring onions are quite sufficient.
3. In order to give a thicker texture to the sauce, add a handful of long-grain rice to cook with the meat. Alternatively, you may wish to use a thicker egg and lemon sauce (see egg and lemon velouté sauce, page 150).
4. Often seasonal vegetables such as artichoke hearts, endives, carrots, celery and leeks are included in the dish. A favourite vegetable in Cyprus, for example, is spinach.

Arni Bouti sto Fourno
ROAST LEG OF LAMB
WITH GARLIC

SERVES
6–8

2 kg (4½ lb) lean leg of lamb
2–3 large garlic cloves, thickly sliced
1 tablespoon dried oregano or thyme
Salt and freshly ground pepper
Juice of 1 lemon
2–3 tablespoons olive oil
1 tablespoon plain flour
2 tablespoons chopped fresh parsley

You choose the amount of garlic in this recipe. A moderate amount of garlic imparts a wonderful and pleasant aroma to the meat. The final sauce is sweet and mellow. A cos lettuce salad (Marouli Salata, see page 50) or a wild greens salad (Horta Salata, see page 53) goes well with this dish.

Preheat the oven to 180°C/350°F/gas mark 4.

Wash the lamb and wipe with a kitchen cloth. Cover a roasting tin with a large piece of foil and place the leg on the foil. Make 5 or 6 incisions into the meat using a sharp knife.

Mix the garlic slices, oregano, salt and pepper, and stuff into the incisions; throw any leftover garlic around the leg. Pour the lemon juice and the oil over the meat and sprinkle on lots of salt and pepper. Close tightly with the foil and roast in the oven for about 2 hours or more until the meat almost falls off the bone.

Transfer the leg to a warm serving dish. Pour the juices and garlic from the tin to a pan, pulp the garlic pieces to a purée, add the flour and cook for 5 minutes, stirring continuously, until the sauce thickens. Taste and adjust the level of seasoning and lemon juice to taste.

Carve the leg into even slices and pour the sauce over them. Sprinkle with chopped parsley and serve with roasted potatoes and a green salad.

Arni Bouti sti Skara
GRILLED LEG OF LAMB

———

SERVES
6–8

The traditional way of roasting a whole lamb in the open air on Easter day is something unique and unforgettable. The lamb is prepared the day before and marinated with lemon, salt and pepper until the next day, when it is pierced by and secured with a long spit called souvla. *Friends, relatives and neighbours then gather for a drink or, a* meze, *or simply to offer advice on the complexity of preparing the marinade, mounting the lamb over the fire, ensuring that the heat is properly distributed along the length of the lamb, or to help rotate the lamb on the spit.*

The timing and the position of the roast are all–important. You start turning at 60 cm (24 in) above the embers and, over a period of four or five hours, the lamb is lowered to 15 cm (6 in), by which time the meat has shrunk and just begins to separate from the bones – and everybody is terribly hungry. Then the real feast begins and lasts for hours until the cool of the evening.

The recipe below is much less demanding. It uses a whole leg of lamb marinated in a typical Greek marinade, then grilled quickly on a barbecue. It is ideal for an open-air party. For maximum flavour, buy a one-year-old leg of lamb from a farm or butcher. It should be short, muscular and a good colour. If you buy from a supermarket, the leg should be hung for a day or two to mature until its colour becomes darker.

3 kg (7 lb) leg of lamb

For the marinade
3 garlic cloves, chopped
1 onion, sliced
Juice of 2 lemons
150 ml (¼ pint) olive oil
10 black peppercorns, crushed
3 bay leaves
2 tablespoons chopped fresh mint
Salt

With a sharp knife, follow the line of the main leg bone and cut along the edge and around it until it can be easily removed. Make a few more cuts until the meat is open and flat. Beat the meat on the fat side with a rolling pin so that it can be roasted evenly. Combine all the marinade ingredients, pour over the meat and leave to marinate overnight.

Next day, remove the meat from the marinade and wipe it lightly with kitchen paper. An outdoor barbecue would be ideal but an oven grill is fine. Place the meat flat under a very hot grill for a few minutes until it is well browned on both sides. Then reduce the heat and grill for 15–20 minutes.

Cut the meat into slices and serve with a yoghurt and cucumber dip (*Tzatziki*, see page 12). Serve the meat with boiled potatoes and a salad as a main meal.

Arni Exohiko

ROAST LAMB COUNTRY-STYLE

SERVES

5–6

2 kg (4½ lb) lean leg of lamb

3–4 garlic cloves, halved

225 g (8 oz) *halloumi, kefalotiri* or Gruyère cheese, cut into 1 cm (½ in) cubes

1 tablespoon plain flour

Salt and freshly ground pepper

4–5 tablespoons olive oil

2 onions, finely chopped

225 g (8 oz) potatoes, peeled and cut into 1 cm (½ in) cubes

1 tablespoon dried oregano or thyme

Juice of 1 lemon

Roasting lamb in the open air without attracting the attention of the Turks was a problem for the Greek bandits during the Greek War of Independence early in the nineteenth century: the aroma of heavy seasoning with mountain herbs would certainly give their position away! The answer was to wrap the meat in paper or put it in an earthenware pot and seal it with mud, then cook it for hours in the smouldering embers of pine logs. This is one of the stories of the origin of this popular dish and of its name. It is known as lamb exohiko *(country-style),* palikari *(as cooked by the brave heroes),* kleftiko *(as cooked by the Greek 'thieves' who used to steal Turkish provisions), or simply* sto harti *(wrapped in paper). This recipe is the urban version, often referred to as* kleftiko spitisio *or the 'home' version.*

Remove the central bone of the leg by cutting around the bone using a small sharp knife. This should leave a hole in the leg for stuffing. Wipe the meat clean and make small incisions all over, inserting the slivers of garlic into them.

Coat the cheese with flour and season with pepper. Heat a little of the oil in a pan and fry the cheese on all sides until it begins to brown. Remove the cheese using a slotted spoon and place in a bowl. Next, fry the onions until golden brown. Add the potato cubes and fry lightly until they begin to brown. Combine the cheese, potatoes and onions, add the herbs, salt and pepper, and mix lightly. Stuff the meat with this mixture.

Preheat the oven to 160°C/325°F/gas mark 3.

Cover a roasting tin with a large piece of foil and place the meat on top. Sprinkle the meat with the lemon juice, 2–3 tablespoons of the olive oil, salt and pepper. Fold the foil over the meat carefully but not too tightly and twist the ends securely so that none of the juice escapes. Bake in the oven for 2–2½ hours.

Bring the whole parcel on to a serving plate and open while hot. Jacket potatoes and roast or fried vegetables (aubergines, whole onions, courgettes) go well with this dish, as does a dry red wine.

Arnisia Paidakia sto Filo
LAMB CUTLETS WRAPPED IN FILO PASTRY

SERVES
4

This popular recipe is a derivation of the previous one (Arni Exohiko, see page 84), using the juiciest part of the lamb, which is first marinated then wrapped in filo pastry and roasted until the meat is pale pink and the filo parcels are golden brown. The meat is either from tender rib cutlets (chops) with the bones removed or cut from the loin to form noisettes which have been skinned, boned and cut into serving portions.

8 lamb rib chops or noisettes, boned, not flattened, about 1 cm (½ in) thick

8 filo pastry sheets, cut in half lengthways

225 g (8 oz) carrots, finely chopped

225 g (8 oz) fresh shelled green peas

1 leek, white part, finely chopped

50 g (2 oz) butter, melted

Salt and freshly ground pepper

1 egg white

For the marinade

2 tablespoons olive oil

Juice of 1 lemon

1 garlic clove, crushed

1 teaspoon dried oregano

Combine all the marinade ingredients, add the meat and set aside for 1–2 hours. Drain the meat and discard the marinade.

Preheat the oven to 200°C/400°F/gas mark 6.

Blanch the vegetables in boiling water for 1 minute, then strain them well. Melt a knob of the butter and sauté the vegetables for a few minutes until soft.

Take a sheet of filo and brush with melted butter. Place a second sheet on top and brush with butter. Place a piece of meat and a spoonful of vegetables at the end of the sheets, about 2.5 cm (1 in) from the base and sides. Sprinkle with salt and pepper. Fold the sides first, then the base of the pastry over the meat and vegetables. Roll up and lightly brush with a dab of egg white to seal the roll. Repeat for the other seven meat portions. Place the parcels on a baking tray, seam side down and brush lightly with butter. Bake in the oven for 10 minutes for pink meat or 20 minutes for well done; the filo pastry should be golden brown and crisp. Serve hot with a green salad with an oil and lemon dressing.

Arni Yiouvetsi
BAKED LAMB WITH PASTA AND CHEESE

SERVES

4–6

1 kg (2¼ lb) shoulder or leg of lamb

3 tablespoons olive oil

1 onion, chopped

3 garlic cloves, chopped

Juice of ½ lemon

900 g (2 lb) ripe tomatoes, skinned, seeded and chopped

2 tablespoons tomato purée

½ teaspoon sugar

1 tablespoon dried oregano

Salt and freshly ground pepper

250 ml (8 fl oz) water

450 g (1 lb) *orzo* or *kritharaki* pasta or short macaroni

600 ml (1 pint) chicken or meat stock or water

100 g (4 oz) Parmesan or feta cheese, grated

A family dish for the winter months that is truly unforgettable. It uses a pasta that looks like flattened grains of rice, called orzo *in Italian and* kritharaki *(small grain of barley) or* manestra *in Greek. The dish is prepared in small individual earthenware pots or in a large and deep casserole called* yiouvetsi, *hence the name of the recipe. The dish is a combination of meat and pasta baked in the oven, including all the juices and gravy. The traditional recipe uses lamb, but other meats such as beef, kid, ox tongue or veal are used in regional dishes. The meat is often flavoured in a mixture with lemon juice, oregano, garlic and pepper, this marinade being also added to the dish. In the absence of* orzo *pasta or* kritharaki, *short macaroni, wide noodles or even cut tagliatelle may be used.*

Preheat the oven to 180°C/350°C/gas mark 4.

Remove any excess fat and cut the meat into serving portions. Heat a little of the oil and fry the meat until browned, then add the onion and garlic and fry until golden brown. Transfer to a roasting dish or an earthenware pot. Sprinkle the meat with the lemon juice, add the chopped tomatoes, tomato purée, sugar, oregano, salt, pepper and water. Cover the pot and bake in the oven for about 1 hour until the meat is tender and the sauce has reduced. Turn the meat over occasionally and add a little water if it gets dry.

Boil the pasta in plenty of salted water for 1–2 minutes only. Drain. Heat the stock or water and add to the meat with the drained pasta. Return to the oven, uncovered, for a further

45 minutes, stirring once or twice, until the liquid is absorbed, adding a little more water during cooking if necessary. A light crust should develop on top of the pasta and the *yiouvetsi* should be moist with no traces of liquid. Serve the meat on top of the pasta and garnish with grated cheese or slices of feta.

Variations

1. If you use macaroni, cook it first separately until almost tender.
2. If you use beef or any fatless meat, increase the amount of oil or use butter.
3. Instead of garnishing with cheese, you may add it 15 minutes before the end and bake until the top is golden brown.

Arni Lemonato me Patates sto Fourno

LEMON LAMB WITH ROAST POTATOES

SERVES

6

This simple and refreshing dish is the traditional Sunday meal of Greece. A green salad and a dry white wine complete the meal.

Preheat the oven to 160°C/325°F/gas mark 3.

Rub the meat with half a lemon. Place it on a large oven dish and sprinkle with salt, pepper and oregano or rosemary. Pour the water around it and cover loosely with a piece of foil. Bake in the oven for about 1 hour, basting the meat occasionally during cooking and adding a little water if it gets too dry.

Add the potatoes around the meat and sprinkle again with a little salt, pepper and oregano. Dot the butter over the potatoes. Pour the juice of 1 lemon over the potatoes and meat and add a little more water, if required. Raise the oven temperature to 200°C/400°F/gas mark 6 and bake without the foil for a further 1 hour or until the potatoes are nicely browned.

1.5 kg (3 lb) leg or shoulder of lamb

2 lemons

Salt and freshly ground pepper

1 tablespoon dried oregano or rosemary

120 ml (4 fl oz) water

1.5 kg (3 lb) potatoes, peeled and quartered

75 g (3 oz) butter, diced

Arni me Melitzanes sto Fourno

ROAST LAMB WITH AUBERGINES

SERVES

6

3 medium aubergines, unpeeled, stems
cut off

Salt and freshly ground pepper

1.5 kg (3 lb) shoulder or middle neck
of lamb

150 ml (¼ pint) olive oil

1 large onion, thinly sliced

1 teaspoon chopped fresh mint

450 g (1 lb) ripe tomatoes, skinned
and roughly chopped

2 garlic cloves, thinly sliced

1 teaspoon ground cumin

1 tablespoon tomato purée

1 tablespoon plain flour

An aubergine stew that is unusual and delicious. You can use all types of aubergine except the very large and spongy ones which have little taste. The mint and cumin complement the flavour of the dish.

Preheat the oven to 160°C/325°F/gas mark 3.

Cut the aubergines lengthways into 1 cm (½ in) slices and sprinkle with plenty of salt. Let them sweat for 30 minutes, then wash them with water and pat dry on kitchen paper.

Meanwhile, cut the lamb into serving portions, removing most of the bones. Heat the oil in a large, heavy pan and fry the onion until soft. Add the meat, salt, pepper and mint and fry until the meat is well browned on all sides. Using a slotted spoon, remove the meat and onion and place in a deep oven-proof dish, leaving the oil in the pan.

Cut the aubergine slices in half and coat them lightly with flour. Reheat the oil and fry them gently on both sides for a few minutes until they begin to brown. Transfer them to the oven dish and lay them evenly over the meat. Add the tomatoes, garlic and cumin. Dilute the tomato purée in a little water and add to the dish.

Bake in the oven for about 1½ hours. The final dish should not be dry, so you may need to add a little stock or water during cooking. Serve with plain yoghurt or a yoghurt and cucumber dip, (*Tzatziki*, see page 12).

Variations

1. This dish can also be cooked on the stove in a flameproof casserole. The procedure is the same; the cooking time is about 1 hour.

2. You may reduce the amount of meat and tomatoes and increase the amount of aubergines, if you wish. You would then need to add more stock during cooking.

Yuvarlakia Avgolemono
MEATBALLS IN EGG AND LEMON SAUCE

I have never heard of anybody who does not like this dish; it is a success every time! It is easy to make and delicious.

Combine all the ingredients for the meatballs in a bowl and mix thoroughly with your hands. Place in the fridge for 1 hour. Wet your hands and shape the mixture into balls, the size of a small egg. If the balls are too small or too large they tend to break up.

Pour the stock into a deep pan, add the butter and bring to the boil. Gently add the meatballs; the liquid should just cover them. Lower the heat, cover the pan and simmer gently for about 45 minutes, removing any scum that rises to the surface. Remove the pan from the heat.

To finish the sauce, whisk the eggs lightly in a bowl, add the juice of half a lemon, season well and whisk again until the mixture is frothy. Combine the stock, a spoonful at a time, with the egg sauce, stirring all the time to avoid curdling the eggs. Pour the final sauce over the meatballs and shake the pan so that the meatballs are thoroughly coated. Adjust the seasoning with salt, pepper and lemon juice to taste. Leave the dish covered for 5 minutes, garnish with dill and serve immediately with boiled potatoes or rice.

Variation
If you wish to have a richer sauce make an egg and lemon velouté (see page 150).

450 g (1 lb) finely minced beef
1 onion, finely chopped
1 egg, beaten
50 g (2 oz) long-grain rice
3 tablespoons finely chopped fresh parsley
1 tablespoon finely chopped fresh dill
Salt and freshly ground pepper

For the sauce
600 ml (1 pint) clear chicken stock
25 g (1 oz) unsalted butter
2 eggs
Juice of 1 lemon

For the garnish
2 tablespoons chopped fresh dill

Moussaka
AUBERGINE AND MINCED LAMB PIE

SERVES
6

4 medium aubergines

2 tablespoons plain flour

Olive oil

1 large onion, finely chopped

3 garlic cloves, chopped

900 g (2 lb) minced lamb

2 tablespoons chopped fresh flatleaf parsley

150 ml (¼ pint) dry red wine

2 tablespoons tomato purée

½ teaspoon ground cinnamon

150 ml (½ pint) chicken stock

½ teaspoon honey

1 tablespoon dried oregano

3–4 tablespoons breadcrumbs

50 g (2 oz) *kefalotiri* or Parmesan cheese, grated

25 g (1 oz) unsalted butter

Salt and freshly ground pepper

For the sauce

75 g (3 oz) butter

6 tablespoons plain flour

600 ml (1 pint) milk

A good pinch of grated nutmeg or ground cinnamon

2 egg yolks

2 tablespoons double cream

Moussaka (pronounced moussakás *by the Greeks and* moussáka *by anybody else) is the generic name for a variety of dishes involving aubergines, courgettes, potatoes, artichokes, even rice, nuts and currants, with or without minced lamb, beef, mutton or other meat. What they all have in common is that they are covered with a thick white sauce, be that béchamel, mornay or even a cheese custard.*

Authentic moussaka does not exist; there are some good, some bad and some very bad versions, especially those served in most restaurants and pubs. The dos and don'ts of a moussaka are too numerous to mention. In general, a moussaka should be creamy and rich but not too heavy, the ingredients should be of good quality and well balanced. The amount of oil should be carefully controlled; it is a misconception that the more oil you use in a moussaka the tastier it will be.

The following recipe consists of aubergines and minced lamb covered with a béchamel sauce. It requires lengthy preparation but the end result is worth the trouble.

Rinse the aubergines but do not peel them, cut off the stems and slice lengthways into 1 cm (½ in) slices. Sprinkle with a lot of salt and leave to sweat for 1 hour. Rinse well and pat dry. This is designed to remove the bitter juices, but most aubergines grown in greenhouses do not need this treatment. Coat each slice lightly with flour. Heat a little oil and fry on both sides until they just begin to turn golden brown. Remove the aubergines from the pan and drain on kitchen paper.

Heat 1 tablespoon of oil in a pan and fry the onion and garlic for about 2 minutes. Add the minced lamb and fry for about 15 minutes until browned. Add the parsley, wine, tomato purée, cinnamon, stock, honey, oregano, salt and pepper, bring to the boil and simmer for 30 minutes or until all the liquid has almost evaporated and the sauce is rich and moist.

To make the sauce, melt the butter, stir in the flour and cook for 1 minute. Whisk in the milk and cook, stirring, until thickened. Season with salt and pepper. Beat the egg yolks, then add a little sauce to the eggs, whisking all the time. Add the rest of the sauce and the cream to the egg mixture and continue whisking until sauce is thick and creamy.

Preheat the oven to 180°C/350°F/gas mark 4.

Butter a large rectangular baking dish. Scatter some breadcumbs on the bottom of the dish and line the dish with aubergine slices. Pour half the meat sauce over and add half the grated cheese. Place another layer of aubergines on top of the cheese, followed by the rest of the meat sauce. Finally, cover with the rest of the aubergines. It makes no difference whether the top layer is aubergines or meat. Pour the sauce over the aubergines and spread with a palette knife. Sprinkle with the rest of the cheese and dot with a little butter. Bake in the oven for 1 hour until the top is golden brown and crusty. Remove from the oven and cool for 15 minutes. Cut into squares or wedges and serve hot.

Variations

1. Feta or Gruyère cheese can also be used; even doubling the quantity of cheese given in the recipe will not over-power the dish.
2. The dish can also be made with courgettes, but in that case do not use aubergines as well. The courgettes should be sliced lengthways and fried on both sides. Avoid adding potatoes.
3. In many Aegean islands such as Chios and Samos, mous-sakas are often covered with a semolina sauce. This sauce is made with 600 ml (1 pint) of milk, 4 tablespoons of fine semolina, 75 g (3 oz) of butter, ½ teaspoon of salt, freshly ground pepper, a pinch grated nutmeg or ground cinnamon and 3 egg yolks. Make the sauce in the same way as the béchamel in this recipe.

Melitzanes Imam
STUFFED AUBERGINES

SERVES

4

There are many different versions of this sumptuous and very popular aubergine dish, originating from almost every country in the Middle East. It probably became known in Greece during the Turkish occupation. The popular story is that it was

4 slim aubergines
150 ml (¼ pint) olive oil
2 onions, chopped
225 g (8 oz) lean minced beef

4 garlic cloves, thinly sliced, not crushed

450 g (1 lb) tomatoes, skinned and chopped, or 1 x 400 g (14 oz) can of chopped tomatoes

1 teaspoon sugar

1 teaspoon dried oregano or thyme

4 tablespoons chopped fresh parsley

Salt and freshly ground pepper

A few black olives (pitted)

made by the cook of a certain Imam – a Turkish priest – who fainted either from ecstasy whilst eating this delicious meal or from shock at discovering the cost of the oil used! This particular recipe comes from my grandmother who was an excellent cook of traditional dishes; she spent half her life in the kitchen cooking for a large family.

Cut the stems off the aubergines but do not peel them. Using a sharp knife, make three slits lengthways in each aubergine, about 2.5 cm (1 in) away from the ends. The depth of the slits should be roughly to the middle of the aubergines. Sprinkle with salt inside the slits and leave for 30 minutes. Wash in running water and pat dry. Heat 3–4 tablespoons of olive oil in a large, deep pan and fry them whole for a couple of minutes on all sides until their purple skin becomes slightly brown. Take them out and place them in an ovenproof dish.

Heat 1 tablespoon of oil in a pan and fry the onions until golden. Add the minced meat and fry for 10 minutes until all the liquid has evaporated. Add the garlic, tomatoes, sugar and oregano or thyme and simmer for 10 minutes. Finally add 3 tablespoons of the parsley, salt and freshly ground pepper and mix well. Leave to cool.

Preheat the oven to 180°C/350°F/gas mark 4.

Open each slit in the aubergines gently and fill with as much of the stuffing as possible, using a small spoon. Put any excess stuffing on the bottom of the dish and arrange the aubergines on top. Pour the rest of the olive oil on top of each aubergine, a little water if you feel they are too dry and a sprinkling of salt. Bake in the oven for 45–60 minutes, basting once or twice during cooking. Garnish with the remaining parsley and the black olives and serve at room temperature.

Variations

1. Quite often the minced meat is omitted to make this a vegetarian dish. The aubergines are then equally delicious when eaten cold.

2. Before you put the dish into the oven, sprinkle the aubergines with 100 g (4 oz) chopped feta cheese and omit the salt. The cheese will melt and mix with the sauce.

3. The dish can also be cooked in a flameproof casserole on top of the oven and is just as delicious. Place the stuffed

aubergines in a wide casserole, add half the amount of olive oil and 250 ml (8 fl oz) of water and simmer over a low heat for about 1 hour.

4. The sugar is added only to reduce the acidity of the tomatoes. If you find this dish too rich you may omit the sugar or even add a little lemon juice.

Pastitsio

MACARONI AND MEAT PIE

SERVES
6–8

A pie of Italian origin – probably pasticcio di maccheroni *– but with Greek ingredients and method of preparation, producing a dish with superior flavour and texture.*

To prepare the meat sauce, heat the oil in a deep pan and fry the onion and garlic for 2–3 minutes. Add the minced meat and cook for another 5 minutes, breaking up any lumps. Add the tomatoes, tomato purée, sugar, parsley, salt and pepper and cook over low a heat for about 15 minutes until the meat is tender. If it gets too dry, cover the pan and continue cooking.

To prepare the cream sauce, melt the butter in a heavy-based pan until it begins to foam. Remove from the heat and stir in the flour. Beat with a wooden spoon until the butter and flour are well combined. Add a little warm milk and stir to a smooth paste. Place the pan over low heat and add the rest of the milk, stirring continuously, until it is amalgamated and the sauce is smooth. Add the seasoning and nutmeg and cook the sauce on a very gentle heat for 10 minutes, stirring continuously. Remove from the heat. Whisk the eggs until frothy, then stir into the sauce with the cheese.

Cook the macaroni for about 5–7 minutes in plenty of boiling, slightly salted water until just cooked but still with a slight bite, *al dente*. Drain and rinse in cold water. Pour over the melted butter. Add 150 ml (¼ pint) of the cream sauce, season with salt and pepper, and toss well.

Preheat the oven to 180°C/350°F/gas mark 4.

Butter a deep flameproof dish well and sprinkle the breadcrumbs on the bottom of the dish. Spread half of the macaroni in the dish followed by all the meat sauce. Spread

450 g (1 lb) thick tubular macaroni

25 g (1 oz) unsalted butter, melted

Salt and freshly ground pepper

2 tablespoons breadcrumbs

100 g (4 oz) *kefalotiri*, Parmesan or *halloumi* cheese, grated

For the meat sauce

1 tablespoon olive oil

1 onion, finely chopped

3 garlic cloves, chopped

700 g (1½ lb) lean minced beef or lamb

900 g (2 lb) ripe tomatoes or 2 x 400 g (14 oz) cans of chopped tomatoes with the liquid

2 tablespoons tomato purée

½ teaspoon sugar

3 tablespoons chopped fresh parsley

Salt and freshly ground pepper

For the cream sauce

50 g (2 oz) unsalted butter

3 tablespoons plain flour

600 ml (1 pint) warm milk

½ teaspoon salt

Freshly ground white pepper

A pinch of grated nutmeg

3 eggs

50 g (2 oz) cheese, grated

the rest of the macaroni on top and then cover with the cream sauce. Level the top with a palette knife and sprinkle with grated cheese. Bake in the oven for 45–60 minutes until the top is nicely browned. Remove from the oven and let it rest for 10 minutes. Cut into squares and serve hot with a Greek salad and cold retsina wine.

Sfougato

COURGETTE AND MINCED MEAT PIE

SERVES

4

3–4 tablespoons olive oil or butter

1 bunch of spring onions, finely chopped

450 g (1 lb) minced beef or lamb

Juice of ½ lemon

900 g (2 lb) small courgettes, peeled and sliced into thin rounds

2 tablespoons chopped fresh parsley

2 tablespoons chopped fresh dill

6 eggs

2–3 tablespoons Gruyère, Parmesan or hard Cheddar cheese, grated

Salt and freshly ground pepper

4 tablespoons toasted breadcrumbs

1 teaspoon dried oregano

2 tablespoons chopped fresh parsley

A few olives

Basically, this is a country pie that is often prepared for picnics. It is made with minced beef or lamb, summer vegetables, eggs and cheese. Popular vegetables to use are courgettes and spinach, but potatoes, aubergines, peppers, leeks and onions are frequently included. Another type of sfougato *that is popular, particularly in Corfu, uses only vegetables.*

Heat the oil or butter and sauté the onions until they begin to soften. Add the minced meat and fry it until it begins to brown. Add the lemon juice, salt and pepper, cover, lower the heat and simmer for 30 minutes until all the water has evaporated.

Add the courgettes, parsley and dill with 2–3 tablespoons of water and continue to simmer for another 15–20 minutes until the courgettes begin to soften but are not completely cooked. Remove from the heat and set aside to cool.

Preheat the oven to 180°C/350°F/gas mark 4.

Mix the eggs, cheese and pepper and whisk until quite fluffy. Fold the egg mixture into the courgettes. Oil a baking dish and sprinkle some breadcrumbs and oregano on the bottom of the dish. Pour the meat and vegetable mixture into the dish and sprinkle some more breadcrumbs on top. Bake in the oven for about 30 minutes until the eggs are lightly set and the top browned. Garnish with chopped parsley and olives and serve hot or cold.

Kreas Kokinisto
MEAT RAGOUT

Kokinisto is the method of braising meat involving long and slow cooking in a red, sweet and slightly sour sauce of tomatoes, vinegar and herbs. Traditionally, less tender cuts of meat are used for this dish: middle neck, shoulder cuts, shanks of lamb or topside, silverside, flank steak and chuck of beef are ideal. There is no need to remove the bone. Kokinisto meat is always served separately with a variety of vegetables which are normally cooked in the meat sauce. Popular vegetables are okra, courgettes, green beans, peas or aubergines.

Cut the meat into serving portions and remove any excess fat.

Heat the oil in a flameproof casserole, add the onion and garlic and fry until soft and translucent. Add the meat pieces and brown well, stirring continuously. Next, add the wine or wine vinegar and bring to the boil. Lower the heat and add the remaining ingredients. Bring to the boil, cover and simmer over a low heat for 1 hour if using lamb or 1½ hours for beef until the meat is quite tender, stirring occasionally. Add a little water if the sauce thickens too much.

1.5 kg (3 lb) lamb or beef, as suggested

2 tablespoons olive oil

1 onion, chopped

2 garlic cloves, sliced

2 tablespoons red wine or balsamic vinegar

900 g (2 lb) tomatoes, skinned and chopped, or 2 x 400 g (14 oz) cans of chopped tomatoes

150 ml (¼ pint) water

2 tablespoons tomato purée

2 bay leaves

½ teaspoon chilli powder or chilli sauce

1 teaspoon dried oregano or thyme

Salt and freshly ground pepper

Arni Kokinisto me Bamies
LAMB RAGOUT WITH OKRA

Okra is an exotic vegetable with a distinctive taste, which is available only in the summer in Greece. Use 450 g (1 lb) of fresh okra and discard any old, brown pods. Wash them well and peel carefully around the top, so that the juices inside do not escape. Do not slice them or cut off the tips. Place in a glass bowl, sprinkle with a little wine vinegar and leave to stand for 1 hour.

Meanwhile, cook the lamb *kokinisto* as described above. Transfer the meat pieces into a serving dish and keep warm. Wash the okra well and add them to the meat sauce in the casserole. Add a little water and cook over low heat for 20–30 minutes until the okra is soft and the sauce has thickened. Avoid stirring the okra often during cooking as this may bruise the pods and make the sauce gluey. Place the okra and the sauce around the meat, sprinkle with chopped fresh parsley and serve warm.

Vodino Kokinisto me Kolokithakia
BEEF RAGOUT WITH COURGETTES

This is a delicious dish from the Peloponnese. Select 900 g (2 lb) small courgettes, about 15 cm (6 in) in length. Cut off the tips but do not peel. Fry them lightly in a little olive oil for 2–3 minutes until brown.

Cook the beef *kokinisto* as described on page 95. Remove the meat, place on a serving plate and keep warm.

Place the courgettes in the casserole and coat them with the meat sauce. Add a little water, if required, and simmer for 10–15 minutes. Place the courgettes and sauce around the meat, sprinkle with chopped fresh dill and serve warm.

Arni Kokinisto me Fasoulakia
LAMB RAGOUT WITH GREEN BEANS

String about 900 g (2 lb) of French beans (preferably snap beans). Cut the long ones in half and wash them in cold water.

Cook the lamb *kokinisto* as described on page 95. Remove the meat pieces, place in a serving dish and keep warm. Add the beans to the meat sauce and cook for 10–15 minutes, depending on the size and type, until they are tender but still a little crisp. The beans will get a little darker and be coated with the sauce. Serve the meat on a bed of beans with the sauce.

Arni Kokinisto me Lahanika
LAMB RAGOUT WITH VEGETABLES

In a similar way, lamb can be combined with seasonal vegetables such as cauliflower, endive and spinach. Lamb and aubergines also make an excellent combination. The cooking time will depend on the type of vegetable and its tenderness.

Sofrito
CORFU-STYLE BRAISED STEAK

SERVES
4

An outstanding and highly aromatic dish from the beautiful island of Corfu, with slices of tender steak braised in generous amounts of mountain herbs, garlic and brandy. It is a recipe in which measurements need not be precise.

900 g (2 lb) fillet of beef or escalope of veal, cut into 2 cm (¾ in) thick slices

Salt and freshly ground pepper

2 tablespoons plain flour

5 tablespoons olive oil

5 garlic cloves, finely chopped

2 tablespoons red wine vinegar

4 tablespoons brandy

1 teaspoon ouzo

A pinch of fresh mint

150 ml (¼ pint) water or meat stock

2–3 tablespoons chopped fresh parsley

Trim the meat of any fat and sinews. Beat lightly with a wooden mallet, then rub well with salt and pepper and coat lightly with flour. Heat a little oil in a heavy-based pan and fry until both sides are well browned. Add the garlic and a little more salt and fry for about 1 minute until the garlic begins to change colour. Add the wine vinegar, brandy, ouzo, mint, water or meat stock, salt and pepper. Bring to the boil, then reduce the heat to the minimum, cover and simmer for about 1 hour until the meat is tender and the sauce has thickened. The dish should have a piquant smell of spirits and garlic. Add the parsley and serve very hot with chips or mashed potatoes. A green salad with plenty of olives and feta cheese is a perfect accompaniment.

Variations

1. Although in this recipe the meat is cooked in the vinegar, it is not unusual to add the wine vinegar at the end of cooking time; this strengthens the sauce.
2. Ideally, cheaper meat cuts should not be used in this dish. However, if you use chuck or stewing steak, cook it in a sealed casserole until the meat is soft.

SERVES

8

1.5 kg (3 lb) boneless meat such as
stewing beef

2 tablespoons plain flour

Salt and freshly ground pepper

2 tablespoons olive oil or 50 g (2 oz)
unsalted butter

150 ml (¼ pint) dry white wine

1 large onion, finely chopped

1 garlic clove, thinly sliced

900 g (2 lb) ripe tomatoes, skinned
and chopped, or 2 x 400 g (14 oz)
cans of chopped tomatoes

1 tablespoon tomato purée

½ teaspoon ground cinnamon

1 teaspoon sugar

A sprig of fresh thyme

1–2 tablespoons chopped fresh parsley

Kapamas

MEAT CASSEROLE WITH TOMATOES AND SPICES

This is the basic recipe for stewing any meat in a rich tomato sauce. It is a highly adaptable recipe for cooking beef, lamb, veal, meatballs and chicken. Seasonal vegetables may be added to produce a rich and aromatic dish, which is a very popular choice for busy housewives.

Trim the meat of most of the fat and cut into about six chunks. Coat with flour, shaking off any excess, and sprinkle with salt and pepper.

Heat half the oil or butter in a pan and fry the meat until well browned. Transfer the meat from the pan to a flameproof casserole, barely cover with water or stock, bring to the boil and simmer until the meat is partly cooked and the water or stock has almost evaporated. Set the heat high and pour the wine over the meat. Cook for a minute and remove from the heat.

Heat the remaining oil or butter and fry the onion and garlic for 1–2 minutes. Add the tomatoes, tomato purée, cinnamon, sugar, thyme and parsley and bring to the boil. Pour the tomato sauce into the casserole with the meat, cover and simmer gently for about 1 hour until the meat is tender. Season with salt and pepper and serve hot.

Kapama Smyrnis

SWEET MEAT CASSEROLE FROM SMYRNA

Prepare the *kapama* as in the basic recipe above but without adding any sugar. Before serving, stir in 1–2 tablespoons of sugar.

Kapama Kyprou
MEAT CASSEROLE WITH AROMATIC VEGETABLES FROM CYPRUS

———

Brown the meat and cook until partly tender, as above. Finely chop a carrot, a celery stick, a small leek, an onion and plenty of parsley and add to the tomatoes. Continue cooking as before. Serve with roast potatoes.

Kapama Makedonias
MEAT CASSEROLE WITH PRUNES FROM MACEDONIA

———

Prunes are often added to meat and game dishes. There is no need to pre-soak the prunes in this dish. The stones can easily be removed when the prunes are soft. Prepare the *kapama* as in the basic recipe. Remove the meat pieces, place 900 g (2 lb) of prunes on the bottom of the casserole, then place the meat on top of the prunes. Add a little water and cook for 10–15 minutes.

Kapama me Lahanika
MEAT CASSEROLE WITH SUMMER VEGETABLES

———

Courgettes and aubergines are ideal for this dish. Cut the courgettes in half, the aubergines into 2 cm (1 in) squares. Fifteen minutes before the end of the cooking time, place the vegetables on top of the meat in the casserole and coat with the tomato sauce. Replace the lid and continue cooking until the meat and vegetables are tender.

Afelia
SAUTÉED PORK WITH CORIANDER

———

1 kg (2¼ lb) pork fillet, cut into 1 cm (½ in) slices

4 tablespoons olive oil

3 tablespoons strained Greek yoghurt

2 tablespoons chopped fresh parsley

For the marinade

90 ml (3 fl oz) olive oil

300 ml (½ pint) dry cider

1 tablespoon coriander seeds, lightly crushed

2 tablespoons lemon juice

10 black peppercorns, crushed

Salt and freshly ground pepper

A coriander marinade is used to improve the blandness of pork. This dish comes from Cyprus where the methods used to breed pigs produce exceptionally tender pork. It is usually served with a pilaf made from bulghar – a form of cracked wheat.

Combine all the marinade ingredients in a glass bowl and mix well. Coat the meat thoroughly with the marinade, place in the fridge and leave overnight.

Remove the meat slices and dry using a kitchen cloth. Reserve the marinade. Heat the oil in a large pan and fry the meat slices on both sides until they begin to brown. Strain the marinade through a fine sieve and pour over the meat. Bring to the boil, lower the heat and simmer gently for 30 minutes until the meat is tender. Place the meat in a warm serving dish, leaving the sauce in the pan.

Add the yoghurt to the sauce and cook over a low heat for 1 minute until the sauce is smooth. Season to taste with salt and pepper. Pour the sauce over the meat, garnish with parsley and pepper and serve with bulghar pilaf, rice pilaf or boiled potatoes.

Pligouri Pilafi
BULGHAR PILAF

———

If you wish to serve this delicious pilaf, melt 75 g (3 oz) of butter and fry a finely chopped onion until pale brown. Add 225 g (8 oz) of bulghar and cook on very low heat for 15 minutes, stirring often. Add enough hot chicken stock to cover the bulghar, bring to the boil, cover and simmer over a low heat for 10–15 minutes until the stock has been absorbed and the bulghar is tender.

Vodino Stifado
BEEF STEW WITH SMALL ONIONS AND ROSEMARY

SERVES
6–8

The secret of this beef stew lies in the combination of aromatic herbs, the slow cooking of the meat and the sweetness of tender small onions. Hare and onion stew (Lagos Stifado, see page 123) and octopus stew (Htapodi Stifado, see page 141) are two other variations.

1.5 kg (3 lb) stewing steak
150 ml (¼ pint) olive oil
1 large onion, finely chopped
1.5 kg (3 lb) pickling onions
 or shallots
4–5 garlic cloves
2 tablespoons white wine vinegar
90 ml (3 fl oz) red wine
2 tablespoons tomato purée
1 sprig of fresh rosemary
½ teaspoon sugar
2 bay leaves
Salt and freshly ground pepper

Cut the meat into serving portions of about 7.5 cm (3 in). Heat half the oil and fry the meat and onion until the meat is well browned. Do not season with salt at this stage. Transfer the contents of the pan to a casserole dish and add the garlic, wine vinegar, wine, tomato purée, rosemary, sugar, bay leaves, salt and pepper. Add enough hot water to cover the meat, then cover and simmer over a low heat for about 1½ hours or until the meat is tender.

Meanwhile, pour boiling water over the pickling onions and leave them to soak for 15 minutes. Drain and peel them and nick a cross in the base of each onion to prevent them from popping out as they cook. Heat the remaining oil and fry the onions gently until golden, then remove with a spotted spoon and add to the meat. Cover and cook over a low heat for about 30–45 minutes, or longer if necessary, without stirring. Do not add extra water. Serve with roast potatoes or saffron rice and a strong red wine.

Variations
1. The rosemary sprigs and bay leaves may be tied with a string and then removed when the dish is served.
2. Instead of frying the onions, boil them in salted water for 2 minutes before adding them to the meat. This makes them sweeter.
3. Cinnamon, ground or whole sticks, is a wonderful spice to add to this beef stew. Add a stick of cinnamon to the meat with the onions and remove it before serving.

Hirino Kidonato

PORK WITH QUINCES

SERVES

6

900 g (2 lb) quinces

Juice of ½ lemon

3 tablespoons olive oil

900 g (2 lb) stewing pork, cleaned and
cut into cubes

1 large onion, chopped

150 ml (¼ pint) dry red wine

Grated rind of ½ orange

2.5 cm (1 in) cinnamon stick

Salt and freshly ground pepper

1 teaspoon sugar or honey

2 tablespoons chopped fresh parsley

Quinces are available in some shops in late autumn, although they are not common. If you can buy them, do not fail to cook this unusual and exquisite dish. Quince trees resemble pear trees and their fruits resemble large, misshapen pears with a fine yellowish fuzz. The fruit is ripe when it is yellow and strongly perfumed. It is ready in late autumn and makes an excellent jam for the winter. It has a sharp taste which complements well the sweet and fatty taste of pork. Quinces from Crete are probably the best in Greece. Lamb or even mutton is an equally good substitute for pork. The main characteristic of this dish is its sweetness so, depending on the ripeness of the quince, you may need to adjust the amount of sugar used.

Peel, core and slice the quinces, then place them immediately into a bowl of water with the lemon juice to prevent discolouration.

Heat the oil in a pan and fry the pork cubes on all sides, then remove from the pan using a slotted spoon. Fry the onion in the pan until soft but not browned. Return the pork cubes to the pan and add the wine and enough hot water to cover the meat. Add the orange rind and cinnamon stick and season with salt and pepper. Bring to the boil then lower the heat and simmer for about 1 hour until the meat is tender. Remove the cinnamon stick and add the sugar and drained quince slices. Add a little more water if necessary, and simmer for another 30 minutes until the fruit is tender. Garnish with chopped parsley and serve.

Hirino me Prassa

PORK STEW WITH LEEKS

SERVES

6

1.5 kg (3 lb) lean pork, most of the
fat removed

Salt and freshly ground pepper

4 tablespoons olive oil

Late winter is the time for slaughtering well-fed pigs in the countryside, and also signals the arrival of leeks in the market. The combination of lean pork and leeks produces one of the most traditional and delicate dishes.

Cut the pork into 6–8 serving portions and season with a little salt and pepper. Heat the oil in a deep flameproof casserole and fry the onions and garlic until soft but not browned. Add the meat and sauté until it turns light golden. Add the wine and the tomato purée diluted in a little water and bring to the boil. Cover the casserole, lower the heat and simmer for about 1 hour, adding a little water occasionally to prevent the meat from drying out.

Wash the leeks well and cut the white parts only into 7.5 cm (3 in) pieces. Blanch them in boiling water for 1 minute, then drain. Add the leeks to the casserole and continue simmering until they are soft and the sauce is reduced. Season to taste with salt and pepper and serve hot.

2 onions, finely chopped
1 garlic clove, crushed
150 ml (¼ pint) dry red wine
2 tablespoons tomato purée
900 g (2 lb) leeks

Hirino me Selino
PORK WITH CELERIAC

Greek celery (*selino*) is smaller, tougher, slightly more bitter and requires longer cooking than its foreign counterpart. If you use celeriac, peel it first, like a potato, and cut into cubes. Add 1 head of celeriac cubes to the casserole when the meat has been simmering for about 30 minutes. If you use ordinary celery, use the head, stalks and leaves and chop them all roughly. Add about 900 g (2 lb) of celery to the casserole 45 minutes after the meat has begun to simmer. In either case, you may need to add a little more water to cover the vegetables.

Hirino me Kolokasi Kyprou
PORK WITH SWEET POTATOES FROM CYPRUS

Kolokasi is a root vegetable that looks and tastes like a Jerusalem artichoke. It is available from Cypriot shops. Peel the *kolokasi* and cut or break it up into pieces. Do not wash it, as it tends to go slimy. You may wipe it with a towel or sprinkle it with lemon juice. Put the pieces into the casserole at the same time as the meat. *Kolokasi* potatoes can also be added to pork with celeriac (*Hirino me Selino*, see page 103).

Hirono me Prasa Avgolemono
PORK WITH LEEKS OR CELERY AND EGG AND LEMON SAUCE

In most recipes with pork it is customary to give a lemony tang to the dish to balance the sweetness of the pork and vegetables by adding fresh lemon juice or an egg and lemon sauce. In this case, omit the tomato purée from the recipe. When the meat is cooked, remove it from the heat, beat 3 eggs and the juice of 1 lemon in a bowl and pour the mixture slowly over the meat and leeks or celery. Shake the casserole to distribute the sauce evenly and leave to stand for 5 minutes for the sauce to thicken.

Katsikaki Kritiko
KID CRETAN-STYLE

SERVES
6

1–1.5 kg (2–3 lb) leg or loin of kid
4–6 garlic cloves, finely chopped
150 ml (¼ pint) brandy
150 ml (¼ pint) lemon and orange juice
1 teaspoon dried oregano
Salt and freshly ground pepper
150 ml (¼ pint) olive oil

The taste of kid or young goat is totally unknown to most English palates, and yet goats provide meat and milk that are enjoyed by many races and cultures: in Spain, Italy, the Arab countries, the Balkans and as far as Texas and Mexico.

In Crete, young goat or kid is often preferred to lamb and is considered to be a delicacy. It competes with lamb at Easter when they are both at their best. The traditional method of cooking kid is to marinate the whole kid and then roast it slowly on an open grill for many hours. This recipe comes from Crete, where kid is marinated in strong fruit juice mixed with mountain herbs. Kid is sometimes obtainable in Italian and continental shops. Lamb can also be cooked in the same way.

Remove any fat, gristle and tendons from the kid and cut into 4–6 pieces, or ask the butcher to do this for you. Mix the garlic, brandy, juices, oregano, salt and pepper in a glass bowl and coat the meat well with this marinade. Cover the bowl and let the meat marinate for at least 24 hours.

Preheat the oven to 220°C/425°F/gas mark 7.

Remove the meat pieces from the marinade and put them in a baking tin. Bring the marinade to the boil in a pan and simmer for 10 minutes. Strain and set aside.

Sprinkle the meat with the oil and pour half of the marinade over the meat. Roast in the oven for 30 minutes. Lower the oven temperature to 160°C/320°F/gas mark 3 and continue cooking for 1½–2 hours, basting frequently until the meat is tender and almost falls off the bone. Add a little hot water during cooking as necessary to ensure that the meat does not dry out. Arrange the meat on a warm platter and spoon over some of the sauce. Serve with noodles or roast potatoes and a green salad.

Kokoretsi
SPICED LAMBS' OFFAL GRILLED ON A SPIT

SERVES

8

Red eggs, Easter soup (Mayiritsa, see page 45) roast lamb (see Arni Bouti sto Fourno, page 82), Kokoretsi and a sweet plaited Easter bread (Tsoureki, see page 186) are all you need for a perfect Easter celebration. Kokoretsi consists of the marinated offal of the paschal lamb, which are made into a long sausage and then grilled at the same time and in the same barbecue as the lamb itself. It is a spicy and salty meze and goes well with ouzo and beer. I must confess that I have a weakness for kokoretsi and would go to any length to visit a restaurant reputed for its kokoretsi. Sadly, I am all too often offered an inferior preparation. I like a kokoretsi to be fragrant with oregano and spices, succulent despite its long grilling and moist with lemon juice.

Remove the fat from the kidneys, peel off the skin and remove the core with a knife or scissors. Remove the skin and pipes from the liver. Cut away the thick muscular arteries and veins from the hearts. Remove any membrane from, but do not break up, the sweetbreads. Wash all the meats well and soak in salted water for 1 hour. Drain and clean thoroughly. Cut them into walnut-sized pieces.

225 g (8 oz) lamb kidneys

225 g (8 oz) lamb liver

2 small lamb hearts

225 g (8 oz) lamb sweetbreads

700 g (1 lb 8 oz) lamb or pig long intestines

1 tablespoon dried oregano

Juice of 2 lemons

2 teaspoons paprika

½ teaspoon ground cumin

4 tablespoons olive oil

2 garlic cloves, crushed

2 bay leaves

2–3 teaspoons sea salt

For the garnish

Cos lettuce leaves

A few radishes

Chopped spring onions

Lemon wedges

In a glass bowl, combine the oregano, lemon juice, paprika, cumin, olive oil, garlic, bay leaves and salt, add the meats and marinate for 1 hour. Discard the garlic and bay leaves and keep the marinade. Thread the meats on to a long spit, alternating the liver, kidneys, hearts and sweetbread pieces.

Wash the intestines well. Turn them inside out using a knitting needle or a thin stick and scrub well with salt, vinegar or wine, then rinse well in water.

Brush the pieces on the spit generously with the marinade, then thread the intestines twice around the meats into a long sausage. Knot the end of the intestines at both ends. Again brush generously with the marinade.

Prepare a medium-hot charcoal and place the spit well above the heat. If the *kokoretsi* is about 5–10 cm (2–4 in) thick you will have to grill it for 2–3 hours. If it is thicker than this, grill for 3–4 hours. While grilling, rotate the spit and lower its position gradually closer to the fire. A rotisserie is ideal for this operation. Baste occasionally with the marinade or with a mixture of oil and lemon juice. The final *kokoretsi* should be well cooked inside and browned on all sides. When done, place a few cos lettuce leaves, a few radishes and finely chopped spring onions on a platter. Slip the *kokoretsi* off the spit on to the platter, cut into slices and serve with plenty of lemon wedges.

Spetsofai
SAUSAGE AND PEPPER CASEROLE FROM PELION

SERVES

4

1–2 tablespoons olive oil

900 g (2 lb) spicy pork sausages such as Spanish chorizo or Italian pork sausages, cut into thick pieces

2 large red peppers, seeded and cut into strips

2 large green peppers, seeded and cut into strips

2 ripe tomatoes, finely chopped, or 1 x 200 g (7oz) can of chopped tomatoes

1 onion, finely chopped

The Pelion mountain is renowned for its natural beauty, its chestnut and olive groves, rushing mountain streams and 24 attractive villages dotted on its slopes. It is east of Volos, the port and market centre of Thessaly. From there, you have the most panoramic view of the provinces of Euboea and the mounts of Ossa and Olympus. Across the sea lies the island of Skiathos, one of the islands of North Sporades.

*The region makes an excellent red wine (*kokkineli*) which can only be consumed locally, as it does not 'travel' well – but nobody complains of that. Separated by a great cavern known* *as the Cave of Chiron is the colourful village of Makrinitsa, from where this dish originates. Its main ingredient is a local pork sausage that is usually made after Christmas. It is laced with red peppers, sliced leeks, orange peel, onions, thyme, oregano and tarragon, and is served as a* meze *grilled or cooked with vegetables.*

3–4 tablespoons red wine
A pinch of sugar
Salt and freshly ground pepper

Heat the oil in a large pan and sauté the sausage pieces and peppers over high heat for about 3–4 minutes until they begin to brown. Remove some of the fat from the pan. Add the tomatoes, onion, wine, sugar, salt and pepper, cover and cook over a moderate heat for 15–20 minutes until the sausages are cooked, adding a little water if the tomato juices are not enough. Serve on a warm platter with plenty of pepper.

Variations

You would find traditional country sausages (*loukanika*) in most villages. The most famous ones suitable for this dish are pork sausages with leeks and oranges from Macedonia, pork and beef sausages with oregano and mint from the Peloponnese and dried black sausages with chilli peppers from Thrace.

Pilioritiko Boubari
SPICY SAUSAGE FROM PELION

———

SERVES
4

A traditional spicy sausage from the beautiful region of Mount Pelion, it is stuffed with chopped lambs' liver and parts of a young lamb such as sweetbreads, spleen and heart. In this recipe, the sausage is served with roast potatoes but it can also be cooked with other vegetables.

225 g (8 oz) minced lean beef
900 g (2 lb) potatoes, peeled and quartered
4 tablespoons oil
Salt and freshly ground pepper
150 ml (¼ pint) water
225 g (8 oz) pork sausage casing

For the stuffing
450 g (1 lb) mixed lambs' liver, sweetbreads and heart
4 tablespoons olive oil
225 g (8 oz) lean minced beef

To make the stuffing, blanch the liver, sweetbreads and heart in boiling water for 1 minute, strain and then clean and chop finely. Heat the oil in a large pan and sauté the onions until translucent. Add the chopped lamb and minced beef and sauté over a low heat for a few minutes. Add the tomatoes and cook for 1–2 minutes, then remove the pan from the heat. Empty the contents of the pan in a bowl and add the dill, rice, salt and

2 onions, finely chopped

1 x 400 g (14 oz) can of chopped
tomatoes, drained

2 tablespoons chopped fresh dill

50 g (2 oz) medium-grain rice

Salt and freshly ground pepper

pepper. Mix well and set aside to cool.

Preheat the oven to 180°C/350°F/gas mark 4.

Clean the sausage casing well. Turn it inside out, scrub well with vinegar and salt, then rinse it well. Place the casing on an electric mincer or fill the casing with the meat mixture by hand, allowing room for swelling. Pierce the sausage with a fork in several places so that the steam can escape whilst cooking and coil it loosely in a spiral on a round ovenproof dish.

Add the potatoes and sprinkle with salt, pepper and the rest of the oil. Pour in the water, cover the dish with foil and bake in the oven for about 30 minutes, then remove the foil and bake for a further hour.

Poulerika ke Kinigi

POULTRY AND GAME

Most tourists to Greece would probably remember two dishes that are frequently served in restaurants: plain roast chicken and chicken cooked in a tomato stew. But the range is far greater than that.

Chicken is eaten all the year round: it is roasted on the spit, stuffed and baked in the oven or casseroled and served with most unusual sauces and vegetables. Chicken pies containing a mixture of cheeses and herbs make a delightful *meze*. Chicken cooked with fresh vegetables, peppers, aubergines or okra is more of a summer fare, whereas chicken stews, ragouts of all sorts and casseroles are the fare of winter. Stuffing chicken or turkey with chestnuts, walnuts, pine nuts and raisins is part of a long tradition, particularly in the Greek islands. This section contains some of these dishes which are prepared throughout Greece.

During the early autumn, flocks of birds pass over Greece from northern Europe on their way to Africa in search of the sun. The hunters' season starts early in September and finishes in November. Birds like French woodcock (*bekatsa*), wild duck (*agriopapia*), pheasant (*fassianos*), partridge (*perdikia*), quail (*ortikia*), thrush (*tsikles*) and wild pigeon (*agrioperistera*) cover the skies in great numbers, particularly in the rural areas in the north, the Macedonian lakes and the plains of Thessaly. The Peloponnesean mountains are also well known for their plentiful game. In the northern regions, small game such as hare (*lagos*) and partridge abound, whereas in the villages of the mountainous areas and east of Tripolis, one can sample specialities of roasted wild she-goat (*giosa*) and kid.

Greeks consider game – especially wild duck and wild boar – plainly roasted with fragrant mountain herbs, cloves, juniper berries, a dish fit for the gods; they are proud to present such a dish to any guest who visits them during the cold months. The spicy game *stifado*, which is painstakingly cooked with loads of sweet onions, is also a popular country dish and a favourite at large family gatherings and village festivals. Pot-roasting hare, rabbit (*kouneli*) or the rare venison (*elafi*) for many hours in wine, aromatic herbs and root veget-

If I must break my fasting, at least let me eat a bird – preferably a turtle-dove.

———

Greek proverb

109

ables produces a rich and sumptuous dish.

There are infinite variations to these dishes from one region and tradition to another, which you can appreciate only by travelling around the country. As cooking in Greece is never an exact science, these dishes represent quite a test of skill and taste to a cook with an adventurous spirit.

Kotopoulo Krasato

CHICKEN IN WINE SAUCE

SERVES

4

1.5–1.75 kg (3–4 lb) chicken
or pieces

2 tablespoons plain flour

3–4 tablespoons olive oil

1 large onion, finely chopped

500 ml (17 fl oz) red wine

3 tablespoons tomato purée

1 garlic clove, crushed

300 ml (½ pint) chicken stock

½ teaspoon sugar

1 teaspoon dried oregano or thyme

1 bay leaf

Salt and freshly ground pepper

2 tablespoons chopped fresh parsley

This is one of the most exquisite stews for chicken, as well as duck, hare, venison or wild boar. It benefits from slow cooking: 1 hour for poultry, 2 hours for duck and 3–4 hours for game is not excessive. In some parts of Greece, cooks add aromatic spices such as cinnamon, cloves and allspice – and the whole neighbourhood then enjoys the aroma of this dish!

Trim the chicken of any fat, the wing and leg tips and excessive skin. Cut into about eight pieces (two legs, two thighs, two wings and two breasts) using a boning knife and poultry shears. Pour boiling water over the chicken and then dry well. Coat the pieces lightly with flour. Heat the oil in a deep, heavy-based frying pan and fry the pieces for about 10 minutes until they are browned on all sides. Remove the chicken, add the onion and sauté until it is soft and translucent. Return the chicken pieces to the pan, raise the heat and add the wine. Boil the wine for about 5 minutes until it is reduced to half its quantity. Lower the heat and add the tomato purée, garlic, stock, sugar, oregano or thyme, bay leaf, salt and pepper. Give it a stir so that the purée is well diluted, cover and simmer over a low heat for 30–45 minutes until the chicken is tender and the sauce slightly reduced. Transfer the chicken pieces to a warm serving dish. Strain the sauce through a fine sieve and discard the herbs. If the sauce is not thick enough, add a knob of butter and whisk gently. Pour over the chicken and sprinkle with chopped parsley. Serve with a plate of fried aubergine slices or peppers in the summer, and rice or pasta in the winter.

Kotopoulo me Spanaki ke Feta

CHICKEN WITH SPINACH AND FETA CHEESE

SERVES

4

The combination of spinach and feta cheese has been the theme of many delicious dishes. Here they are used as a stuffing for chicken breasts.

To make the stuffing, place the spinach in a pan with a pinch of salt and sauté for 2–3 minutes until the water has evaporated and the spinach wilted. Let it cool and then chop it finely. Heat the oil and fry the onion until golden brown. Add to the spinach, with the feta cheese and a little salt and pepper, and mix well.

Make a cut into the side of each chicken breast to form a pocket and fill with the mixture. Secure with cocktail sticks. Heat 2 tablespoons of oil in a pan and fry the stuffed breasts on both sides until browned. Add the stock and wine, bring to the boil, lower the heat and simmer gently for 15 minutes. Transfer the chicken to a hot serving dish and reserve the wine mixture.

Melt the butter in a pan and combine well with the flour. Add the wine mixture, the yoghurt, dill and parsley and bring to the boil. Lower the heat and cook for 2–3 minutes until the sauce begins to thicken. Season with salt and pepper. Pour the sauce over the breasts, remove the cocktail sticks and serve with a green salad and chilled retsina wine.

4 large chicken breasts, skinned

2 tablespoons olive oil

150 ml (¼ pint) chicken stock

150 ml (¼ pint) dry white wine

25 g (1 oz) unsalted butter

1 tablespoon plain flour

3 tablespoons strained Greek yoghurt

2 tablespoons chopped fresh dill and parsley

Salt and freshly ground white pepper

For the stuffing

450 g (1 lb) spinach, stalks removed, washed and drained

1 tablespoon olive oil

1 small onion, finely chopped

100 g (4 oz) feta cheese, washed well

Salt and freshly ground pepper

Kotopoulo me Bamies

CHICKEN WITH OKRA

SERVES

4

Bamies, *ladies fingers, okra and gumbo are all names of the same vegetable. Select okra that are bright green, small and in season. If you intend to keep them for a day or two, sprinkle them with lemon juice or vinegar. Rinse them well before using them.*

Wash the okra well. Peel carefully with a sharp knife around the top so that the juices inside do not escape. Do not cut off the tips or slice them. Place in a glass bowl and sprinkle over

450 g (1 lb) okra

1 tablespoon white wine vinegar

Salt and freshly ground pepper

1.5–1.75 kg (3–4 lb) chicken

600 ml (1 pint) chicken stock

450 g (1 lb) tomatoes, skinned and chopped

1 tablespoon tomato purée

150 ml (¼ pint) red wine
½ teaspoon sugar
1 tablespoon chopped fresh rosemary
1 tablespoon chopped fresh parsley

the wine vinegar. Season and set aside for 2–3 hours.

Clean the chicken. Cut off the ends of wings and legs and the skin of the neck. Place the whole chicken in a deep flame-proof casserole. Pour in the chicken stock to cover the bird and simmer for 30–45 minutes until it is cooked but still quite firm.

Wash the okra well and add them to the casserole with the tomatoes, tomato purée, wine, sugar and rosemary. Cook gently for about 20–30 minutes until the okra are soft and the sauce has thickened. Transfer the chicken carefully to a serving dish. Place the okra and some of the sauce around the chicken. Sprinkle with chopped parsley and serve with rice or roast potatoes.

Kotopoulo Lemonato
CHICKEN IN LEMON SAUCE

SERVES
4

1.5–1.75 kg (3–4 lb) chicken
2 lemons
3–4 tablespoons olive oil
Finely chopped rind of 1 lemon
½ teaspoon dried oregano or thyme
600 ml (1 pint) chicken stock
Salt and freshly ground pepper
3 eggs
1 tablespoon chopped fresh dill

A very simple dish, full of lemon, delicate and invigorating.

Cut the chicken into about eight pieces (two legs, two thighs, two wings and two breasts) using a boning knife and poultry shears. Rub the pieces with the juice of a lemon and set aside to marinate for 1 hour.

Heat the oil in a deep, heavy-based frying pan, add the chicken pieces and cook over a moderate heat for about 10 minutes until they are browned on all sides. While they are cooking, season with salt and pepper. Add the juice of half a lemon, the chopped rind, oregano or thyme and enough chicken stock to cover the chicken. Cover and simmer over a low heat for 45–50 minutes until the chicken is tender. Transfer the chicken pieces to a warm plate.

Strain the liquid using a fine sieve back into the pan. Whisk the eggs in a large bowl for about 2–3 minutes. Take a ladleful of the chicken sauce and pour into the beaten eggs in a single stream, whisking continuously. Repeat with another ladleful until the sauce is well integrated. At this stage adjust the sauce with extra lemon juice and seasoning, if necessary. Pour the sauce over the chicken pieces and sprinkle with some chopped dill.

Kotopoulo Gemisto me Kastana
CHICKEN STUFFED WITH CHESTNUTS

———

SERVES

4

Chicken or turkey stuffed with chestnuts is a traditional Christmas dish in Greece, as in many other countries. The stuffing can be prepared a day in advance and kept in the fridge.

To prepare the stuffing, make cuts on the sides of the chestnuts using a sharp knife, cover with water and bring to the boil. As soon as they start to boil, remove from the heat without draining. Take out one chestnut at a time, peel off the shell and remove the skin. Place all peeled chestnuts in boiling water or chicken stock and boil for 10–15 minutes until soft but firm and whole. Drain, reserving the stock, and set aside.

Heat the oil and fry the onion and garlic until soft but not browned. Thinly slice the chicken liver and heart, add to the onions and simmer for 3 minutes. Stir in the rice and mix well with the rest of the ingredients. Add enough of the reserved chicken stock to cover the rice, the cognac or ouzo, salt and pepper, and cook over a low heat for 7–10 minutes until all the liquid has been absorbed. Remove from the heat.

Reserve a few whole chestnuts for garnish and chop the remainder roughly. Mix with the rice and add the oregano and sultanas.

Preheat the oven to 180°C/350°F/gas mark 4.

Wash the chicken well. Rub it inside and outside with the juice of half a lemon, salt and ground pepper. Spoon some of the stuffing loosely into the neck cavity and secure the neck skin to the back with a skewer. Spoon the rest of the stuffing into the body cavity and insert the legs so that the opening is partly sealed. Place the bird, breast side up, in a roasting tin. Rub it again with the juice of half a lemon and spread half the butter generously over the breast and legs. Cover loosely with foil and place 3–4 tablespoons of water in the dish to keep the bird moist whilst cooking. Bake in the oven for about 2 hours, ensuring that the bird does not become dry. Lift the foil and baste occasionally. When done, the juices from the bird should run clear. Remove the foil for the last 10 minutes and increase the oven temperature to 220°C/425°F/gas mark 7 until the chicken is golden brown. Remove from the oven and

225 g (8 oz) chestnuts
600 ml (1 pint) chicken stock
3–4 tablespoons olive oil
1 onion, finely chopped
1 garlic clove, crushed
1.5–1.75 kg (3–4 lb) chicken, including giblets
100 g (4 oz) long-grain rice
3 tablespoons cognac or ouzo
Salt and freshly ground pepper
1 teaspoon dried oregano
A handful of sultanas
Juice of 1 lemon
3 tablespoons chopped fresh parsley

leave to stand for 15 minutes before serving. Place on a large platter and garnish with chopped parsley and the whole chestnuts sautéed in the remaining butter.

Variations

1. Turkeys are cooked in the same way but need a greater quantity of stuffing. They also need additional fat or pork sausage meat in the stuffing, which helps to lubricate the bird.

2. Popular garnishes also include stewed apricots, plums and quinces.

Kotopoulo me Piperies ke Kremidia
CHICKEN WITH PEPPERS AND ONIONS

SERVES

6

150 ml (¼ pint) olive oil

900 g (2 lb) onions, thinly sliced

2 garlic cloves, crushed

700 g (1½ lb) green peppers, seeded and sliced into rings

1.5–1.75 kg (3–4 lb) chicken, without giblets

450 g (1 lb) tomatoes, skinned and chopped, or 1 x 400 g (14 oz) can of chopped tomatoes

1 tablespoon tomato purée

150 ml (¼ pint) red wine or 2 tablespoons red wine vinegar diluted to the same quantity in hot water

1 bay leaf

3 tablespoons chopped fresh parsley

Salt and freshly ground pepper

3 tablespoons double cream

This recipe uses traditional summer ingredients in an exquisite wine and tomato sauce. The Greeks use the small and sweet variery of green and red peppers which are very tender and often grilled and eaten whole. A small hot chilli pepper is sometimes added to give an extra punch to the dish.

Heat the oil in a flameproof casserole and fry the onions, garlic and peppers for 2–3 minutes, stirring frequently, until the onions are soft and translucent. Remove all the ingredients using a slotted spoon and set aside.

Wash the chicken well, remove any excess fat and cut into eight portions (two legs, two thighs, two wings, two breasts). Pat dry on kitchen paper. Fry them in the casserole until browned on all sides. You may have to do this in two batches. Add the fried peppers and onions, the tomatoes, tomato purée, wine, bay leaf, parsley, salt and pepper. Cover and simmer over a low heat for about 45–50 minutes or until the chicken is tender and the sauce has reduced to half its original volume. Remove from the heat, stir in the cream and serve with rice or small roast potatoes.

Kotopoulo Psito me Yiaourti
GRILLED CHICKEN WITH YOGHURT

The use of yoghurt to marinate the chicken is well known in the East and in all Mediterranean countries. Yoghurt does not, however, flavour the chicken as much as it tenderizes it and makes it juicy. In this recipe, yoghurt is mixed with an oil-lemon-garlic marinade and poured over the cooked chicken.

Combine the marinade ingredients in a deep glass bowl. Do not skin the chickens. Place the chickens, poussins or chicken pieces into the bowl and mix well with the marinade. Marinate for 2 hours or longer, turning the chickens over several times to cover with the marinade.

Remove the chickens and sprinkle them with more salt and pepper. Preheat the grill to medium and place the chickens about 10 cm (4 in) from the heat. Grill for 12–15 minutes, brushing them often with the marinade, until light brown. Test the flesh with a skewer; if the juices run clear the chickens are done. Place them on a serving dish. Heat the marinade in a pan for 3 minutes, then remove from the heat and cool. Mix in the yoghurt and pour over the chickens. Set aside for 30 minutes and then serve with saffron rice or a vegetable dish.

2 baby chickens or 4 poussins or chicken breasts

225 g (8 oz) strained Greek yoghurt

For the marinade

5 tablespoons olive oil

3 garlic cloves, crushed

Juice of 1 lemon

1 teaspoon dried oregano or thyme or marjoram

Salt and freshly ground pepper

Kotopoulo me Anginares ke Bizelia
CHICKEN WITH ARTICHOKES AND PEAS

Small globe artichokes, fresh peas and new potatoes form a perfect combination. They go well with chicken or spring lamb in this delicious dish.

Wash the chicken and cut off the ends of wings, legs, the skin of the neck and any excess fat. Cut into eight pieces (two legs, two thighs, two wings and two breasts). Pat dry on kitchen paper, then rub with salt and pepper. Heat the oil in a heavy-based pan and fry the chicken pieces until they are browned on all sides.

1.5–1.75 kg (3–4 lb) chicken, without giblets

Salt and freshly ground pepper

3–4 tablespoons olive oil

6 globe artichokes or 450 g (1 lb) of tinned artichoke hearts, drained

Juice of 1 lemon

450 g (1 lb) small potatoes, peeled

1 large onion, finely chopped

25 g (1 oz) butter

450 g (1 lb) tomatoes, skinned and chopped

2 tablespoons tomato purée dissolved in a little stock

1 garlic clove, thinly sliced

1 teaspoon sugar

1 bay leaf

90 ml (3 fl oz) dry white wine

1 kg (2¼ lb) fresh peas in their shells or 450 g (1 lb) frozen garden peas

Transfer to kitchen paper to drain, then place in a deep flame-proof casserole large enough to contain all the ingredients.

Prepare the artichokes as described on page 67. Keep them in water and the lemon juice until you are ready to use them. If you are using tinned artichoke hearts, drain and wash them well. Remove some of the oil and fat in the pan, cut the artichokes in half and add them to the pan. Fry them lightly for a few minutes until they become soft, then transfer them to the chicken using a slotted spoon. Add the potatoes to the pan and fry them lightly until they begin to brown, then transfer them to the chicken. Add the onion and butter to the pan and fry gently, stirring frequently, for 5 minutes until softened. Add the tomatoes, tomato purée, garlic, bay leaf, sugar, wine and a little salt and pepper, cover and simmer for 30 minutes, stirring frequently.

Meanwhile, shell the peas and add them to the chicken. When the sauce is ready, pour it over the chicken and vegetables and simmer over a low heat for 45–60 minutes until the chicken is tender and the sauce is quite thick. Serve with a medium dry white wine.

Kotopoula sti Souvla
SPIT-ROASTED CHICKEN

In this popular way of roasting, nothing but free-range or home-grown chickens will do. When choosing a bird, check that the 'dressed weight', that is the weight after plucking and drawing, including the giblets, is no more than about 900 g (2 lb). These small birds are often known as double poussins, and are the best for spit-roasting. They are young (up to three months old), plump and require little if any oil or fat to enhance their flavour. When roasted, they are succulent with a delicious flavour and a rich brown glaze.

Choose two or three young chickens for four to six people, wash them well, dry them inside and out and place them in a deep glass or earthenware bowl. Mix 150 ml (¼ pint) of dry white wine, 4–5 tablespoons of olive oil, 3 crushed garlic cloves, 1 teaspoon of dried thyme, salt and pepper in a bowl, then pour the mixture over the chickens. Leave them to marinate for a few hours or overnight in the fridge. During this time, spoon the marinade over the chickens two or three times.

Prepare the fire in a barbecue and allow the coals to burn down to a medium-low heat so that the chickens will cook well inside and not burn on the outside. Ideally the barbecue should be equipped with a revolving spit so that the chickens can roast evenly. Take out each chicken from the marinade and push it onto the spit. Tie the legs and wings with a wire, if necessary, and turn the spit frequently until the chickens are done; this will take about 1–1½ hours depending on the size of the birds. Baste frequently with the reserved marinade and do not allow the chickens to dry. Remove the chickens from the spit and place on a warm serving dish. Sprinkle with chopped parsley and serve hot with lemon wedges.

Papia me Elies
DUCK WITH OLIVES

SERVES

4

Some of the best game can be found in the hunting grounds of Macedonia and Thrace; it is proudly displayed in the big shopping markets of Thessaloniki and Alexandroupolis in the winter. Wild duck is prized above other birds for its rich and succulent flavour; it can be cooked in a variety of ways, the most popular being with vegetables such as celery, leeks and spinach or, as in this recipe, with tomatoes and olives.

Wild duck or mallard is the species from which all domesticated ducks originate. They are greedy birds that feed on all vegetable and animal matter, including frogs, worms and fish, with the result that their flesh often has a fishy taint. Greek cooks take special care in preparing wild duck. The bird will be hung for two or three days, then plucked and drawn. Next it will be cleaned well, marinated with vinegar, and then the inside will be rubbed with salt or burnt with a red-hot poker or a glowing piece of charcoal.

This recipe, which comes from the Peloponnese, uses a domesticated duck cooked in an aromatic sauce mixed with large olives; the best in Greece are the green olives with a pleasant nutty flavour from Nafplion.

Select a flameproof casserole large enough to contain the duck

1.5 kg (3 lb) duck

3–4 tablespoons olive oil or butter

2 onions, finely chopped

450 g (1 lb) tomatoes, skinned and finely chopped

150 ml (¼ pint) dry white wine

1 garlic clove, crushed

225 g (8 oz) large, pitted green or black olives

2 bay leaves

½ teaspoon ground cloves and ground cinnamon (optional)

1 sprig of fresh rosemary

Salt and freshly ground pepper

150 ml (¼ pint) hot chicken stock or water

and all the other ingredients. Clean the duck and remove any excess fatty parts from the cavity, the neck, tail and under the wings. Prick the duck all over with a fork.

Heat the oil or butter in the casserole and brown the duck on all sides. Remove the duck from the dish, then add the onions and garlic and fry until soft. Place the duck back in the casserole, breast side up, and add all the remaining ingredients except the olives. Bring to the boil, lower the heat, cover and cook for 1 hour until the duck is almost tender. Add the olives, salt and pepper to taste, and continue cooking for a further 20 minutes until the duck is done and the sauce is thick. Place the duck on a warm serving dish. Remove the bay leaves, rosemary and as much fat as possible from the sauce. Pour the sauce around the duck and serve hot.

Papia me Maroulia ke Bizelia
DUCK WITH COS LETTUCE AND FRESH PEAS

SERVES

4

1.5 kg (3 lb) duck

Salt and freshly ground pepper

2–3 tablespoons olive oil or butter

3 large onions, finely chopped

1 garlic clove, crushed

100 g (4 oz) smoked bacon, rind removed, sliced into small pieces

1 large cos lettuce, sliced into 2.5 cm (1 in) pieces

900 g (2 lb) shelled fresh or frozen peas

1 teaspoon dried oregano

½ teaspoon sugar

150 ml (¼ pint) hot chicken stock or water

1 tablespoon chopped fresh dill

This is traditional country cooking at its best. The whole duck and both vegetables are cooked together until tender.

First clean the duck and remove any excess fatty parts from the cavity, the neck, tail and under the wings, then prick it all over with a fork. Season well with salt and pepper. Heat the oil or butter in a large flameproof casserole and brown the duck on all sides. Remove from the pan, then add the onions, garlic and bacon and fry until golden brown. Return the duck to the casserole and add the lettuce and peas around it. Add the oregano, sugar and half the chicken stock or water, bring to the boil, lower the heat, cover and simmer gently for about 1 hour until the duck is tender. If necessary, add a little more stock during cooking, but the dish should be cooked with the minimum of liquid and stirring.

Remove the duck to a serving dish and cut into serving portions. Surround with the vegetables and garnish with chopped dill and pepper.

Perdikia Krasata
PARTRIDGES IN WINE

Partridges, commonplace in rural areas, are cooked in three ways: in wine (krasata), *in a tomato sauce* (kokinista) *or served with a lemon sauce (*lemonata).

In Britain, two types of partridge are common: the grey and the red-legged partridge. The hen weighs about 350–400 g (12–14 oz) and the cock slightly more. In Greece, the mountain partridge is of the grey kind and a little heavier. The partridge season starts in early September and finishes by the end of February. Older birds are first braised or cooked for a long time in a casserole in order to bring out their flavour. Younger partridges should be hung for five to seven days, although the Greeks do not particularly like the 'high' condition of the birds. Most partridges sold in supermarkets abroad can be assumed to be young; they should still have their head, their beak should be darkish and sharp, their legs yellowish and their bones relatively soft.

4 partridges, plucked and well washed

Salt and freshly ground pepper

1 tablespoon dried oregano

2–3 tablespoons oil or butter

250 ml (8 fl oz) white wine

1/2 tablespoon lemon juice

1 x 400 g (14 oz) can of tomatoes, chopped and sieved (optional)

300 ml (1/2 pint) strained Greek yoghurt (optional)

Rub the partridges inside and out with a little salt, pepper, oregano and oil. Set aside for 1 hour to marinate.

In a pan large enough to hold the birds, melt a little oil or butter and brown the partridges on all sides. Transfer the birds and their juices to a flameproof casserole and add the wine, lemon juice and tomatoes. Cover and cook over a low heat for about 1 hour, basting occasionally, until the birds are tender. Add a little water if they become too dry.

Transfer the birds to a warm serving dish. Boil the sauce until reduced to half its original volume. Check the seasoning, but do not use an excessive amount of salt. To make a richer sauce, add the yoghurt to the final sauce and mix lightly. Pour a little sauce over each bird and serve with mashed or chipped potatoes.

Variation
Older birds should be cooked in a covered pan in the oven at 160°C/325°F/gas mark 3 for about 2 hours, ensuring there is sufficient liquid in the pot during cooking. Mix the sauce with the yoghurt and serve as before.

Ortikia se Klimatofila
ROAST QUAILS WRAPPED IN VINE LEAVES

SERVES

2

4 quails or small pigeons

Salt and freshly ground pepper

25 g (1 oz) butter

8 large vine leaves, rinsed and drained

4 thick slices of fat, smoked bacon

Quails are white-fleshed birds with a gamey flavour. They are tender and need to be cooked for a short time only in the oven. The flesh is rather dry, so pork fat or bacon is placed on the breast or around the bird. Pigeons can be cooked in the same way, but for a little longer. Vine leaves impart a special lemony fragrancy to quails or pigeons cooked in this dish. Vine leaves in brine are readily available in supermarkets.

Preheat the oven to 220°C/425°F/gas mark 7.

Rub the birds well with salt and pepper. Spread the breasts with a thin layer of butter and wrap each with 2 vine leaves. On top of the vine leaves place a bacon slice to cover, and truss securely with string. Roast in the oven for 10 minutes. Remove from the oven, remove the vine leaves and bacon and place the birds back in the oven for a further 8–10 minutes, until golden brown. Serve with garlic bread, a country salad and a full-bodied red wine. Forget the knife and fork and eat quails with your fingers; it is traditional to serve quails with a finger bowl. They are delicious as a *meze* or main dish.

Ortikia me Pilafi
QUAILS WITH RICE

SERVES

2

25 g (1 oz) butter

1 onion, finely chopped

1 garlic clove, finely chopped

4 quails

900 ml (1½ pints) chicken stock

6 black peppercorns, crushed

Salt

225 g (8 oz) long-grain rice

A handful of grated *kefalotiri* or Parmesan cheese

1 tablespoon chopped fresh parsley

A very simple but delicious dish, which can be further enhanced by adding a cinnamon stick for the last 10 minutes of cooking.

In a flameproof casserole large enough to contain all the birds, melt the butter and fry the onion and garlic until soft. Add the quails and fry lightly on all sides until they begin to brown. Pour in 300 ml (½ pint) of the stock, add the peppercorns and season with salt, if necessary. Cover and simmer gently for 1 hour or until the birds are tender.

Add the rice and the remaining stock. Bring to the boil, lower the heat to minimum, cover and cook for 12–15 minutes until the liquid is fully absorbed by the rice. Remove from the heat and leave to stand, covered, for 10 minutes. Sprinkle with a handful of grated cheese and a little chopped parsley and serve hot.

Variation

Just after browning the birds, pour in a small cup of cognac and set alight. Add a glass of red wine, 225 g (8 oz) of peeled and chopped tomatoes, and then continue with the recipe.

Bekatses sto Fourno
ROAST WOODCOCKS

Woodcock is just as delicious as quail and partridge, provided it is young and hung for two or three days but no longer, otherwise it quickly loses its flavour. Allow one or two birds per person. Clean and truss the birds, remove and discard the livers and gizzard. Rub well with salt, pepper and oregano. Tie a piece of pork fat over the breasts and brush the birds all over with olive oil.

Cook in a hot oven preheated to 200°C/400°F/gas mark 6 for 20–30 minutes. Serve each bird with slices of lemon. If you wish to serve them with a sauce, use the oils left over in the oven dish, mix them with a glass of sweet red wine and 1–2 tablespoons of tomato purée. Cook this sauce for 10 minutes, then pour it hot over the birds.

Alternatively, wrap the birds with smoked bacon and pierce with a skewer. Barbecue over a hot fire, but not too close to the flame, basting often with a mixture of oil, salt, pepper and oregano. Serve on a bed of fried vegetables such as peppers, mushrooms, onions or spinach.

SERVES

2

4 woodcocks

3 tablespoons olive oil

3 onions, finely chopped

2 bay leaves

1 teaspoon dried oregano

250 ml (8 fl oz) red wine

About 300 ml (½ pint) water or chicken stock

Salt and freshly ground pepper

A knob of butter

Bekatses Krasates
WOODCOCKS IN WINE

Nothing brings out the distinctive flavour of woodcock better than wine and olive oil.

Clean and truss the birds, remove and discard the livers and gizzards. Wash the birds well and pat dry on kitchen paper. Heat the oil in a deep pan and fry the birds on all sides until golden brown. Transfer to a large flameproof casserole.

Fry the onions in the oil left in the pan until soft. Empty the contents of the pan into the casserole. Add the bay leaves, oregano, wine and enough water or chicken stock just to cover the birds. Cover with the lid and cook gently for about 45 minutes until they are tender. Transfer them to a hot serving dish.

Boil the sauce until reduced by half, then strain through a fine sieve. Season with salt and pepper, add a knob of butter and pour the sauce over the birds.

SERVES

2

700 g (1½ lb) pheasant

Salt and freshly ground pepper

2 tablespoons plain flour

2 tablespoons olive oil

25 g (1 oz) butter

150 ml (¼ pint) dry white wine

150 ml (¼ pint) water

100 g (3 oz) mixed almonds and pine nuts

1 tablespoon white wine vinegar

Juice of 2 oranges

1 orange, sliced

Fasianos me Amygdala ke Koukounaria
PHEASANT WITH ALMONDS AND PINE NUTS

Whereas almonds are probably the cheapest nuts in Greece, pine nuts are expensive and rare, as they are not grown commercially. Both nuts should be added to this dish at the end so that their flavour is preserved. The strong aroma of oranges and the distinctive flavour of these nuts combine to produce this exquisite dish, which originates from Crete. Hen pheasants are smaller than the cocks, but tastier.

Cut the pheasant into large pieces, season with salt and pepper and coat very lightly with flour. Heat the oil and butter and fry the pieces until they begin to brown. Pour the wine and water into the pan, add salt and pepper, bring to the boil, cover and simmer for about 45 minutes until the bird pieces are soft. Remove them with a slotted spoon and keep them warm.

Pass the sauce through a fine sieve back into the pan. Add

the almonds and pine nuts, wine vinegar and the orange juice. Bring the sauce fast to the boil and boil until reduced by half. Pour the sauce over the pheasant, garnish with orange slices and serve on a hot plate with a rice pilaf or roast potatoes.

Lagos Stifado
HARE AND ONION STEW

SERVES

4

Hare, rabbit, lean beef, venison or even snails may be used in stifado. This strongly spiced and flavoursome dish is ideal for the cold winter months. The meats are always marinated and cooked with small whole onions or pickling onions.

Cut the hare into serving portions, first by cutting off the legs, then cutting the body into half down the backbone, and cutting each half into three to four equal portions. Mix all the ingredients for the marinade in a large glass bowl. Add the meat and leave to marinate overnight in an airy place, turning the pieces occasionally.

Remove the hare pieces from the marinade and dry them well. Drain the marinade using a fine sieve and reserve.

Dust the meat with flour. Heat the oil and fry the meat until nicely browned. Place the pieces in a flameproof casserole, add the strained marinade, tomatoes, tomato purée, the oil from the frying pan, the sugar, salt, pepper and water. Bring to the boil, then simmer over a low heat for about 1 hour.

Meanwhile, pour boiling water over the pickling onions and leave for 15 minutes to soak. Peel and nick a cross in the base of each onion to prevent the centres popping out as they cook. Then add to the casserole with the garlic and bay leaves. Cover and cook for a further 45–60 minutes until the onions are soft. Serve hot with rice pilaf, fried potatoes or a green salad.

Variation
Slow cooking is what brings out the best in a *stifado* dish. After frying the meat, place it with the peeled onions and the rest of the ingredients in a glazed earthenware dish and cook in a slow oven at 150°C/300°F/gas mark 2 for 3–4 hours, adding water as necessary.

2 kg (4½ lb) hare, skinned

2 tablespoons plain flour

2 tablespoons olive oil

900 g (2 lb) ripe tomatoes, skinned and diced

1 tablespoon tomato purée

1 teaspoon sugar

Salt and freshly ground pepper

300 ml (½ pint) water

1 kg (2¼ lb) pickling onions

3 garlic cloves, sliced

3 bay leaves

For the marinade

1 onion, finely chopped

2 tablespoons olive oil

1 garlic clove, crushed

2 bay leaves

1 teaspoon juniper berries, crushed

1 teaspoon black peppercorns, crushed

1 tablespoon dried thyme or oregano

1 tablespoon coriander seeds, crushed

300 ml (½ pint) red wine or 2 tablespoons cider vinegar and water

Lagos me Karidia
HARE IN WALNUT SAUCE

2 kg (4½ lb) hare, skinned

2 tablespoons plain flour

3 tablespoons olive oil

50 g (2 oz) butter

1 onion, finely chopped

2–3 garlic cloves

Juice of ½ lemon

90 ml (3 fl oz) brandy or sweet sherry

300 ml (½ pint) stock or water

1 bay leaf

½ teaspoon ground cinnamon

Salt and freshly ground pepper

100 g (4 oz) walnuts, crushed

For the marinade

150 ml (¼ pint) white wine vinegar

150 ml (¼ pint) water

2 celery sticks, chopped

½ lemon, sliced

A little chopped fresh oregano
or thyme

A traditional way of tenderizing hare and then cooking it slowly in a rich sauce. The addition of walnuts dates back to ancient times when walnut trees were introduced to Greece from Persia. The combination of honey and walnuts became the basis of a number of classical desserts and biscuits. In many Aegean islands, this dish is made with chicken.

Mix the marinade ingredients in a glass bowl. Wash and cut the hare into serving pieces, add to the marinade and leave to stand in a cool place for one or two days. Discard the marinade, dry the hare pieces well and coat lightly in seasoned flour.

Heat the oil and butter in a deep pan and fry the hare pieces for about 10 minutes until browned on all sides. Transfer them to a flameproof casserole. Add the onion and garlic to the oil in the pan and fry for 2–3 minutes, then transfer the contents of the pan to the casserole. Add the lemon juice, brandy, stock or water, bay leaf, cinnamon, salt and pepper. Bring to the boil, cover and cook over low heat for 2–3 hours.

Transfer the hare pieces to a warm serving plate. Strain the sauce through a fine sieve into a pan, add the walnuts and cook over a medium heat for 1–2 minutes. Pour the sauce over the hare and serve with a green salad and a fruity red wine.

Kounelaki Riganato
ROAST RABBIT WITH
OREGANO SAUCE

1.5–1.75 kg (3–4 lb) young rabbit

1 tablespoon white wine vinegar

1 tablespoon salt

600 ml (1 pint) water

2 garlic cloves, sliced

½ tablespoon dried oregano

Salt and freshly ground pepper

Juice of 1 large lemon

*Rabbit (*kouneli*) and hare (*lagos*) are cooked in a similar way, that is, either as a stew with onions (Lagos Stifado, see page 123) or sometimes in a wine and lemon sauce. Young rabbits, however, can be tender, especially after being marinated for hours, and may be roasted or grilled, just like chicken. A simple acidic marinade cleans away any traces of blood, breaks down the meat fibres and makes the flesh white. Rabbit has an affinity with garlic, and this recipe uses garlic and oregano as* *a stuffing. The Greeks use mountain* rigani, *which is a more pungent herb than oregano.*

Mix the wine vinegar, salt and water, pour over the rabbit and leave to marinate for 10 hours or overnight. Wash the rabbit well, remove any blood and wipe dry with a kitchen cloth.

Preheat the oven to 230°C/450°F/gas mark 8.

Mix the garlic, oregano, salt and pepper in a bowl. Using a sharp knife, make incisions in the rabbit and stuff the garlic and oregano into the incisions. Place the rabbit in a roasting dish and roast in the oven for about 5–8 minutes, then reduce the oven temperature to 180°C/350°F/gas mark 4. Beat together the lemon juice, oil and any leftover garlic and pour it over the rabbit. Roast for about 2 hours, basting frequently with the liquid in the dish, until the rabbit is tender. Remove the rabbit to a warm serving plate, cut into serving portions and sprinkle with chopped parsley.

Make a gravy by stirring the butter, flour and wine or stock into the juices remaining in the roasting dish and cook until the gravy is smooth. Serve the rabbit with the gravy and a creamy rice pilaf. A dry light red wine is perfect with this dish.

150 ml (¼ pint) olive oil
1 tablespoon chopped fresh parsley

For the gravy
25 g (1 oz) butter
1 teaspoon plain flour
3–4 tablespoons red wine or stock

Thalassina

FISH

The sea has always played a vital role in Greek daily life. It provides food, a means of communication and transport, commerce and the livelihood of fishermen and their families.

The sea is and has always been a source of cultural inspiration to the Greeks. Most of the wonderful ancient tales and myths are based on the struggle of man against the sea. Stories of sea gods and monsters were nothing but an expression of the awe and fear of the Greek explorers who navigated the Mediterranean seas for 3000 years. In the words of the Byzantines, the sea was 'uniting, rather than dividing' (*synappei mallon i temnei*) the Greeks. It was this uniting force, along with the desire for commerce and trade, that enabled them to marshal the biggest navy of 1000 ships during the Trojan wars.

Now more than ever, Greeks rely on their own sea as the main supply of fish. There is hardly any fish-farming and, despite pollution and over-fishing, hardly any fish are imported. Those professional fishermen who do not serve the tourist industry still take their boats out at dawn and return with fish in the morning. They sell their catch to top restaurants or customers on the quayside, then spend the rest of the day mending their nets in the harbour or repairing their boats. In the great fish markets of Athens, Piraeus and Thessaloniki you can find a variety of seasonal fish, displayed in various categories, that are always fresh, some even sold live. Red mullet is the pride and joy of any fishmonger; they eclipse in beauty and price the larger fish and even the occasional lobster.

I could be described as being fanatical about fish, and given the choice between fish and meat, I would always choose fish. Our family house was only a few metres from a fishing harbour, and I was taught by my grandmother to get up early in the morning, go down to the harbour and wait for the boats to come in. I knew most of the fishermen by name, as well as their agents who handled their daily catch. I was supposed to strike a deal and come home with a kilo of fresh fish that would 'make my grandmother proud'. Her taste was always difficult to please; she would inspect the fish, make sure that the eyes were sparkling, the gills were red, the scales firm and the

In the city of Torone you must buy belly steaks of sharks; sprinkle them with cumin, a little salt, green olive oil, and fry over embers. Not many men know this divine food, and none of those who are cowards and are paralysed because the creature is a man-eater. But every fish likes human flesh if it can get it.

———

Athenaeus

tail slightly twisted. If something was suspect, back to the harbour I would go, properly instructed this time, or else.

Most Greek fish dishes are straightforward. Fresh fish is simply fried or grilled and served with olive oil and fresh lemon juice, the emphasis being on the freshness of ingredients and spontaneity of cooking. Medium-sized fish are usually marinated beforehand, and small fish are coated with seasoned flour and fried whole. Sauces for fish are very few: elaborate sauces and packet sauce mixes or bottled sauces are considered imported concoctions and are avoided. Instead, a garnish of lemon slices, fresh parsley, some olives or a side salad accompany most fish dishes.

Barbounia sto Fourno
BAKED RED MULLET

SERVES

4

4 x 900 g (2 lb) mullet, scaled and cleaned

Juice of ½ lemon

120 ml (4 fl oz) olive oil

2 onions, thinly sliced

4 garlic cloves, sliced

1 green or red pepper, seeded and sliced into rings

4–5 tablespoons chopped fresh parsley or coriander or rosemary

2–3 bay leaves

10 black peppercorns

5 allspice berries

2–3 cloves

300 ml (½ pint) dry white wine

Salt and freshly ground pepper

Red mullet is highly esteemed in Greece for its flavour and delicacy, although it is very expensive. Very small ones are fried in a little olive oil or grilled whole (see page 22). Larger ones, averaging 100–225 g (4–8 oz) in weight, are baked or fried with flavourings of thyme, rosemary, tomatoes and olives.

To Prepare Red Mullet

Red mullet should be scaled with care as the skin is very fragile. Remove the gills, gut the fish and wash thoroughly. The Greeks do not usually gut small fresh mullet as they have a gamey and rich flavour (the French call red mullet the 'woodcock of the sea', and they cook it in the same way). Some say the liver and cheeks also give it a special taste, but I discard these.

Preheat the oven to 200°C/400°F/gas mark 6.

Place the fish in an oven dish and sprinkle with lemon juice. Heat the oil in a pan and fry the onions and garlic for about 3 minutes until soft. Add the remaining ingredients, raise the heat and cook until the wine has almost evaporated. Pour the onion sauce over the fish and cook in the oven for about 30 minutes. Remove the bay leaves and serve hot with a country salad (*Horiatiki Salata*, see page 50).

Barbounia sto Harti
RED MULLET BAKED IN FOIL

This simple method of baking fish can also be used for trout, swordfish, tuna, bonito, grey mullet, snapper or bream.

Allow one large mullet per person. For each fish, cut a piece of greaseproof paper or silver foil into an oval shape that is large enough to enclose a fish. Prepare the fish as described on page 128. Make 2 or 3 cuts across the fish using a sharp knife and place each fish on its foil. Drizzle some olive oil and lemon juice over the fish, sprinkle on a little fresh thyme or chopped fresh parsley and season generously with salt and freshly ground pepper.

Preheat the oven to 180°C/350°F/gas mark 4. Wrap the fish in the foil, crimping the edges of the foil together by making small pleats in it, so that none of the flavour escapes. Place on a baking tray and bake in the oven for 20–30 minutes, depending on the thickness of the fish.

To serve, unwrap the foil carefully and place the fish and its juices on a hot plate. Serve with a country salad (*Horiatiki Salata*, see page 50). If you prefer a thick sauce to go with the fish, pour the sauce from the foil into a pan and add 1 tablespoon of cornflour. Heat gently, stirring continously, until the sauce has thickened.

Pestrofa sto Harti
TROUT BAKED IN FOIL

SERVES
4

Trout is fished mostly in the lakes and rivers of northern Greece. There is excellent trout in the lakes of Ioannina – the capital of Epirus – and the Kalamas river that feeds it, but for how long it is difficult to guess; pollution from fertilizers, chemicals and waste is increasingly becoming a real threat to fishing.

Trout is usually fried, grilled or baked in foil, as in the previous recipe for red mullet. Alternatively, during spring and summer, trout is served stuffed with seasonal vegetables such as carrots, celery, fennel and wild mushrooms.

4 tablespoons olive oil

2 onions, finely chopped

1 celery stick, finely chopped

100 g (4 oz) mushrooms, finely chopped

1 tablespoon chopped fresh parsley

1 garlic clove, crushed

2 tablespoons water

Juice of 1 lemon

Salt and freshly ground pepper

4 medium trout, scaled and cleaned

1 teaspoon dried oregano

Preheat the oven to 180°C/350°F/gas mark 4.

Heat 2 tablespoons of olive oil in a pan and fry the onions, celery, mushrooms, parsley and garlic for 5 minutes, then add the water and half the lemon juice and simmer for a further 5 minutes. Season with salt and pepper.

Fill the trout with the stuffing and place each separately on a piece of greaseproof paper or foil which is large enough to enclose the fish. Sprinkle each fish with a dash of lemon juice, olive oil, the oregano, salt and pepper, and wrap with the foil. Bake in the oven for about 20 minutes. Serve the fish with its juices, with a salad of your choice and a light rosé or retsina wine.

Kefalos Gemistos

STUFFED GREY MULLET

SERVES

4

1 kg (2¼ lb) grey mullet, scaled and cleaned

2 small onions, chopped

450 g (1 lb) ripe tomatoes, skinned and chopped

1 celery stick, finely chopped

300 ml (½ pint) dry white wine

2–3 tablespoons olive oil

For the stuffing

100 g (4 oz) white breadcrumbs

A little milk to soak the breadcrumbs

100 g (4 oz) whiting

25 g (1 oz) butter

50 g (2 oz) mushrooms, finely chopped

2 tablespoons chopped fresh parsley

Salt and freshly ground pepper

Grey mullet is a round and firm fish with a fine flavour that is often underestimated. It can be grilled, stuffed and baked in the oven or poached with fresh vegetables. Smaller mullets are tastier than large ones. Grey mullet is often compared to red mullet, and for this reason it is unfortunate that this fish carries the name 'mullet' in English. In Greek it is called kefalos *or 'big head'. Both names are inappropriate.*

In the past, the roe of grey mullet was smoked to form the basis of the original taramasalata. *Alas, all the innards of grey mullet are nowadays thrown away.*

Preheat the oven to 180°C/350°F/gas mark 4.

Soak the breadcrumbs in the milk, then squeeze dry. Boil the whiting in a little water until the flesh flakes, then skin it and remove the flesh from the bones. Melt a little butter in a pan and fry the mushrooms gently until soft. Combine the breadcrumbs, whiting flesh, mushrooms, parsley, salt and pepper in a bowl and mix well. Stuff the mixture into the cavity of the mullets.

In a pan, fry the onions, tomatoes and celery for 5 minutes, then transfer to an ovenproof dish large enough to take the mullet. Lay the fish on the vegetables, pour over the wine and a little olive oil and bake in the oven for 30 minutes, basting frequently, until tender.

Psari Plaki
BRAISED FISH

Plaki *is a general term for baking or braising fish in the oven with vegetables. The term also applies to roasting vegetables on their own, such as potatoes or beans. Fish* plaki *is often baked with lots of garlic or lemon slices and then served on a bed of vegetables with a sauce.*

*The recipe below uses tomatoes and potatoes and a moderate amount of garlic. Any large fish could be used, such as sea bass, grey mullet or red snapper. The fish is baked whole and makes an impressive presentation. Other fish, such as fresh cod, mackerel, haddock or halibut can also be used provided they are filleted or cut into steaks. The ideal Greek fish for this dish is pandora, a Mediterranean type of sea bream (*lithrini*, known as* pageot rouge *in France) which has a rose pink colour, firm flesh and can grow up to 40 cm (16 in) in length.*

150 ml (¼ pint) olive oil

1.5–1.75 kg (3–4 lb) fish or filleted
fish, cut into serving portions, scaled
and cleaned

Juice of 1 lemon

1 large onion, thinly sliced

2 garlic cloves, thinly sliced

3 large tomatoes, coarsely chopped

150 ml (¼ pint) dry white wine

3–4 tablespoons chopped fresh parsley

4 bay leaves

Salt and freshly ground pepper

2 medium potatoes, peeled and sliced
1 cm (½ in) thick

Preheat the oven to 180°C/350°F/gas mark 4.

Brush a baking dish with a little of the olive oil, place the fish in the middle and, using your fingers, rub it inside and out with salt, pepper and half the lemon juice.

Heat half the oil in a pan and fry the onion and garlic until soft but not browned. Add the tomatoes, wine, parsley, bay leaves, salt, pepper and the rest of the lemon juice and simmer over a low heat for 15 minutes. Remove the bay leaves and pour the mixture over the fish, ensuring that the tomatoes and herbs are on top of the fish. Arrange the potatoes around the fish, pour on the rest of the olive oil and bake in the oven, uncovered, for 30–40 minutes until the potatoes are tender and the fish is flaky. Place the fish on a warm platter, surround with the vegetables and serve with crusty bread and a dry white wine.

Gavros Plaki
BAKED ANCHOVIES

900 g (2 lb) anchovies or large sardines, cleaned, gutted, heads removed

4 garlic cloves, thinly sliced

2 large tomatoes, skinned and thinly sliced

1 lemon, peeled and thinly sliced in rounds

150 ml (¼ pint) olive oil

2–3 tablespoons chopped fresh parsley

1 tablespoon dried thyme

Salt and freshly ground pepper

Large anchovies (gavros), *sardines* (sardeles) *or whitebait* (marida) *can grow up to 20 cm (8 in) in length. They have an elongated silvery body with pointed snout. They are very tasty fish suitable for this dish which is baked in the oven.*

Preheat the oven to 200°C/400°F/gas mark 6.

Cut the fish open with a sharp knife and remove the backbone. Arrange the fish in an ovenproof dish and insert a slice of garlic, a slice of tomato and a round of lemon between each fish. Use a round earthenware dish and arrange the dish like the spokes of a wheel; it makes a nice presentation. Sprinkle the fish with oil, parsley, thyme, salt and pepper and bake in the oven for 15–20 minutes until tender.

Psari Plaki Spetsiotiko
BAKED FISH FROM THE ISLAND OF SPETSAI

1 x 1.5 kg (3 lb) fish such as grouper, sea bream, sea bass or grey mullet, scaled and cleaned

Salt and freshly ground pepper

Juice of 1 lemon

150 ml (¼ pint) olive oil

1 tablespoon plain flour

2 onions, thinly sliced

2 garlic cloves, finely chopped

450 g (1 lb) tomatoes, skinned and sliced

1 tablespoon tomato purée

120 ml (4 fl oz) dry white wine

2–3 tablespoons chopped fresh parsley or dill

Spetsai is a low, wooded, undulating island off the coast of Peloponnese, and a short distance by boat from Athens. Historically, it has produced more admirals and brave sailors than most other islands in Greece; it is a prosperous island with excellent facilities for underwater fishing.

Season the fish with salt and pepper. Make deep cuts into the fish with a sharp knife, and place it on a well-oiled baking dish. Pour over the lemon juice and half the olive oil, sprinkle with the flour and set aside to marinate for 1 hour.

Preheat the oven to 180°C/350°F/gas mark 4.

Heat the rest of the oil in a pan and sauté the onions and garlic until soft. Add the tomatoes, tomato purée, wine and parsley, cover and simmer for about 15–20 minutes until the sauce thickens. Pour the sauce over the fish and bake in the oven for about 1 hour for large fish or 40 minutes for smaller ones, basting once or twice. If the fish gets dry add some more wine – there should be a little sauce remaining when the fish is cooked.

Variation

The fish is often covered with breadcrumbs and baked until the breadcrumbs produce a thick crust. Omit the flour in the recipe and cover the fish with 25 g (1 oz) of fresh bread-crumbs; then let it marinate, as above. Before baking the fish, pour another 25 g (1 oz) of breadcrumbs on top of the sauce.

Psari Marinato
MARINATED FISH

SERVES
4

A variety of marinades are devised nowadays to enhance the flavour of meat or fish, whereas in the past marinades were used as preservatives, similar to brines, spices and salt.

This dish uses a marinade which used to meet the needs of the islanders in the past: to preserve, handle and then distribute fish in the absence of freezing facilities. Fish such as red mullet, sardines, mackerel and cod were mostly marinated in this way and preserved in large quantities for a week or more. This recipe comes from the Cyclades islands, right at the centre of the Aegean Sea. The original sauce is made using copious amounts of vinegar, which I have reduced in this recipe to make it more palatable. The dish can be prepared a day in advance.

1–1.5 kg (2–3 lb) fresh fish such as red mullet, plaice, sole, skate, cod fillets, scaled and cleaned

Salt

Lemon juice

2 tablespoons plain flour

300 ml (½ pint) olive oil

For the sauce

2 tablespoons plain flour

3–4 tablespoons white wine vinegar

3 tablespoons tomato purée

2–3 garlic cloves, crushed

Salt and freshly ground pepper

300 ml (½ pint) water

1 teaspoon sugar or honey

A sprig of fresh rosemary

Sprinkle the fish with salt and lemon juice and leave to marinate for 1 hour.

Dust the fish lightly with flour and fry in hot (but not smoking) oil until pale golden. Transfer the fish to a deep platter.

Strain the oil into a bowl and wipe the frying pan clean with kitchen paper. Pour half the oil back into the pan. Heat the oil again and add 2 tablespoons of flour, stirring with a wooden spoon until the mixture becomes light brown in colour. Add the wine vinegar, tomato purée, garlic, salt, pepper and water. Whisk the mixture until smooth and simmer on low heat for 15–20 minutes until the sauce thickens. A few minutes before serving, add the sugar or honey and rosemary and pour the sauce over the fish. It is best to let the dish cool slightly before serving.

SERVES

4

3–4 tablespoons olive oil

1 onion, finely chopped

1 tablespoon plain flour

150 ml (¼ pint) dry white wine

150 ml (¼ pint) fish stock

1 garlic clove, chopped

2 bay leaves

3–4 fresh sage leaves or a pinch of dried sage

4 tablespoons chopped fresh parsley

Salt and freshly ground pepper

900 g (2 lb) skinned eel, head removed, and cut into 5 cm (2 in) pieces

Heli Yiahnisto
STEWED EEL

Huss, dogfish, rockfish, rock salmon and eels form an ugly family of fish, but have a delicious flavour that is often hidden in soggy batters and unpleasant vinegars. Fresh eel has a long muscular body with a rich and delicate flavour; its high oil content makes it suitable for frying or grilling. The type of eel commonly found in Greek waters, around rocky areas with crevices, is the conger (known as mougri*). It can grow up to 3 m in length and has grey skin with a slightly lighter belly. It can live to a depth of 100 m.*

To Prepare Eels

If you are squeamish about live eels ask your fishmonger to kill and skin whole eels and chop them into pieces about 5 cm (2 in) long. If you wish to skin the eel yourself, hold it down firmly with a towel on a flat surface, and with a sharp knife make an incision around its neck just below the head. Grip the skin with a pair of pliers and then peel it off all in one go. Cut off and discard the head. Slit the belly and remove the intestines, then wash it well. If you wish to bone it, press it flat and remove the backbone all in one piece.

Chunks of eels are always cooked in wine, especially a good dry wine or sherry, and aromatic herbs. Traditional eel stews also contain tomatoes. The following recipe, however, contains no tomatoes and comes from the island of Chios.

Heat the oil in a pan and fry the onion until soft but not browned. Add the flour and mix with a wooden spoon until it is absorbed by the oil. Gradually add the fish stock and wine, stirring continuously until the sauce is smooth and begins to boil. At this stage, add the garlic, bay leaves, sage and 3 tablespoons of parsley. Season with salt and pepper and simmer for 2–3 minutes over a low heat until the sauce begins to thicken. Add the eel pieces, cover the pan and simmer for 20 minutes, by which time the fish will be tender and the sauce a rich white colour. Transfer the fish on to a warm plate, pour the sauce over it and garnish with the remaining parsley.

Heli Yiahnisto me Domates
STEWED EEL IN TOMATO SAUCE

Once eels have been skinned and boned (see page 134) they can be fried, grilled, stewed, poached or smoked, just like many similar fish. An interesting method of cooking eel is to wrap them in vine leaves and roast them over an open charcoal fire. The traditional Greek way of cooking eel, however, is to stew them in a rich wine and tomato sauce.

Heat the oil in a pan and fry the onion and garlic until soft but not browned. Sieve the tomatoes and discard the juice, then add them to the pan with the bay leaves, sage, salt and pepper, and simmer over low heat for 15 minutes until the sauce is rich and thick. Add the eel pieces, wine and 2 tablespoons of the parsley, cover and simmer on low heat for 20–30 minutes. Garnish with the remaining parsley, remove the bay leaves and serve hot with a dry white wine.

150 ml (¼ pint) olive oil

1 onion, finely chopped

1 garlic clove, chopped

450 g (1 lb) fresh tomatoes, skinned and chopped, or 1 x 400 g (14 oz) can of chopped tomatoes

2 bay leaves

2–3 fresh sage leaves or a pinch of dried sage

Salt and freshly ground pepper

900 g (2 lb) skinned eel, head removed, cut into 5 cm (2 in) pieces

150 ml (¼ pint) dry white wine

2–3 tablespoons chopped fresh parsley

Palamida sto Fourno
BONITO BAKED WITH VEGETABLES

For this recipe, fresh bonito (palamida) or tuna (tonos), cut into fairly thick slices or steaks, is surrounded with summer vegetables, then baked in the oven.

Preheat the oven to 180°C/350°F/gas mark 4.

Heat half the oil in a deep pan and fry the onions until soft. Add the aubergine cubes and fry them at high heat for a few minutes on all sides until they begin to brown. Transfer the contents of the pan to a shallow ovenproof dish.

Season the steaks with salt and pepper, then coat them in flour. Add 2 tablespoons of oil to the pan and fry the steaks on both sides for 2–3 minutes. Remove the steaks with a slotted spoon into the ovenproof dish. Add the pepper, tomatoes, carrots, garlic, bay leaves, chilli and herbs and pour over the rest of the oil. Add 2–3 tablespoons of warm water, season with salt

150 ml (¼ pint) olive oil

2 onions, finely chopped

1 aubergine, stem cut off then cut in cubes or chunky pieces

4 x 200 g (7 oz) bonito or tuna steaks

Salt and freshly ground pepper

2 tablespoons plain flour

1 pepper, seeded and roughly chopped

450 g (1 lb) ripe tomatoes, quartered

2 carrots, chopped

1 garlic clove, thinly sliced

2 bay leaves

1 small chilli pepper, chopped

1–2 teaspoons fresh thyme or basil

and pepper and mix the vegetables well with the oil. Cover the dish loosely with a sheet of foil, then bake in the oven for 45 minutes. Serve warm with either fresh bread or boiled rice.

Bakaliaros Pastos Skordalia
FRIED SALT COD WITH GARLIC SAUCE

SERVES

4

700 g (1 ½ lb) dried salt cod
300 ml (½ pint) warm milk
Toasted breadcrumbs for coating
Oil for deep-frying

Greeks are rather partial to imported salt cod, in spite of the long soaking and preparation it requires. Its strong aroma, when fried into crisp balls and served with a garlic sauce and a glass of retsina wine, makes it unusual and very typical of the ambience of a Greek taverna. Fresh cod, particularly in this recipe, is not a good substitute.

Rinse any loose salt off the cod and then soak it in cold water for 12–24 hours, changing the water 5–6 times. The longer you soak it, the less salty it becomes. Drain and cut the cod into serving pieces, discarding the tails and fins. Carefully remove the skin and any bones so that the pieces are still intact. Cover with cold water and bring slowly to the boil, then drain immediately. Arrange the pieces on a plate and pour the milk over them. Leave for an hour, until the milk has been completely absorbed.

Remove each piece and coat with breadcrumbs, then fry in hot oil until golden and crisp. Using a slotted spoon, remove the pieces on to kitchen paper to drain, then transfer to a serving dish. Serve hot with a garlic sauce (*Skordalia*, see page 151), a beetroot salad (*Panzaria Salata*, see page 55) or wild greens salad (*Horta Salata*, see page 53). A bottle of retsina is a must with this dish.

Variation
A simple batter would add more flavour to the cod. Soak and de-salt the cod pieces as above. Beat 2 eggs with 2 tablespoons of water in a bowl until fluffy. Season with freshly ground pepper. Blend 75 g (3 oz) of self-raising flour to a paste with 5 tablespoons of water and whisk with the eggs until the batter is smooth. Leave to stand for 30 minutes, then dip each piece into the batter and fry in hot oil, as before.

Bakaliaros Yiahni
COD STEW WITH TOMATOES AND PEPPERS

SERVES

4

This is a simple traditional summer meal, which can be prepared with either salt or fresh cod.

If you use salt cod, prepare it as described on page 136. If you use fresh cod, wash it well and cut into serving pieces but do not remove the skin. Wipe the pieces with kitchen paper and lightly coat in flour.

Heat the oil in a flameproof casserole until very hot, and fry the cod on all sides until golden. Remove with a slotted spoon on to kitchen paper to drain.

In the same oil, fry the onions, pepper and garlic for about 5 minutes, stirring constantly, until they begin to soften. Add the tomatoes, wine vinegar, bay leaf and pepper, cover and simmer for 30–45 minutes until the sauce has reduced.

Add the cod pieces, cover and simmer gently for a further 15–20 minutes. Transfer the cod to a serving dish, pour the sauce around it and serve.

700 g (1 1/2 lb) cod
2 tablespoons plain flour
120 ml (4 fl oz) olive oil
450 g (1 lb) onions, thinly sliced
1 large green pepper, seeded and sliced into rings
2 garlic cloves, crushed
450 g (1 lb) tomatoes, skinned and finely chopped, or 1 x 400 g (14 oz) can of chopped tomatoes
1 tablespoon white wine vinegar
1 bay leaf
Freshly ground pepper

Garides me Feta Saltsa
PRAWNS IN FETA CHEESE SAUCE

SERVES

2

Sadly, it is hard to find fresh large prawns anywhere in Greece outside the big cities, and even there the prices are astronomical. It is cheaper and easier to buy them frozen from supermarkets or even fishmarkets. When in Greece, you should be completely on your guard against prawns (garides), scampi (karavides) or even the rare oysters (stridia) served in pretentious tavernas and seaside restaurants, where they are often tasteless, cooked to destruction or coated with some repellent batter.

The Greeks have a variety of simple and wonderful recipes for seafood. They range from their favourite way of grilling to slow baking in a mixture of summer vegetables and fresh herbs which complement the prawn's delicate flavour.

6 tablespoons olive oil
5 spring onions, finely chopped
2 garlic cloves, thinly sliced
450 g (1 lb) tomatoes, skinned and chopped
1/2 teaspoon sugar
150 ml (1/4 pint) dry white wine
1 teaspoon dried oregano
Salt and freshly ground pepper
700 g (1 1/2 lb) large prawns, cleaned and prepared
100 g (4 oz) feta cheese, crumbled
3 tablespoons chopped fresh parsley

To Prepare Prawns

Uncooked prawns are usually shelled, apart from the small tail piece. Just throw them into a boiling *bouillon* (a stock made of vegetables, wine and herbs) for up to 10 minutes until they turn pink, and they will be perfectly cooked. Select large unshelled prawns. Shell them yourself by pulling off the head and then the legs. Leave the tail on and peel off the body shell. Avoid the pre-shelled frozen variety, which looks pretty but has little flavour. If you buy frozen ones, allow them to defrost, then drain off the liquid. In all cases, prawns should be deveined; this involves removing the black intestine on the back of large prawns, either by pulling it out or cutting it off. Precooked prawns are ready to eat cold. You need to cook them for 3–4 minutes to make them piping hot.

Preheat the oven to 200°C/400°F/gas mark 6.

Heat 4 tablespoons of the oil in a deep pan and fry the onions and garlic until translucent. Add all the remaining ingredients, except the prawns, feta cheese and parsley and simmer for 15 minutes. Add the prawns and cook for a further 8–10 minutes. Transfer the prawns to an ovenproof dish, preferably an earthenware dish, add the crumbled feta cheese, sprinkle with the remaining olive oil, add the parsley and bake for 5–10 minutes until the cheese just begins to melt.

Variation

If you wish to omit the feta cheese, proceed by adding 2 tablespoons of brandy to the wine and tomato sauce and serve immediately.

Garides me Rizi
PRAWN PILAF

This very popular dish is cooked with the minimum of liquid.

Heat the oil and fry the onion and garlic for 2–3 minutes until soft. Add the rice and cook for 1 minute, stirring once or twice. Add the tomatoes, sugar, lemon juice, oregano or coriander and water and season with salt and pepper. Bring to the boil, lower the heat, cover and simmer gently for about 10–12 minutes. Add the prawns and cook for a further 3–5 minutes until the rice is cooked but firm. Crumble the cheese over the prawns, cover the pan while it is hot and leave to rest for 5 minutes until the cheese begins to melt. Garnish with chopped parsley and serve hot.

4 tablespoons olive oil

1 onion, chopped

2 garlic cloves, thinly sliced

100 g (4 oz) long-grain rice

450 g (1 lb) tomatoes, skinned and chopped

1 teaspoon sugar

1 tablespoon lemon juice

2 teaspoons dried oregano or 1 teaspoon chopped fresh coriander

300 ml (½ pint) water

Salt and freshly ground pepper

700 g (1½ lb) large prawns, cleaned and prepared (see page 138)

100 g (4 oz) feta cheese

3 tablespoons chopped fresh parsley

Garides Ladolemono
PRAWNS IN LEMON SAUCE

Place the onion, carrot, bay leaf, wine, water, salt and pepper in a flameproof casserole. Bring to the boil, then simmer for 15 minutes. Add the prawns and cook for about 4–5 minutes, then remove them to a serving plate and discard the sauce in which they were cooked.

Combine the sauce ingredients and pour over the prawns. Garnish with fresh salad vegetables.

1 onion, sliced

1 carrot, chopped

1 bay leaf

150 ml (¼ pint) dry white wine

150 ml (¼ pint) water

Salt and freshly ground pepper

700 g (1½ lb) large prawns, cleaned and prepared (see page 138)

For the sauce

2 tablespoons olive oil

Juice of 1 lemon

For the garnish

Fresh salad vegetables such as lettuce leaves and tomatoes

Htapodi Krasato
OCTOPUS IN WINE

1 kg (2¼ lb) octopus

4 tablespoons olive oil

2 onions, finely chopped

300 ml (½ pint) red wine

225 g (8 oz) tomatoes, skinned
and chopped

2 tablespoons tomato purée

1 celery stick, chopped

2 bay leaves

1 teaspoon dried oregano

Salt and freshly ground pepper

There is probably no more sinister creature in the sea than an octopus, especially for those of us who were brought up with the adventure stories of Jules Verne, or the Japanese monster movies depicting love affairs between a giant octopus and a fish-girl! In fact, the octopus is a gentle creature, living in coastal areas and caves; its only defence is a sac of ink which it squirts when threatened. It grows to up to 50 cm (20 in) in length and has a rubbery flesh covered with a purplish membrane. The Greeks will beat an octopus on a flat rock to tenderize it and then hang it to dry in the sun. You would not need to do that, as the octopus sold abroad is of a different kind and already tenderized.

To Prepare Octopus

To remove the head cut well below the eyes in the part that unites all the tentacles. If the octopus has long tentacles, you will need to blanch it in boiling water for 10 minutes, then skin it. If you also wish to use the head, turn the pouch-like head inside out, discard all the innards and cut out the beak of the mouth and the eyes. If you wish to tenderize it, put all the pieces in a plastic bag and beat them with a wooden mallet. Alternatively, simmer in water for 1 hour, then peel off the skin.

Prepare the octopus and cut into 2.5 cm (1 in) pieces. Heat the oil in a deep pan and fry the onions until they change colour, then add the octopus pieces and fry them for 5 minutes until all the pieces turn white and the juices run out. Add the remaining ingredients. Cover the pan and simmer for 2 hours, stirring occasionally, until the sauce has reduced to half of its original quantity. Serve hot.

Htapodi Pilafi
OCTOPUS PILAF

———

Prepare the octopus as described on page 140, using the same ingredients. When ready, remove the bay leaves and add 225 g (8 oz) of long-grain rice and enough warm water to make the sauce in the pan up to 600 ml (1 pint). Cover the pan with a napkin to absorb any steam, cover with the lid and simmer over a very low heat for 12 minutes until all the liquid has been absorbed and little holes appear on the surface of the rice. Allow it to rest, still covered, for 10 minutes, then give it a good stir and serve on a warm plate with plenty of freshly ground pepper and chopped fresh parsley.

Htapodi Stifado
OCTOPUS STEW WITH PICKLING ONIONS

———

SERVES
4

This is a slightly elaborate dish but absolutely delicious.

Prepare the octopus as described on page 140. Leave the octopus whole. Heat the oil in a deep pan and fry the onions until they change colour. Add the whole octopus and all the remaining ingredients except the small onions, cover and simmer for 1 hour, stirring occasionally. Leave to cool.

Meanwhile, peel the small onions carefully, leaving them whole.

When the dish is cool, remove the octopus and chop it into 5 cm (2 in) pieces. Strain the sauce in the pan using a fine strainer, then return it to the pan. Add the octopus pieces, the peeled onions and the garlic and simmer gently, covered, for about 1 hour until the onions are cooked. Stir in chopped parsley, salt and a generous amount of pepper and serve at once.

1 kg (2¼ lb) octopus

4 tablespoons olive oil

2 onions, finely chopped

450 ml (¾ pint) red wine

450 g (1 lb) tomatoes, skinned and chopped

2 tablespoons tomato purée

1 celery stick, chopped

2 bay leaves

1 teaspoon dried oregano

4 garlic cloves

Salt and freshly ground pepper

350 g (12 oz) small pickling onions

1 tablespoon chopped fresh parsley

Kalamarakia Gemista
STUFFED SQUID

SERVES

4

1 kg (2¼ lb) squid about 7.5 cm (3 in) long

150 ml (¼ pint) olive oil

1 large onion, finely chopped

Salt and freshly ground pepper

75 g (3 oz) long-grain or basmati rice

1 red pepper, seeded and finely chopped

2 tablespoons chopped fresh parsley

2 tablespoons chopped fresh dill

A pinch of chilli or cayenne pepper or a few drops of tabasco sauce

1 tablespoon pine nuts

150 ml (¼ pint) red wine

225 g (8 oz) tomatoes, skinned and finely chopped

Whereas small squid are delicious when fried (see page 21), the larger variety is best stuffed and baked in the oven; this is the way in which squid of about 10 cm (4 in) or longer are cooked in most Mediterranean countries. The ingredients for the stuffing vary and may include cheeses, salted anchovies, nuts of all sorts, boiled eggs, breadcrumbs and other ingredients. This recipe uses rice.

Clean the squid as described on page 21 and reserve the tentacles. Wash well and chop the tentacles very finely.

Preheat the oven to 180°C/350°F/gas mark 4.

Heat the oil in a pan and fry the onion until translucent. Add the chopped tentacles, salt and pepper and fry for a few minutes until any water has evaporated. Add the rice, pepper, parsley, dill, chilli or cayenne and pine nuts and mix well. Add a small glass of warm water, cover and simmer over a low heat for 5–7 minutes until the rice is half cooked. Strain the mixture and reserve the liquid.

Fill the squid with this stuffing, allowing room for the rice to expand, and close the openings with cocktail sticks. Arrange evenly in a round baking dish.

Prepare the sauce by bringing the reserved liquid, wine and chopped tomatoes to the boil in a pan. Simmer for 1–2 minutes, then pour the sauce over the squid. Bake in the oven for about 1 hour, basting occasionally, until the squid are tender. Remove them with a slotted spoon and place on a platter. Thicken the sauce by boiling it rapidly until reduced, then pour it over the squid. Garnish with chopped parsley and slices of lemon. Serve warm or, as the Greeks prefer to eat it, cold with a glass of ouzo.

Soupies me Spanaki
CUTTLEFISH WITH SPINACH

Cuttlefish can be as delicate in flavour as octopus and squid, provided it is cooked slowly. Cuttlefish can grow up to 25 cm (10 in) long and weigh up to 900 g (2 lb). They are covered with grey or black skin and have arms and tentacles growing from the head. Like squid, the eyes, the yellowish deposit under the head and the central bone must be removed, although the ink sac may be retained in some recipes. Very young cuttlefish can be floured or battered and fried just like squid (see page 21); the larger ones need to be cooked for 2 to 3 hours.

To Prepare Cuttlefish

First wash the fish well, then cut it from just below the head to the tail using a sharp knife. Remove the central bone and all the innards, including the ink sacs if appropriate, which you must lift carefully without breaking or you will be covered in ink. Remove the inner membrane and discard everything except the tentacles and the body. Next, wash the bag of the body, turn it inside out and remove any grit or sand. Rub the body with your fingers to remove the outer skin and then rinse again.

Prepare the cuttlefish, retaining an ink sac if you wish. Chop the tentacles and cut the body into squares. Wash and drain in a colander.

In a pan large enough to contain all the ingredients, heat the oil and fry the onions and fennel, reserving the feathery leaves, over a low heat until soft, then stir in the cuttlefish, season with pepper and fry for 10–15 minutes until it begins to brown. Add the wine and water. Squeeze the ink sac, if using, to expel some of the ink into the pan. Cover the pan and simmer over a low heat for about 1 hour until the cuttlefish is tender.

Add the spinach, raise the heat to medium and cook for about 15–20 minutes, stirring often, until the spinach has wilted and most of the liquid has evaporated. Add the dill, mint, any fennel leaves, more salt and pepper, and cook for a further 1 minute. Season to taste. Transfer on to a platter, sprinkle with feta cheese and serve warm.

900 g (2 lb) cuttlefish, preferably small to medium in size

150 ml ($\frac{1}{4}$ pint) olive oil

1 bunch of spring onions, cut in half

1–2 fennel bulbs, trimmed and thinly sliced, including the feathery leaves

Salt and freshly ground pepper

150 ml ($\frac{1}{4}$ pint) dry white wine

150 ml ($\frac{1}{4}$ pint) warm water

1.5 kg (3 lb) spinach, stems removed, coarsely chopped

2–3 tablespoons chopped fresh dill

1 teaspoon chopped fresh mint

50 g (2 oz) feta cheese, chopped

Soupies me Prasines Elies

CUTTLEFISH WITH GREEN OLIVES

SERVES

4

900 g (2 lb) cuttlefish, preferably small to medium size

150 ml (¼ pint) olive oil

1 large onion, finely chopped

2–3 garlic cloves, halved

Salt and freshly ground pepper

150 ml (¼ pint) dry red wine

2 tablespoons tomato purée

2–3 bay leaves

225 g (8 oz) pitted green olives

1 lemon, cut into wedges

Olives are a versatile ingredient with which to cook beef, lamb, rabbit, chicken and duck. Most dishes with olives are of peasant origin and exact quantities do not often apply. Olives have an uncanny affinity with garlic and nuts and with strong wine sauces. This unusual dish can equally be made with octopus or squid.

Prepare the cuttlefish as described on page 143, retaining an ink sac if you wish. Chop the tentacles and cut the body into squares. Wash and drain in a colander.

Heat the oil in a pan and sauté the onion until soft. Add the cuttlefish pieces, garlic, salt and pepper and simmer over a low heat for about 15–20 minutes until all the water has evaporated. Add the wine, tomato purée, bay leaves and some of the ink, if using, stir and bring to the boil. Lower to medium heat and cook for 30–45 minutes until the cuttlefish is tender. Season to taste.

Meanwhile, boil some water in a pan and add the olives. Remove from the heat and set aside for 5 minutes. Drain and wash them well in warm water. When the fish is done, add the olives and continue cooking for a further 10 minutes. Transfer to a serving dish and garnish with lemon wedges

Midia Pilafi

MUSSEL RICE PILAF

SERVES

4

900 g (2 lb) fresh mussels in the shell

90 ml (3 fl oz) olive oil

1 onion, sliced

1 garlic clove, crushed

1 x 200 g (7 oz) can of chopped tomatoes

1 tablespoon tomato purée

1 small chilli pepper, seeded and chopped, or ½ teaspoon cayenne pepper

Mussels are extremely popular and versatile: they can be fried, made into soup, cooked (yiahni) in a rich wine and tomato sauce, baked (plaki) with vegetables or stuffed with garlic and fine herbs.

Mussels with rice is a traditional Mediterranean dish, full of colour and taste. On the whole, Greek mussels are plump and succulent with a delicate flavour of the sea. They are often served in restaurants in their shells, just to differentiate them from the poor quality of bottled mussels.

Prepare the mussels as described on page 25. Strain the liquid in which the mussels were boiled through a fine muslin, and reserve.

Heat the oil in a deep pan and fry the onion and garlic until soft but not brown. Add the mussels and sauté them for 1–2 minutes only. Add the tomatoes, tomato purée, chilli and parsley and cook gently for 5 minutes until the sauce begins to thicken. Empty the contents of the pan into a bowl.

Put the rice into the pan and stir it about until it looks transparent. Pour in the reserved cooking liquid and add enough hot stock or water to cover the rice. Bring to the boil, lower the heat to the minimum, cover the pan and simmer for about 10 minutes until the rice is nearly cooked.

Add the mussels and sauce to the rice, season with salt, pepper and more parsley and add a little more stock if necessary. Give it a stir and simmer until the rice is done. Remove the pan from the heat, cover it with a cloth and the lid and leave to rest for 15 minutes. Fluff up the rice with a fork and serve at once. Top with crumbled feta cheese, if you wish.

Variations

1. It is not uncommon to include other sea creatures such as scallops, clams, crayfish, crabs, prawns and squid. Each is cooked separately in a little water which is then strained and reserved for the pilaf.
2. An interesting variation is to add more vegetables to the dish. Leeks are a favourite, also celery and peppers of all colours.
3. Many Greeks, especially those from Istanbul, prefer a more spicy pilaf. A pinch of ground cinnamon, allspice, cumin and pine nuts are often added to the rice.

2 tablespoons chopped fresh parsley

Salt and freshly ground pepper

For the pilaf

225 g (8 oz) long-grain rice

150 ml (¼ pint) hot chicken or vegetable stock

50 g (2 oz) feta cheese, crumbled (optional)

Saltses

SAUCES

Compared to many other countries, apart from France, Greece can boast of one or two sauces that are internationally renowned: the versatile egg and lemon sauce, *avgolemono*, and the delicious garlic sauce with walnuts, *skordalia*.

It is said that the Ancient Greeks invented the art of making sauces: Hariades of Athens invented the white sauce that was probably equivalent to the French béchamel sauce; Lamprias invented the brown sauce that was based on cooked flour. A fish sauce that was probably a relish of dried fish or caviare was also popular; and many other sauces made, with honey, vinegar, cumin, cheeses, herbs, even fragrant rose petals, are known from ancient literature. Later on, the Romans imparted some of that knowledge of making sauces to the French, particularly sauces for roast meat and flavouring sauces for bread and grain-pastes.

Unlike the French, however, modern Greeks have lost the art of inventing new sauces. The everyday sauce (*saltsa*) is usually made from the juices left in the pan after cooking meat, fish or vegetables. It will then be added to the dish so that it blends well with the main ingredients. Most Greek sauces and salad dressings are based on such magical ingredients as good quality olive oil, garlic, lemon and nuts, to which we must add the wonderful mountain herbs, oregano, thyme and dill, the rich and creamy yoghurts, the sun-rich tomatoes and the wonderful peppers.

A Few Tips on Eggs

Keep fresh eggs in a cool place for up to a week. A fresh egg should sink in cold water. Egg yolks are useful for thickening soups and sauces; one egg yolk will thicken about 200 ml (7 fl oz) of liquid. Once integrated, the liquid should not be allowed to boil again or the eggs will curdle. The egg whites are normally whisked and used for lightening. Store whites in a fridge, but bring them back to room temperature before whisking them.

When you cook lentils, do not add perfume.

———

Athenaeus

Saltsa Domatas
TOMATO SAUCE

MAKES
750 ml (1¼ pints)

2 tablespoons olive oil

1 onion, finely chopped

900 g (2 lb) ripe tomatoes, skinned and chopped, or 2 x 400g (14 oz) cans of chopped tomatoes

2 tablespoons tomato purée

2 garlic cloves, chopped

1 celery stick, finely chopped

1 carrot, finely chopped

1 bay leaf

1 teaspoon dried basil

½ teaspoon sugar or honey

Salt and freshly ground pepper

1 tablespoon butter (optional)

A traditional sauce suitable for all kinds of pasta, fried potatoes and aubergines. It is made with fresh tomatoes and herbs in the summer and preserved tomato purée in the winter.

Heat the oil in a deep pan and fry the onion and garlic until soft but not browned. Add the remaining ingredients, cover and simmer for about 45 minutes, stirring frequently, until the sauce begins to thicken. Remove the bay leaf and press the sauce through a fine sieve. The sauce is now ready to use. For a creamier sauce, add a knob of butter and simmer for 1–2 minutes.

The sauce may be kept in sterilized jars in the fridge for up to 3 months; pour a little olive oil on the surface of the sauce to seal it in the jar.

Saltsa Domatas me Kima
TOMATO SAUCE WITH MINCED MEAT

MAKES ABOUT
1.2 litres (2 pints)

1 tablespoon butter

450 g (1 lb) lean minced beef or lamb

750 ml (1¼ pints) tomato sauce (*Saltsa Domatas*, see above)

This is a typical tomato sauce with minced beef or lamb, which is suitable for moussakas, pastichios and pasta dishes.

Melt a knob of butter in a deep pan and fry the minced meat well, breaking up any lumps. Add the sauce, mix well and bring to the boil. Lower the heat and simmer gently, uncovered, for 20–30 minutes.

Aspri Saltsa
BÉCHAMEL SAUCE

———

This useful and creamy sauce is derived from the French béchamel maigre *sauce in which hot milk is the liquid used. The amount of flour and butter determines the thickness of the sauce. It forms the base of several other sauces and is used in covering moussakas and pasta dishes.*

Bring the milk to the boil, then remove from the heat. Melt the butter in a heavy-based pan until it foams, then remove from the heat and stir in the flour. Add a little milk and whisk until a smooth paste is formed with no lumps. Place the pan over a low heat and add the rest of the milk, whisking continously until the milk is amalgamated and the sauce is not lumpy. If the sauce is still lumpy press it through a fine sieve, or use a liquidizer. Add the salt, pepper and nutmeg and cook the sauce over a very gentle heat for 10 minutes, stirring continously. If the sauce is prepared in advance, cover it with a knob of butter which will melt over the top to prevent any skin forming.

To reheat the sauce, always use a *bain-marie* or warm the sauce in a heatproof bowl set over a pan of simmering water.

MAKES
300 ml (½ pint)

300 ml (½ pint) milk
40 g (1½ oz) butter
3 tablespoons plain flour
½ teaspoon salt
Freshly ground white pepper
A pinch of grated nutmeg

Aspri Saltsa me Tyri
BÉCHAMEL SAUCE WITH CHEESE

———

Prepare the béchamel sauce as above. Remove from the heat and add 90g (3oz) of crumbled feta cheese or finely chopped hard Cheddar. Pour immediately over pasta dishes.

149

Avgolemono Saltsa
EGG AND LEMON SAUCE

MAKES
300 ml (½ pint)

300 ml (½ pint) clear stock
2 large eggs
Juice of ½ lemon

Egg and lemon sauce is widely used in Greece and is delicate and simple to make, using only eggs, lemon juice and plenty of stock; it requires no herbs or spices. It is lighter than a Hollandaise egg sauce which uses butter and little stock.

Always use a clear meat, fish, chicken or vegetable stock. Good quality stock cubes may be used, but they tend to have a rather boring flavour; they are acceptable as a seasoning with other ingredients.

A light consistency is achieved using whole eggs. A thicker sauce may use egg yolks only and, occasionally, plain flour or cornflour. The amount of lemon juice will depend on the type of dish: meat and fish dishes may need more lemon juice than vegetable dishes.

Heat the stock in a small pan, then remove it from the heat. Whisk the eggs in a large bowl for 1–2 minutes, then whisk in the lemon juice. Gradually add half the hot stock, a spoonful at a time, while whisking continuously. Pour the remaining stock into the egg mixture and shake the bowl. Cover and leave to stand for 5 minutes. Do not reheat. The sauce should now be thickened and ready to use.

Creamy Egg and Lemon Sauce 1
This variation is a richer sauce which is ideal for soups and lamb casseroles. Separate 2 eggs and whisk the egg whites in a bowl until they form stiff peaks. Beat the egg yolks with a fork and combine with the lemon juice and egg whites. Gradually add the stock, as before, only more carefully this time in order to avoid poaching the egg whites. Serve immediately while the sauce is hot.

Creamy Egg and Lemon Sauce 2
This variation of the above sauce is ideal for chicken dishes. Use 4 egg yolks or 3 whole eggs and the juice of a large lemon. The procedure is the same as in the basic recipe.

Egg and Lemon Velouté Sauce
This sauce has a thick, rich consistency and is ideal for

cooked meatballs (*Yuvarlakia*, see page 89). Melt 25 g (1 oz) of unsalted butter in a heavy-based pan and mix in 1 tablespoon of plain flour or cornflour, stirring continuously over a low heat until the mixture is smooth. Pour in the stock and simmer for about 4–5 minutes, allowing the sauce to reduce a little. Remove from the heat. Lightly whisk 3 egg yolks, add the juice of half a lemon, salt and pepper and combine with the stock, as in the basic recipe.

Skordalia
BASIC GARLIC SAUCE

———

A delicious sauce with velvety texture and fine flavour, this is a perfect accompaniment to grilled fish, shellfish, mussels, chicken, rabbit, fried courgettes, aubergines, boiled broccoli and beetroot. Ideally, it should be made with a mortar and pestle, resulting in a sauce grain that is not too smooth. This recipe uses an electric blender. Mix the sauce with the stock of the dish or garnish it with olives and serve as a side meze.

Soak the garlic cloves in the wine vinegar overnight. Discard the vinegar. Blend the garlic with a little salt in a blender or pound in a mortar until smooth. Soak the bread in water, then squeeze dry using your hands. Blend the bread and garlic mixture, then pour on the oil and vinegar, a little at a time, whisking until the sauce is thick and fluffy. Do not overmix in the blender. Adjust the seasoning with salt, pepper and wine vinegar to taste.

Variations
1. An interesting variation originating in the Greek islands uses half the quantity of bread and half boiled potatoes. Boil the potatoes in their skin, peel when cool and blend them with the bread until smooth. Proceed as above.
2. For a creamier *skordalia*, add 2 egg yolks during the blending process. This produces an egg-garlic sauce suitable for poached fish, similar to the French *aïoli*, known in the Ionian Islands as *aliada*.

MAKES
300 ml (½ pint)

3–6 garlic cloves
2–3 tablespoons white wine vinegar
Salt and freshly ground white pepper
6 slices stale white bread, crusts removed
120 ml (4 fl oz) virgin olive oil

Skordalia me Karidia
GARLIC AND WALNUT SAUCE

MAKES
450 ml (¾ pint)

4 slices stale white bread, crusts removed

3 garlic cloves, crushed

250 g (9 oz) ground walnuts

150 ml (¼ pint) virgin olive oil

3 tablespoons white wine vinegar or lemon juice

Salt and freshly ground white pepper

This variation of the basic skordalia *should ideally be made with young green walnuts used for pickling. In this recipe, ground walnuts, which form the basis of many Middle Eastern sauces, are used. The amount of garlic may be adjusted to suit your taste; personally, I like more garlic than that given in this recipe. This is the traditional Greek recipe. The addition of a little cream or yoghurt will produce a smoother texture. The sauce freezes well. Add a small amount of the sauce to meat, chicken or fish stock to enhance its basic flavour.*

Soak the bread in a little water, then squeeze dry. Blend the bread, garlic and walnuts in a blender or pestle and mortar. Pour in the oil, a drop at a time, whisking continuously until it is thoroughly blended. Finally add the wine vinegar or lemon juice and season with salt and pepper. Mix well and adjust its flavour, if necessary, to taste. If the sauce curdles, add 1–2 tablespoons of warm water and mix again. Taste all the time to see if it blends well.

Skordalia me Amigdala
GARLIC AND ALMOND SAUCE

MAKES
300 ml (½ pint)

4 slices stale white bread, crusts removed.

4–5 garlic cloves, crushed

100 g (4 oz) ground almonds

Salt and freshly ground white pepper

150 ml (¼ pint) virgin olive oil

3 tablespoons white wine vinegar or lemon juice

The combination of almonds and garlic produces an excellent, rich sauce which is best served with vegetable dishes and fried fish.

Soak the bread in a little water, then squeeze dry. Blend the bread, garlic, almonds, salt and pepper in a blender or pestle and mortar. Pour in the oil, a drop at a time, whisking continuously. Finally, add the wine vinegar or lemon juice and extra seasoning, if needed. The sauce should have the consistency of mayonnaise. If the sauce curdles, add 1–2 tablespoons of warm water and mix again. Taste all the time to see if it blends well.

Mayonneza
MAYONNAISE

———

2 egg yolks, at room temperature

½ teaspoon mustard powder

300 ml (½ pint) virgin olive oil, at room temperature

1 tablespoon lemon juice or white wine vinegar

Salt and freshly ground pepper

Do not hurry in making a mayonnaise; in fact, it is best done using a wooden spoon, a pudding basin and lots of muscle power. It is essential that the eggs and oil are at room temperature. If the mayonnaise fails or curdles, start again in another bowl with a fresh egg and half the oil, then gradually add the curdled mayonnaise and then the rest of the oil.

Whisk the egg yolks and mustard to a purée. Add the oil, a drop at a time, whisking constantly to ensure that is completely amalgamated with the egg yolks. This can also be done in a blender. As the sauce becomes thicker and creamier, add the rest of the oil in a single, steady stream. When all the oil has been added, you should have a very thick mixture. Stir in the lemon juice. This will thin the sauce and make it a little paler. Add 1–2 teaspoons of water if you wish to alter the consistency; only trial and error will tell you that. Finally, season to taste with salt and pepper. You can use this mayonnaise on salads, boiled potatoes, cold meats or fried fish.

Additional Flavours to the Basic Mayonnaise

There is no end to enhancements of the basic mayonnaise. Here are a few the Greeks try:

1. Add a few spoonfuls of chilled, strained yoghurt to produce a lightly sour sauce that is perfect for meatballs, salads, boiled artichokes or asparagus.
2. Add 5 or more crushed garlic cloves; an ideal mayonnaise for any garlic freak!
3. Core and finely chop 225 g (8 oz) of black and green olives. Mix with chopped fresh parsley and add to the mayonnaise. Ideal with any grilled fish or chicken.

Ladolemono
OIL AND LEMON DRESSING

2 parts virgin olive oil

1 part lemon juice

Chopped fresh parsley or other fresh herbs (optional)

Salt and freshly ground pepper

A simple dressing used for brushing fish and shellfish for grilling, for flavouring salads and cooked vegetables, and adding, often indiscriminately, to every meze *in the book!*

Place all the ingredients in a glass jar and shake vigorously. This dressing can be used immediately or kept in the jar for later use.

Ladoxido
OIL AND VINEGAR DRESSING

MAKES

85 ml (3 fl oz)

3 tablespoons virgin olive oil

2 tablespoons white wine vinegar

1 tablespoon water

A little chopped fresh parsley or dried oregano (optional)

Salt and freshly ground pepper

1 teaspoon mustard powder (optional)

This is mainly a dressing for salads. The kinds of herbs and mustard added depend on the type of salad and personal taste.

Whisk all the ingredients until well blended.

Kokines Piperies Saltsa
RED PEPPER SAUCE

MAKES

1 kg (2¼ lb)

450 g (1 lb) red peppers

90 ml (3 fl oz) olive oil

900 g (2 lb) ripe tomatoes, skinned, finely chopped and strained

3 garlic cloves, crushed

1 tablespoon chopped fresh parsley, dill or chives

A pinch of hot paprika

Salt and freshly ground pepper

A delicious red sauce, the degree of hotness being determined by the amount of paprika used. The sauce is suitable for grilled meatballs, rissoles, chicken dishes, omelettes and boiled or steamed fish.

Scorch the peppers under a grill or over a gas fire, then wrap them in clingfilm while still hot. Set aside to sweat for 10 minutes. Peel off the skin, remove the stems and core and then chop them very finely.

Heat the oil in a pan and add the tomatoes, garlic and parsley. Simmer gently over a low heat for 30 minutes, stirring often. Add the peppers, paprika, salt and pepper and continue simmering until the sauce is blended and smooth. Store in a jar and place in the fridge for later use.

Saltsa Psariou
SAFFRON SAUCE FOR FISH

———

MAKES
750 ml (1¼ pint)

150 ml (¼ pint) clear fish stock
½ teaspoon saffron strands
150 ml (¼ pint) sweet white wine
450 g (1 lb) red peppers
4–5 tablespoons virgin olive oil
2 tablespoons white wine vinegar
Salt and freshly ground pepper

This variation of the previous sauce is particularly good for grilled or baked fish. Brush the fish with the sauce before grilling, then serve the rest of the sauce separately. Saffron is rarely used in Greek cooking. Some people believe it to be an aphrodisiac. It is grown in some places in Macedonia and Crete and sometimes used as a dye.

Put the stock, saffron strands and wine in a small pan and bring to the boil. Continue boiling until the sauce is reduced by half. Meanwhile, grill the peppers until soft, peel and seed them, then chop them finely.

Put the saffron sauce, half the chopped peppers and the remaining ingredients in a blender and blend at high speed for 30 seconds. Pour into a pan and add the rest of the peppers. Cook over a low heat for 1–2 minutes, stirring continuously until the sauce is well blended.

Saltsa Yiaourti me Skordo
YOGHURT AND GARLIC SAUCE

———

MAKES
250 ml (8 fl oz)

2 garlic cloves, crushed and pressed
with a pinch of salt
250 g (9 oz) strained Greek yoghurt
2 tablespoons olive oil
Salt and freshly ground pepper
Chopped fresh dill, parsley, mint or
chives

This pungent sauce is often cooked with vegetable dishes or served separately with fried fish. The yoghurt may be substituted by soured cream.

Combine the garlic and salt, yoghurt, olive oil, salt and pepper in a bowl. Cover and chill for 1 hour before using. Keep in the fridge for later use. Mix chopped dill, parsley, mint or chives into the sauce before serving.

Psomia ke Pittes

BREADS AND PIES

Greeks love bread: they eat bread with every meal, bread is used for the Holy Communion on Sundays and in many religious celebrations, people show their hospitality to friends and strangers by offering aromatic sweet breads to them, and they invite them to dinner or supper by simply saying 'come to eat bread with us'.

This love of bread is not new; it goes back to prehistoric times, notably to Minoan Crete (3000–1100 BC), when most plains and hillsides were cultivated for their excellent wheat and barley. Later, during the Classical Age, bread played an entirely different role in the everyday life, worship and nutrition of the Greeks. The first usable bread-oven was invented at the time of Pericles in the fifth century BC. It was preheated, open at the front, and eventually became the model for all culinary uses for many centuries to come. It was used by rich families to bake bread at home and by city bakers to bake bread for both the rich and poor. The bread for the rich was usually well made with fine flours and designed into round loaves; the staple food of the countryside and of poor people was thick pancakes made from cheap barley flour. From the simple bread, *maza*, made from coarse-ground cornmeal, to the most refined and soft bread, *semidalite*, made from fine wheat flour, there were many other breads made from combinations of wholewheat, bran and rye flours to suit the taste and pocket of everybody. The method of baking bread was equally varied. Most breads were baked in the oven; refined breads, however, were grilled in the grate or baked over a coal fire; others were placed in special vessels over boiling water or cooked in hot oil.

The art of bread-making was in mixing the various kinds of flour and bread dough to produce shapes of loaves that were attractive and were good enough to be used for special family occasions or public festivals. Athenaeus describes some 72 exciting pastries and breads made from refined flour, oil and honey, for what must have been the equivalent to modern croissants, baps, sweet rolls, cakes and cookies. Mentioned under the general term of 'breads', they included suet pastries, cheese breads, wafer-thin and crispy breads made with wine, pepper

Without bread and wine, love runs cold.

——

Greek proverb

and milk, and small square breads seasoned with anise, poppy seeds, cheese and olive oil.

The art of making good bread soon spread abroad, first to the Greek colonies on the Mediterranean coasts, then to the Romans and Gauls. During the reign of Augustus in 30 BC, there were 329 bakeries in Rome run by Greek craftsmen bakers. It was during that time that the flaky pastry we know today as filo was invented, and various pies containing cheeses and honey were made with it. The *patisserie* that was first established in Ancient Greece was based on olive oil – butter was then considered the food of barbarian cattle breeders. It was not until the Middle Ages that fat or butter was added to make pastry more pliable.

The art of bread-making and the customs of the Classical period, particularly those relating to consumption and quality of bread, continued during the Byzantine times (324–1453). From the very beginning, however, shortages of bread and other foodstuffs became the major problem of the new Byzantine Empire. With the ever–increasing migration of people from the country to the capital, Constantinople, the state was forced to control the supply of wheat, the distribution of flour to the city bakers and even the price of bread in the market. The most popular bread of the poor, called *kivarion*, was made with bran and mixed flours, and the most refined one consumed by rich merchants, called *katharon*, was made from fine soft wheat flours. Pitta breads were very popular. They were usually prepared with flour ground by hand-mills and baked on heated flat slabs. Many sweet breads and cakes originate from that period; these were made with honey, milk, grape must, fruits, seeds and all kinds of nuts.

During the Turkish occupation (1453–1821) life in Greece was not easy. Living standards deteriorated and poverty forced most Greeks to use strong-flavoured, hardy grains for the every-day bread. Barley bread became the most basic commodity. It was usually made from the whole grain with only the outer husk removed, and required steeping in a lot of water and several hours' cooking in the oven. It was said that 'barley bread needs to be kneaded by the river and baked in the forest'. Breads made from white wheat flour were a luxury and reserved for special occasions: the church mass, weddings, baptisms and the festive celebrations of Christmas and Easter. A great variety of mixed-flour breads, rusks, dry biscuits and highly decorated commemorative breads and pies originate from that period, and many are still made in the same way today.

In the history of modern Greek folklore, bread has a somewhat magical and often outlandish significance: a loaf of bread placed under the pillow is said to provide peaceful sleep and protection from harmful night fairies; bread is often blessed by the priest and placed on the chest of infants to ward off evil spirits, provide a cure for any illness and give protection against the 'evil eye'. The custom of placing cereals and grains with the dead in order to propitiate the demons – in the belief that life continues after death – is still practised in Cyprus and the Dodecanese islands, as it was in Ancient Greece. Bread may be the staff of life, but in northern Greece people believe that the yeast that makes the bread rise is the light of life. On Christmas Eve, the daughter of the house will prepare the yeast (*prozymi*) by mixing it with flour and water, then light a candle and recite three times, 'Christ is born today, let the light make this yeast rise'. If the yeast has risen by next morning, it will be used to make bread for the rest of the year; if it collapses, it is considered a very bad omen. In farming communities, bread is sculptured into all sort of shapes and dedicated to farm animals, farmhouses and farm implements; bread made in the shape of a shoe, for example, will be symbolic for the labour in the farm, while bread made in the shape of a hand will represent the hand of Christ blessing the farmer.

Traditional pies, *pittes*, made from thin filo pastry are an art for which Greece is famous. In rural areas, the technique of stretching the dough using a long and thin rolling pin (*plastri*), and then tossing and spinning it in the air until it is as thin as a leaf (hence the name filo) and almost transparent, requires dexterity and years of experience. Housewives learn this technique from their mothers and pass it on to their daughters. Combining cheeses, spinach or leeks with three, four or even more different kinds of wild greens to produce delicious pies of a unique flavour is also an art that is often kept secret. On the other hand, women with a particular instinctive talent for decorating breads and pies for special occasions (baptisms, weddings, social events), known in Crete as *xobliastres*, are often engaged to produce such artistic masterpieces which are highly admired as gifts or kept as decorations in the house.

In most traditional pies, the filling used is always between two layers of pastry. In the main, it consists of vegetables, eggs, cheeses and occasionally chicken, game or minced meat, mixed with a lot of fresh herbs such as fennel leaves, dill and parsley. Commercial cheeses that are salty and sharp are often moderated by combining them with delicious local cheeses in a perfect mix to produce a creamy filling with a mild and buttery taste. Almost without exception, the fat used is good quality olive oil, except in sweet recipes where clarified butter is also used.

In major towns, shortage of time and lack of experience in drawing out thin pastry force the housewife to use commercial filo pastry. It is versatile and easy to control; it can be used in almost all savoury and sweet pies and requires little extra care in handling and preparation. It has very little flavour of its own and that is probably its strength, in that a variety of oils, fats and butters may be used to add the flavour required. It can be folded into most attractive shapes such as triangles, coils, rolls and squares. It can be fried or baked to a crispy texture that cannot be achieved with home-made pastry.

Filo pastry

Filo is available either fresh or frozen. It is usually sold in 450 g (1 lb) packets of 20–30 sheets, depending on thickness. The size of the sheets also varies, but a packet will line a baking dish of about 33 x 23 cm (13 x 9 in). If you use a round or square dish, trim the filo so that the edges hang over the dish. The edges should then be brushed with oil and folded in. Cut filo through the entire stack of sheets you require using a sharp knife or a pair of scissors, and then always lightly brush each sheet separately with oil or melted butter.

How to Handle Filo Pastry

When exposed to air, filo dries very quickly and becomes brittle, so it should be kept covered with a dry towel all the time – a wet towel will cause the filo sheets to stick together. In order to handle filo properly, you need two dry kitchen towels and one slightly damp.

1. If the filo is fresh, remove its wrap and open out on a dry kitchen towel. Cover with another dry towel and then place a dampened towel on top.
2. If the filo is frozen, remove its wrap and cover with a dry towel and then with another lightly dampened towel. Leave to thaw for 1 hour, then handle as for fresh filo.

Fats Used with Filo

Olive oil is suitable for savoury vegetable, cheese and meat pies. Always use good quality olive oil. Corn and vegetable oils do not add much to the flavour of the dish. Butter is mainly used with sweet recipes and should always be clarified. To do this, melt the butter and heat slowly without browning. Remove from the heat and allow to stand for a few minutes, then skim off the froth leaving any settled milk solids in the pan. Clarified butter may be kept in the fridge for subsequent use. A light coating of melted butter is required on each filo sheet to enable it to brown when baking. Margarine can also be clarified and used in equal proportions with butter. Butter and oil can also be used in equal quantities; they should be mixed and then slightly warmed.

Cheese Mixtures

Nearly all pies use creamy, good quality feta cheese. The best is made from sheeps' milk and the next best from cows' milk. Feta made from goats' milk has often a pungent flavour when heated, and should be avoided. *Halloumi* cheese is sweet and mellow and is excellent when mixed with feta. Other cheeses which melt well when heated are grated Gruyère and white Cheddar. Dry *kefalotiri* is a good substitute for feta cheese, but as an alternative use grated Parmesan or white Cheshire. A good blend of sharp and mild cheeses, such as feta with unsalted mozzarella, *halloumi* or even most curd and cottage cheeses, are ideal for most Greek pies.

Baking Dishes

Home-made pastry is usually rolled out into large squares that will fit into special round or square, shallow dishes. Use a strong and rigid baking dish and avoid tin or uncoated iron dishes. Pizza pans of various sizes are ideal.

MAKES

1.25 kg (2¾ lb) loaf

150 g (5 oz) semolina flour, finely
ground

400 ml (14 fl oz) lukewarm water

25 g (1 oz) fresh yeast or 2½
teaspoons dried yeast

450 g (1 lb) strong white (bread) flour

150 g (5 oz) strong wholewheat
(bread) flour

2 teaspoons salt

2 teaspoons sugar or honey

3–4 tablespoons virgin olive oil

2 tablespoons ouzo (optional)

Sesame seeds

Horiatiko Psomi
COUNTRY BREAD

*Country bread is made with special 'country', or 'yellow' as it is
known, flour, which is a mixture of bread flours (strong wheat
white and strong wholemeal flour) plus 30–35 per cent fine
semolina flour. It is also made with* prozymi *– a sour dough
starter, not yeast – which does the work of leavening. The
bread has a dense texture, a wonderful aroma and an attractive light yellow colour. It is easily digestible and can be eaten
with almost all meals. The tradition of making bread using a
leavening starter dates back to ancient times when millet flour
was mixed with grape juice, and then kneaded and allowed to
ferment. Some 40 years ago, fresh yeasts were practically
unknown, and today* prozymi *is mostly used in the country and
commercial yeasts in the towns. In this recipe white flour is
mixed with wholewheat flour and a small proportion of fine
semolina. With fresh yeast or active yeast, the dough is kneaded
twice. If you wish, you may add a teaspoon of aniseed or a
little ouzo for extra flavour.*

How to Make *Prozymi*

This is a small piece of fermented dough from the previous
baking, and kept in a bowl of flour. It is usually softened in
warm water and then incorporated into the new mix. If you
want to prepare it from scratch for 1 kg (2¼ lb) of plain flour,
use 250 g (9 oz) of strong plain flour, 15 g (½ oz) of fresh yeast
or 2 teaspoons of dried yeast and 450 ml (16 fl oz) of water.
Mix the yeast with a little water, add to the flour with the rest
of the water and beat the mixture with a wooden spoon until
well blended. Cover with clingfilm and leave to ferment in a
warm place for 24 hours. For better results, let the mixture ferment for 2–3 days, depending on the degree of pungency
required, after which add a little flour and water to form a
thick pulp ready for use.

To make a country bread, mix the semolina with half the
water and set aside to soak for 30 minutes. In a small bowl,
blend the yeast with a little water, cover and leave to rest for
10 minutes until it doubles in size.

Sift the flours into a large warmed bowl and make a well in
the centre. Add the semolina, the yeast mixture and the

remaining ingredients. Using your fingers, mix the flours and liquid ingredients well until you have an elastic dough which leaves the sides of the bowl. Transfer on to a well-floured board and knead the dough by stretching and folding in its edges, using the palm of your hands. Continue kneading for about 10 minutes until the dough becomes elastic and springs back when pressed with your finger. Place the dough in a warm, oiled bowl, cover with an oiled plastic bag and place in a warm place for about 2 hours (longer if placed in a cooler place) until the dough has risen to at least double its original volume.

Turn the dough out on a floured surface and knead it for about 1–2 minutes, then smooth over the top. Lightly oil a large baking tray and sprinkle with sesame seeds. Place the dough in the middle of the tray, dampen its surface with a little water using your hands and sprinkle more sesame seeds on top. Cover it with an oiled plastic bag and let it rise again in a warm place until doubled in size.

Preheat the oven to 230°C/450°F/gas mark 8.

Make a few cuts on the surface of the bread using a sharp knife dipped in flour or a few holes using a fine skewer, then bake it in the oven for 10 minutes. Reduce the oven temperature to 200°C/400°F/gas mark 6 and bake for a further 40–45 minutes until the bread sounds hollow when tapped on the underside. Remove from the tray and allow to cool on a wire rack.

Mavro Psomi
BLACK BREAD

———

Substitute the white and semolina flours with 600 g (1 lb 5 oz) of strong wholewheat flour. Add a good pinch of ground cloves to the ingredients and ½ teaspoon of instant coffee. After the first rising, shape the dough into two long loaves. Instead of using sesame seeds, dust with flour or brush with milk or egg wash. Bake in a preheated oven at 230°C/450°F/gas mark 8 for 30–35 minutes. This bread is crisp with a faint aroma of cloves; it can be eaten with all meals and with garlic sauces, and makes excellent croûtons.

Kathimerino Psomi

DAILY BREAD

1.25 kg (2¾ lb) loaf

500 ml (17 fl oz) milk

25 g (1 oz) fresh yeast or 1 tablespoon dried yeast

100 ml (3 fl oz) lukewarm water

2 tablespoons sugar

1 kg (2¼ lb) strong white flour

1 tablespoon salt

4 tablespoons olive oil

A little, milk, water or beaten egg

Sesame seeds or grated nutmeg (optional)

The everyday bread the Greeks love is also called polytelias *or* de luxe. *It is a pure white, sumptuous bread made with milk and highly refined flour. It is usually made commercially and bought from the local bakery piping hot early in the morning.*

Bring the milk to the boil, then cool until it is warm to the touch (40°C). Mix the yeast with the water and sugar until completely dissolved, then leave to rest in a warm place for about 15 minutes until little bubbles begin to form.

In a large bowl, mix the flour, salt, olive oil, milk and yeast to form a firm dough, adding more flour if it is too sticky to handle. Transfer on to a well-floured board and knead the dough for about 15 minutes, by stretching using the palm of your hands and then folding in its edges. Use extra flour if the dough is too sticky. Shape the dough into a ball, place inside an oiled plastic bag and leave to rise in a warm place until it has doubled in size.

Remove from the bag and knead it again for about 2 minutes. Shape into a single loaf, two loaves or several rolls; dust each lightly with flour or leave plain. Place on an oiled ovenproof tray, cover and leave to rise for about 1 hour until doubled in size.

Preheat the oven to 230°C/450°F/gas mark 8.

Brush each loaf with milk, water or egg and sprinkle with sesame seeds or grated nutmeg, if you wish. Bake in the oven for 10 minutes, then lower the oven temperature to 180°C/350°F/gas mark 4 and bake for 40 minutes for a single loaf or 30–35 minutes for smaller loaves until the crust is deep golden brown and the bottom sounds hollow when tapped. Remove from the tray and allow to cool on a wire rack. Serve warm or cold.

Elioti
OLIVE BREAD FROM CYPRUS

MAKES

900 g (2 lb) loaf

A country bread made in the villages of Cyprus with local sweet olives, not pickled and often unpitted. Fresh herbs are also added depending on the season: dill, mint, thyme or parsley. Ideal olives are the shrivelled black olives from Thassos or Lesbos; those to be avoided are Kalamata or green olives. This bread is an ideal accompaniment to ouzo, wine, yoghurt and cucumber dip (Tzatziki, see page 12) and fish meze.

2–3 spring onions, finely chopped

225 g (8 oz) black olives, pitted and coarsely chopped

2 tablespoons finely chopped fresh dill or mint

2–3 tablespoons olive oil

For the dough

300 ml (10 fl oz) lukewarm water

15 g (½ oz) fresh yeast or ½ tablespoon dried yeast

1 tablespoon sugar

450 g (1 lb) strong white flour

½ tablespoon salt

2 tablespoons olive oil

Make the dough as described on page 164. Let it rise for the first time, then knock back and flatten the dough with your hands or using a rolling pin. Brush the surface with oil and spread with the onions, olives and herbs. Knead for about 2–3 minutes until the olives are evenly dispersed in the dough. Form into a round loaf, place on an oiled ovenproof tray, cover and leave to rise in a warm place for about 1 hour until double in size. Preheat the oven to 180°C/350°F/gas mark 4.

Bake the loaf in the centre of the oven for 45–50 minutes until the crust is deep golden brown and the bottom sounds hollow when tapped.

Tyropsomo
CHEESE BREAD

Omit the herbs and replace the olives by an equal amount of crumbled feta or Gruyère cheese. Form the dough into an oblong shape, brush with egg wash and sprinkle with sesame seeds. Excellent with wines: use it to clear the palate between drinking different types of wine.

300 ml (½ pint) milk

75 g (3 oz) unsalted butter

3 tablespoons plain flour

A pinch of grated nutmeg

200 g (7 oz) feta cheese, washed and crumbled

150 g (5 oz) *halloumi* cheese, grated

3 eggs, lightly beaten

1 small onion, finely grated

Freshly ground pepper

250 g (9 oz) filo pastry

4–5 tablespoons olive oil

Tyropita sto Tapsi
CHEESE PIE

Northern Epirus is famous for the best cheese pies. They are made with a very thin egg batter and filo pastry covered with cheese, and eaten hot for lunch with local red wines. This recipe is a variation that is commonly made with filo pastry.

Preheat the oven to 180°C/350°F/gas mark 4.

Bring the milk to the boil, then remove it from the heat. Melt the butter in a pan over a low heat and stir in the flour. Add a little milk and whisk until you have a smooth paste, then add the rest of the milk, whisking continously until the milk is fully incorporated. Cook over a low heat for 10 minutes, stirring continously. Remove from the heat and add the nutmeg, cheeses, eggs, onion and pepper and mix well.

Lightly brush a sheet of filo pastry with oil and place in a greased baking dish. Line with half the filo sheets, brushing each one with oil and ensuring that the edges are overhanging the dish. Spread the cheese mixture evenly over the pastry, then cover with the remaining filo sheets, brushing each one with oil. Trim the edges even, then fold in the ends to seal in the pie. Score with a knife through the top filo sheets into squares, brush with more oil and sprinkle with little water. Bake in the oven for about 1 hour until golden brown. Let the pie stand for 10 minutes, then cut through the scored lines and serve hot.

MAKES ABOUT

70

450 g (1 lb) feta cheese, washed and crumbled

350 g (12 oz) Gruyère, white Cheddar or cottage cheese, grated

3 eggs, lightly beaten

2 tablespoons chopped fresh parsley or dill

Tyropitakia
SMALL CHEESE PASTIES

These are little triangular cheese pasties that make an excellent meze. *They are wrapped in filo pastry, or sometimes in puff pastry, and are deep-fried or baked in the oven. Make these pasties in advance, freeze them and then bake when required. The pastries must be eaten warm; cold or reheated pasties are not very pleasant.*

Preheat the oven to 180°C/350°F/gas mark 4.

Combine the cheeses, eggs and parsley or dill, season with pepper and nutmeg and blend well. Lay the filo stack on a flat surface and cut lengthways in three strips about 10 cm (4 in) wide. Cover the strips with a damp cloth to avoid drying. Brush a strip with melted butter and place a heaped teaspoon of cheese filling on one end of the strip. Fold the corner of the strip over the filling until it meets the opposite edge to form a triangle. Continue to fold the pastry over in triangles until you meet the top end of the strip. Brush with melted butter and place, seam side down, on a greased baking tray. Repeat with the remaining pastry and filling. At this stage you can freeze the pasties for later use. Bake in the oven for 30–40 minutes until the triangles are puffed and golden brown. If you use frozen pasties, bake straight from the freezer for 10 extra minutes. Serve hot.

Freshly ground pepper
½ teaspoon grated nutmeg
450 g (1 lb) filo pastry (20–25 sheets)
225 g (8 oz) butter, melted or olive oil

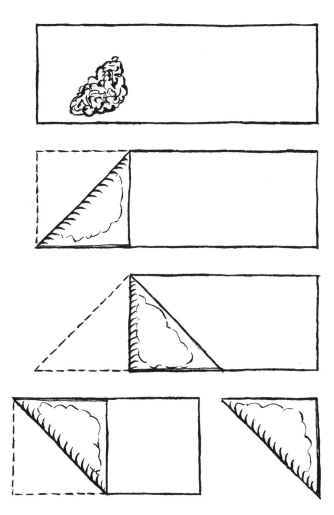

Spanakopita

SPINACH AND CHEESE PIE

900 g (2 lb) spinach, washed, stems removed, coarsely chopped

1 bunch of spring onions, trimmed and chopped

150 ml (¼ pint) olive oil

225 g (8 oz) feta cheese, washed and crumbled

4 eggs, lightly beaten

3 tablespoons chopped fresh dill and parsley

Salt and freshly ground white pepper

250 g (9 oz) filo pastry, about 12 sheets

A pinch of grated nutmeg

Spinach is available almost throughout the year, and spinach pies filled with cheese are probably the most popular Greek pies of all. They are ideal for picnics as they can be served cold; perfect for Sunday lunch or for an evening buffet. Spinach blends well with leeks and most edible wild greens – purslane, dandelion, rocket – which add a touch of bitterness.

Preheat the oven to 180°C/350°F/gas mark 4.

Heat 3 tablespoons of oil and fry the onions until soft but not browned, then tip the contents into a bowl. Add the spinach to the pan, without extra water, and cook for about 3 minutes until the spinach has wilted. Transfer to a colander and squeeze it until all moisture has drained off. Mix the onions and drained spinach with the cheese, eggs, dill and parsley, salt and pepper (remembering that feta cheese is salty) and mix all these ingredients well.

Brush a 4 cm (1½ in) deep baking dish with oil and lay in a sheet of filo, brushing it with oil. The sheet should overhang the edges of the dish. Repeat with 5 more filo sheets, then spread the filling to fill the dish nicely, and cover with the rest of the filo, brushing each sheet with oil, including the top sheet. Score the top sheets with a razor-sharp knife into diamonds or squares or prick the top with a fork to allow the steam to escape during cooking. Trim the edges, and fold them over the top or flute them with your fingertips, brushing them with oil to make them stick. Sprinkle or spray the top with a little water to prevent the pastry curling, and bake in the oven for about 45 minutes or until the top is golden brown and crisp. Serve warm or cold.

Variations

1. Use 1 lb (450 g) of leeks as an additional vegetable. Wash the leeks and cut the white parts only into thin slices; discard the green parts or use them for soup. Blanch the leeks in boiling water, then drain well. Sauté the leeks in a knob of butter until transparent, then combine with the spinach and the other ingredients.

2. Flaky or shortcrust pastry can replace the filo. It should

be rolled out as thin as possible.

3. The quantity of feta can be halved and both cottage cheese and grated Parmesan can be added.

4. There is another version of the spinach pie, made with spinach, onions, wild greens and lots of fresh herbs. It is usually eaten during Lent, when people live mainly on vegetables.

Spanakoboureka
SPINACH AND CHEESE ROLLS

Shaping spinach and cheese mixtures into triangles (see page 167) or rolls is easy. For rolls, take a sheet of filo and brush it lightly with melted butter. Place a second sheet on top and brush it with butter. Place 1–2 tablespoons of filling at one end of the sheet, 2 cm (1 in) away from the edges. Fold in the sides and then the base over filling, then roll up towards the middle of the sheet. Brush with melted butter and continue folding and rolling to the end of the sheet. Place join side down on a flat baking dish, brush with butter and bake in a preheated oven at 180°C/350°F/gas mark 4 for 25–30 minutes to allow the inside to cook well. The rolls should then be crisp and golden brown. Do not turn them over while baking. In Thrace and the island of Samos these rolls are twisted into snail-like coils, before baking.

Prasopita
LEEK PIE

SERVES
10–12

Leek pies are just as delicious as spinach pies. Leeks are sautéed in butter for 10 minutes and then mixed with the same ingredients as those listed for the spinach and cheese pie (Spanakopita, *see page 168). This particular pie is said to originate from a little-known area north of Ioannina in Epirus, where it is usually made with home-made pastry. It is a real challenge to stretch the pastry as thin as possible. If you use filo pastry, however, use*

900 g (2 lb) leeks
75 g (3 oz) unsalted butter, melted
75 g (3 oz) arborio or other medium-grain rice
5 eggs, lightly beaten
250 g (9 oz) strained Greek yoghurt
300 ml (½ pint) milk

3–4 tablespoons olive oil

250 g (9 oz) feta cheese, washed and crumbled

250 g (9 oz) Gruyère cheese, grated

Salt and freshly ground pepper

For the pastry

450 g (1 lb) plain flour

1 egg, lightly beaten

1 tablespoon olive oil

½ tablespoon white wine vinegar

½ teaspoon salt

300 ml (½ pint) lukewarm water

25 g (1 oz) unsalted butter, melted

10 sheets on the bottom of the dish and 10 on top. Alternatively, use shortcrust pastry rolled out very thinly.

First prepare the pastry. Sift the flour into a large bowl, make a well in the centre and pour in the egg, oil, wine vinegar, salt and a little of the warm water. Mix in the flour a little at a time until you have a soft dough, adding more water if necessary. Transfer to a well-floured surface and knead the dough for 10 minutes until it is very soft and pliable. Cut into 2 balls, one slightly larger than the other. Cover with a wet towel and leave to rise in a warm place for 1 hour.

Sprinkle a surface with flour and, using a long rolling pin, roll out one ball in all directions as thinly as possible. Rotate the dough on the surface while rolling, rather than turning it over. Brush with melted butter and stretch the dough with your hands, pulling it evenly in all directions. Repeat the process with the other ball. The larger sheet goes to the bottom of the dish. Cut to the size required and brush again with melted butter just before you are ready to use it.

Cut and discard the roots and the rough outer leaves of the leeks. Wash them well to get rid of any grit, then slice them into 1 cm (½ in) rounds. Heat 25 g (1 oz) of the butter and sauté the leeks over a low heat for about 10 minutes until softened.

Boil the rice in plenty of water for 10 minutes, drain, then rinse and drain again. In a large bowl, mix the leeks, rice, eggs, yoghurt, milk, oil and remaining butter. Mix well, add the cheeses and season with a little salt and pepper.

Preheat the oven to 180°C/350°F/gas mark 4.

Brush a large baking dish with melted butter and lay the bottom sheet so that it hangs over the edge of the dish. Trim to size and spread the filling evenly over the pastry. Cover with the top sheet of pastry, then fold in the edges, pressing them with your fingers to seal the pie. Score the surface with a sharp knife into squares or diamonds, brush the top with butter and sprinkle with a little water. Bake in the oven for about 1 hour until the top is crisp and golden.

Variation

A favourite and unusual pie is made with leeks and minced meat. Reduce the amount of leeks and add an equal amount of lean minced lamb or beef. Brown the meat with a knob of butter, add a little wine, then simmer over a low heat for 20 minutes until the wine has evaporated. Add the meat to the rest of the ingredients of the filling.

Kolokithopita

COURGETTE AND CHEESE PIE

When courgettes are plentiful at the end of the summer, a feta cheese and courgette pie makes a delicious lunch or a snack for picnics.

700 g (1½ lb) courgettes

250 g (9 oz) feta cheese, washed and crumbled

3 eggs, lightly beaten

3–4 spring onions, finely chopped

2 tablespoons double cream

1 tablespoon chopped fresh dill

Salt and freshly ground pepper

250 g (9 oz) filo pastry

90 ml (3 fl oz) olive oil or melted butter

Top and tail the courgettes and shred them coarsely. Sprinkle with salt and place in a colander for 1 hour to drain.

Squeeze courgettes with your hands to remove as much water as possible. Combine the courgettes with the cheese, eggs, spring onions, cream, dill, a little salt and pepper and mix well with a fork.

Preheat the oven to 180°C/350°F/gas mark 4.

Lightly brush a sheet of filo pastry with oil and place on a greased baking dish measuring about 25 x 32 cm (10 x 13 in). Line with half the filo sheets, brushing each sheet with oil and ensuring that the filo edges hang over the dish. Spread the courgette mixture evenly over the pastry. Fold the overhanging sheets over the filling, then cover with the remaining filo sheets, brushing each one with oil. Trim the edges even, then fold in the ends to seal the pie. Score with a knife through the top filo sheets into squares, brush with more oil and sprinkle the surface with a little water. Bake in the oven for about 1 hour until crisp and golden brown. Allow the pie to stand for 10 minutes, then cut through the scored lines and serve hot or warm.

Variations

1. If you wish to give your pie a rustic look, instead of the shiny appearance of the filo pastry, prepare a light batter by whisking the remaining oil with 1–2 tablespoons of plain flour and 3–4 tablespoons of water. Pour or brush this batter over the surface, before baking the pie.

2. The pie can also be made with marrow or pumpkin in the winter. This pie is not normally covered with pastry. The somewhat bland flavour of this vegetable is enhanced by

adding more cream, sugar, cinnamon, nutmeg and raisins and leaving out the cheese. If it becomes too wet, add some breadcrumbs to the mixture. This is known as *Kolokithopita Glikia*, sweet courgette pie.

Kreatopita Makedoniki

MEAT PIE FROM MACEDONIA

SERVES

6–8

900 g (2 lb) lean beef, veal or lamb

3 tablespoons olive oil

450 g (1 lb) onions, finely chopped

150 ml (¼ pint) water

2 tablespoons cornflour

90 ml (3 fl oz) milk

4 eggs, lightly beaten

100 g (4 oz) hard Cheddar, Parmesan or Gruyère cheese, grated

½ teaspoon grated nutmeg

Salt and freshly ground pepper

250 g (9 oz) filo pastry

100 g (4 oz) butter, melted

The north of Greece is famous for its meat pies: Macedonia for its lamb pies, Thrace for its pork pies and Epirus for its veal or beef pies. Meat pies are typically made for annual celebrations: weddings, birthdays, Carnival Sunday in the spring, New Year's Day. For this recipe from Macedonia, use either tender leg or shoulder of lamb, lean minced beef or veal.

Remove any gristle, fat and bones from the meat and chop it into very small pieces. Heat the oil and fry the meat and onions over a medium heat until the meat is browned. Reduce the heat, add the water and simmer until the meat is tender. Whisk the cornflour with the milk in a bowl and pour it into the pan. Mix the sauce and the meat and cook for 1–2 minutes until the sauce thickens. Remove from the heat and allow it to cool for 10 minutes. Combine the eggs, cheese, nutmeg, salt and pepper with the meat and mix well.

Preheat the oven to 180°C/350°F/gas mark 4.

Lightly brush a sheet of filo pastry with melted butter and place in a greased baking dish measuring about 25 x 32 cm (10 x 13 in). Line with half the quantity of filo sheets, brushing each sheet with butter and ensuring that the filo edges are overhanging the dish. Spread the meat mixture evenly over the pastry. Fold the overhanging sheets over the filling, then cover with the remaining filo sheets, brushing each one with butter. Trim the edges even, then fold in the ends to seal the pie. Score with a knife through the top filo sheets into squares, brush with more butter and sprinkle the surface with little water. Bake in the oven for about 1 hour until the top is crisp and golden brown. Allow the pie to stand for 10 minutes, cut through the scored lines and serve hot or warm.

Kotopita
CHICKEN PIE
———

This rich and unusual pie is made with either filo or puff pastry; the thin, almost transparent filo pastry, however, gives it a uniquely crisp texture.

Heat the oil in a deep pan and fry the onions until soft but not browned. Add the chopped leeks and simmer for 5 minutes. Add the chicken pieces and enough water to cover, bring to the boil and simmer for about 1 hour until the chicken is very tender. Remove the chicken pieces from the pan using a slotted spoon. When cool enough to handle, bone the chicken, discarding all skin, bones and fatty parts. Dice the chicken pieces into cubes.

Boil the sauce in the pan until reduced to half its original quantity. Blend the flour to a paste with a little cold water and pour this mixture in the sauce. Add the milk or cream to the pan and cook, stirring frequently, until the sauce thickens. Remove from the heat and leave to cool. Stir in the chicken pieces, the cheese, eggs, nutmeg and salt and pepper and mix well until the cheese has melted.

Preheat the oven to 180°C/350°F/gas mark 4.

To assemble the pie, melt the clarified butter in a pan. Brush a shallow 25 cm (10 in) square baking dish with butter. Line it with 2 sheets of filo pastry, brushing one each with a little melted butter, so that their edges are overhanging the dish. Cover with another 3 sheets of filo, brushing each one with melted butter. Spread the filling evenly over the pastry. Fold over the overlapping filo edges. Cover with the remaining filo pastry, brushing each sheet with butter. Fold in the ends to seal in the pie. Brush the top sheet generously with the remaining butter. Using a sharp knife, score into squares or diamonds. Sprinkle the top with a little water to prevent the pastry from curling up and brush with the beaten egg yolk to glaze. Bake in the oven for 1 hour until golden brown and crisp on top. Remove from the oven and leave to cool for 15 minutes. Cut the pie into the shapes previouly scored and serve with a country salad (*Horiatiki Salata*, see page 50).

4 tablespoons olive oil

2 onions, sliced

2 leeks, white parts only, finely chopped

900 g–1.5 kg (2–3 lb) chicken, cut into 4–6 pieces

1 tablespoon plain flour

60 ml (3 fl oz) full-fat milk or cream

3 tablespoons grated Parmesan or *kefalotiri* or cream cheese

3 eggs, lightly beaten

½ teaspoon grated nutmeg

Salt and freshly ground pepper

50 g (2 oz) clarified butter, melted

450 g (1 lb) filo pastry

1 egg yolk, beaten, to glaze

Pita me Thalasina
SEAFOOD PIE

175 g (6 oz) unsalted butter

3 tablespoons plain flour

300 ml (½ pint) milk

½ tablespoon Dijon mustard

250 g (9 oz) Gruyère, Parmesan or *kefalotiri* cheese

Salt and freshly ground pepper

1 onion, finely chopped

225 g (8 oz) prawns, cooked and peeled

225 g (8 oz) crab meat, roughly chopped

225 g (8 oz) cooked white fish

1–2 tablespoons chopped fresh parsley

250 g (9 oz) filo pastry

As fish and seafood pies go, the islands of the Aegean Sea have a long tradition of creating excellent pies with the freshest of ingredients: prawns, crabs, mussels, lobsters and a variety of white fish. Unfortunately, there is little demand for fish pies nowadays in restaurants and pies with fresh shellfish are made only at home.

Shellfish should always be very fresh. Any white fish, such as cod, monkfish or trout should be filleted, cooked briefly in salted water, drained, and then any bones removed and the flesh crumbled into chunks. If you use shortcrust or puff pastry, allow the filling to cool completely before assembling the pie, otherwise the fat in the pastry will melt.

Melt 3 tablespoons of the butter over a low heat, then whisk in the flour until the the mixture is smooth. Add the milk, whisking continuously, until the milk is amalgamated and there are no lumps. Cook for 10 minutes, stirring, then add the mustard, cheese, salt, plenty of freshly ground pepper and stir until the cheese has melted. Remove from the heat.

Melt a further 3 tablespoons of the butter and fry the onion for 3 minutes until soft. Add the fish and sauté over a low heat for 10 minutes, stirring gently. Combine the fish and parsley with the cheese cream.

Preheat the oven to 180°C/350°F/gas mark 4.

Brush a sheet of filo pastry with melted butter and place it in a greased baking dish measuring about 25 x 32 cm (10 x 13 in). Line with 3 more filo sheets, brushing each one with butter and ensuring that the filo edges are overhanging the dish. Spread half of the mixture evenly over the pastry, then cover with 3 more filo sheets, brushing each one with melted butter. Spread with the rest of the mixture and then fold the overhanging sheets over the filling. Cover with the remaining filo sheets, brushing each one with butter. Trim the edges evenly and then fold in the ends to seal the pie. Score with a knife through the top filo sheets into squares, brush generously with the remaing butter and sprinkle the surface with a little water. Bake in the oven for about 40 minutes until crisp and golden brown. Allow the pie to stand for 5 minutes, then cut through the scored lines and serve hot or warm.

Topikes Pites
REGIONAL PIES

―――――

*Apart from the familiar triangular pies (*trigona*) and those baked on a tray (*sto tapsi*), there are many wonderful regional specialities, both savoury and sweet, which are made with local cheeses, yoghurts, nuts and other ingredients. The dough is always home-made and the little pies are formed into the most imaginative shapes.*

Bougatses are individual square parcels covered with crisp filo pastry and filled with meat or cheese. Sweet *bougatses* filled with custard or sweet or soured cream flavoured with oranges and spices, make an excellent accompaniment to afternoon coffee.

Bourekia pies, containing cheese, cream, spinach or chicken, are usually shaped into long, fat cigars. The *bourekia* from Thrace are egg and yoghurt pies with a filo topping made into unusual shapes of ribbons, bow ties or flattened flowers.

Flaounes are traditional Easter pasties from Cyprus, originating probably from the Ancient Greek fig cakes (*palafi*) or the Byzantine cheese cakes (*plakountes*). The word 'flan' is derived from *flaounes*. The pasties are filled with cheeses from Paphos (similar to Cheddar), minced lamb, sugar or raisins.

Kalitsounia from Crete are small pies filled with the local *kefalograviera* cheese or cream cheese (*anthotyro*), mixed with orange juice and cinnamon, shaped into half-moons, rolls or squares, fried in oil and then sprinkled with sugar. Almost every region of Crete produces its own version of *kalitsounia*.

Klostopites from Thessaly are long rolls filled with cream cheese and grilled aubergines or local wild greens, and then coiled in a round baking tray.

Lyhnoi from Crete are tartlets filled with fresh cottage cheese, shaped into small discs and then covered with sesame seeds.

Meletinia are sweet cheese tartlets – a speciality of the island of Santorini. They are filled with a custard made with sweet *mizithra* cheese, semolina flour, ground mastic and sugar.

Peinirli are snacks shaped into little boats filled with cheese, and topped with hard-boiled eggs, a piece of ham, bacon, mushrooms, peppers or salami.

Roumeliotikes Pites from central Greece are made with 5 or 6 layers of filo pastry and filled with eggs, feta cheese and lots of butter.

Skaltsounia are nut and honey pasties prepared all over Greece. The flavour of the local honey is what distinguishes one from the other. They are filled with walnuts, almonds, apricots, orange zest and spices.

Yuslemedes from Lesbos are well–known tarts filled with *mizithra* (cottage cheese), shaped into half-moons and then deep-fried in oil.

Frouta ke Glykismata

FRUITS, SWEETS
AND CAKES

There are a suprising number of fruit trees in every Greek village, which in the springtime blossom to a spectacular display of colours. The fragrance in the air is breathtaking. From the time the first fruits appear in the market, and then throughout the season, fruit is on everyone's table. It is customary to share the fruits of one's garden with one's neighbour: a bowl of figs or cherries in the summer or a bag of chestnuts in the winter is a delightful gift. It is also customary to finish a meal with fresh fruits of the season, since the Greeks rarely have heavy sweets, puddings or cakes for dessert. Probably the heaviest dessert in the winter is baked apples or quinces sprinkled with walnuts, brandy and sugar.

Fruits are a treat for anyone who visits Greece. Melons (*peponia*) from Crete, the size of a rugby ball, appear as early as Easter; oranges (*portokalia*) from the groves of Peloponnese and Crete are best around Christmas; heavily scented, small and rounded pears (*ahladia*) appear in June; large and juicy peaches (*rodakina* or *yarmades*) are available from July to September; delicious water melons (*karpouzia*) are stacked by every roadside in the summer from June onwards; people often eat pomegranate (*rodia*) seeds by the handful, while taking a stroll; figs (*sika*) are best during their short season from August to September; the early apricots (*verikoka*) in May are sweet and sharp and are invariably used for making jam and spoon preserves; in late May, the first black sweet cherries (*kerasia*) tell you that the summer fruit season has arrived; grapes (*stafilia*) have a long season (from June to December) and are cheap and full of the Greek sun; apples (*mila*) are available the year round, but the best (the small and yellow *firikia*) will be found in the northern mountains, where temperatures are cooler.

With an abundance of fresh fruit in the market, the Greek attitude to fruit is rather casual. Fruits are rarely preserved and hardly used in cooking. Plain fruit jams are made and kept for the winter. Syrupy 'spoon sweets' (*glyka tou koutaliou*) are a speciality of Greece and most households have a reserve of

*To say a few words is sugar;
to say none at all is honey.*

———

Greek proverb

these traditional sweets for their guests. They are usually made with a whole preserved fruit and served with a glass of cold water or liqueur. The most popular spoon sweets are *visino* (black cherries), *neranzi* (slices of orange peel), *neranzakia* (tiny green oranges), *anthos* (lemon blossom), *triandafillo* (rose petal), *fraoula* (strawberry-flavoured grapes), *sika* (early green figs), *domataki* (small, unripe tomatoes), *melitzanaki* (tiny aubergines), *kidoni* (diced quince), *mastiha* (sugar paste, see page 189) and many more. Most spoon sweets are a family tradition, and cannot be made successfully from recipes; commercial ones, on the other hand, are excellent and can be obtained from confectionery or grocery shops in Greece or continental shops in Britain.

Walk into a large bakery shop or confectionery shop (*zaharoplastion*) in Greece and you will be startled by the display of elaborate cream and chocolate cakes, sweet desserts, inviting rolls of nut-filled pastry (*Baklava*, see below), shredded pastry (*kadaifi*), syrupy pies sprinkled with cinnamon and nutmeg (*Galaktoboureko*, see page 180), elaborate gâteaux, delicious doughnuts and tarts filled with fruits, nuts and honey, piles of almond shortbreads drenched in icing sugar (*kourabiedes*, see page 181), honey puffs (*loukoumades*), coffee biscuits (*koulourakia*) of all sorts and shapes, and the excellent ice-cream. Many of these marvels of confectionery art date back to Ancient Greek and Byzantine times.

This section contains a small selection of typical sweet recipes, which are the favourite of most Greek homes.

Baklava
NUT-FILLED PASTRY

MAKES
30

450 g (1 lb) filo pastry, at room temperature

150 g (5 oz) unsalted butter, melted

For the nut filling

225 g (8 oz) shelled walnuts, roughly chopped

50 g (2 oz) blanched almonds, roughly chopped

Perhaps the most celebrated of all Greek pastries, baklava is a superb dessert that is easily recognizable by its layers of thin filo pastry and its nut filling – all drenched in syrup. If you wish to reduce the sweetness, add more lemon juice and rind and leave the honey out when making the syrup. You can also make a lighter syrup by increasing the amount of water. It is worth making it at home; the recipe is quite simple. For information on how to handle filo, see page 160.

Preheat the oven to 160°C/325°F/gas mark 3.

Mix all the filling ingredients. Grease the bottom of a baking tin and lay the first sheet of filo. Brush with melted butter and place 3 more filo sheets on top, brushing each one with butter. Spread half of the nut mixture over the pastry. Next, place 4 filo sheets over the mixture, brushing each one with butter. Spread with the rest of the nut mixture. Finally, place 7 or 8 filo sheets on top, brushing each one with butter, except the top sheet. Score the surface with a sharp knife into diagonal or square pieces, no deeper than the top layer of nuts. Sprinkle the top with a few drops of water to prevent it curling in the oven. Bake in the oven for 1½ hours. If the top is browning too much, cover with foil, but do not reduce the cooking time. Remove the *baklava* from the oven and allow it to cool completely.

Meanwhile, make the syrup by placing all the syrup ingredients in a pan and heating for 2 minutes until the sugar has dissolved. Simmer over a low heat for 8–10 minutes, without stirring. Discard the cinnamon and lemon rinds. Pour the hot syrup over the *baklava* and set aside to cool for a few hours or overnight until the syrup has been fully absorbed.

Cut through the scored shapes with a sharp knife and serve with coffee and a glass of iced water.

Variations

1. Use one type of nuts for the filling, preferably walnuts. In this case, use lemon juice and cloves only in the syrup. If you use chopped almonds only, flavour the syrup with rose water and brandy or the rind of an orange.
2. You can increase the oven temperature to 180°C/350°F/gas mark 4 and bake for half the stated time. Make sure, however, that the pastry is evenly browned at top and bottom.
3. For a more aromatic syrup, leave the spices in the syrup and chill overnight.

50 g (2 oz) roasted hazelnuts, roughly chopped
75 g (3 oz) caster sugar
½ teaspoon ground cinnamon
A pinch of ground cloves

For the syrup
450 g (1 lb) caster sugar
400 ml (14 fl oz) water
2 tablespoons clear honey
1 tablespoon lemon juice
1 x 10 cm (4 in) cinnamon stick
A thin strip of lemon rind

MAKES
10–15

1 litre (1¾ pints) full-fat milk

5 eggs

175 g (6 oz) caster sugar

50 g (2 oz) fine semolina

1 teaspoon vanilla essence

1 teaspoon grated lemon rind

25 g (1 oz) unsalted butter

12 sheets filo pastry

100–175 g (4–6 oz) butter, melted

For the syrup

225 g (8 oz) caster sugar

600 ml (1 pint) water

1 teaspoon lemon juice

1 tablespoon brandy

For the covering

Icing sugar

Ground cinnamon

Galaktoboureko
VANILLA CREAM PIE

Second only to baklava, *this traditional custard cream pie is much loved by the Greeks. It is served in the morning, afternoon or very late after dinner. It looks attractive and inviting at pastry shops and is usually eaten fresh on the day it is made. It is sweet, firm and scented with vanilla essence, lemon, cinnamon, cloves, nutmeg, oranges and brandy.*

Preheat the oven to 190°C/375°F/gas mark 5.

Heat the milk to near boiling point, then remove from heat. Beat the eggs and sugar in a bowl until thick and creamy. Add the semolina, vanilla essence and lemon rind and mix well. Add the milk to the egg mixture, a little at a time, whisking continuously. Add the butter and mix well for 3–4 minutes until the butter has melted and the custard is thick.

Brush a 22 x 30 cm (9 x 12 in) baking dish with melted butter and cover it with 1 or 2 sheets of filo pastry so that it overhangs the dish on all sides. Add 5 more sheets, brushing each sheet with melted butter. Pour the custard into the tin and spread evenly. Turn the edges of the pastry over to cover the filling. Cover with the remaining 6 filo sheets, brushing each one with melted butter. Cut off the excess filo pastry and score through the top layers into squares or diamonds, using a sharp knife. Sprinkle a few drops of water on top of the pie to prevent the filo from curling during baking. Bake in the oven for 40–45 minutes. The top of the pastry should be golden brown and the custard set.

Meanwhile, prepare the syrup. Bring the sugar and water to the boil, add the lemon juice and brandy and simmer over low heat for 15–20 minutes until the syrup lightly coats the back of a spoon.

Remove the pie from the oven, pour the syrup evenly over it, then leave to cool. Cut through the scored marks and dust with icing sugar and ground cinnamon.

Yiaourtopita
YOGHURT CAKE

———

A very pleasant and light cake, this can be served with whipped cream and roasted almonds.

Preheat the oven to 180°C/350°F/gas mark 4.

Cream together the butter and sugar until light and fluffy. Add the egg yolks, one at a time, beating continuously after each addition. Sift the flour with the bicarbonate of soda and salt and fold into the butter mixture. Add the vanilla essence and beat well until the mixture is thoroughly blended. Add the yoghurt. Whisk the egg whites in a deep bowl until they form stiff peaks, then fold into the butter and yoghurt mixture. Grease and line a 23 cm (9 in) square cake tin and pour half of the mixture into the tin. Sprinkle over the nuts, then pour in the rest of the mixture. Bake in the oven for about 1 hour until golden and firm to touch. Remove the cake from the tin and place it on a wire rack to cool. Before serving, cut the cake into square or diamond shapes and dust with icing sugar.

250 g (9 oz) unsalted butter, softened

250g (9 oz) caster sugar

5 eggs, separated

450 g (1 lb) self-raising flour

1 teaspoon bicarbonate of soda

A pinch of salt

$\frac{1}{2}$ teaspoon vanilla essence

225 g (8 oz) strained Greek yoghurt

75 g (3 oz) walnuts or almonds, peeled and finely chopped

Icing sugar

Kourabiedes
SHORTBREADS WITH ALMONDS

———

Much loved on all occasions, particularly at Christmas and on New Year's Day, these creamy shortbreads are covered with icing sugar and served with afternoon coffee. They melt in your mouth. At weddings, it is customary to serve kourabiedes *and sugared almonds to all the guests. For extra flavour, you can use toasted almonds.*

Cream the butter and margarine with the icing sugar until pale and soft, then add the ouzo or cognac, vanilla essence and almonds. Mix the flour and baking powder, then fold it into the mixture to make a soft but firm dough. Adjust the consistency of the mixture by adding more ouzo or more flour. Cover the dough and chill for 30 minutes.

Preheat the oven to 160°C/325°F/gas mark 3.

100 g (4 oz) unsalted butter, at room temperature

100 g (4 oz) margarine, at room temperature

75 g (3 oz) icing sugar plus extra for dusting

2–3 teaspoons ouzo or cognac

1 teaspoon vanilla essence

100 g (4 oz) almonds, blanched and chopped

450 g (1 lb) plain flour

1 teaspoon baking powder

A little diluted ouzo or rose water

Roll the dough out to about 1 cm (½ in) thick, cut into pieces and shape them into small balls, ovals, pears, S-shapes or crescents. Lightly brush 2 non-stick baking trays with melted butter and dust with flour. Place the *kourabiedes* 5 cm (2 in) apart on the trays to allow for expansion. Bake in the oven for 20–25 minutes until firm and very pale gold; they should not be overcooked. Transfer to a wire rack to cool.

Sprinkle the shortcakes with diluted ouzo or rose water and dust liberally with icing sugar. Arrange them on a plate and dust with more icing sugar. They can be stored in an airtight container for 1 month; their flavour improves with time.

Karidopita
WALNUT CAKE

SERVES

8–10

225 g (8 oz) unsalted butter

450 g (1 lb) caster sugar

5 eggs, separated

1 teaspoon ground cinnamon

450 g (1 lb) plain flour

3 teaspoons baking powder

½ teaspoon bicarbonate of soda

Grated rind of ½ orange

225 g (8 oz) walnuts, roughly chopped

4 tablespoons milk

For the syrup

350 g (12 oz) sugar

600 ml (1 pint) water

1 cinnamon stick

3 tablespoons brandy or dark rum or fruit liqueur

Mountain walnuts grow in abundance in Greece and are gathered in October. They are very cheap to buy and even cheaper when unshelled. Tender green walnuts make an excellent spoon sweet.

Preheat the oven to 200°C/400°F/gas mark 6.

Beat the butter and sugar until pale and creamy. Add the egg yolks, one at a time, whisking continuously. Whisk the egg whites in a bowl until they form soft peaks. Fold half the whites into the butter mixture, add the ground cinnamon and combine gently using a spatula. Mix in the flour, baking powder, bicarbonate of soda, orange rind, milk and walnuts until all the ingredients are well blended. Fold in the remaining egg whites and pour the mixture in a well-buttered 23 cm (9 in) deep square cake tin. Sprinkle the chopped walnuts over the cake and bake it in the oven for about 40 minutes or until a fine skewer inserted comes out clean.

Prepare the syrup by boiling the sugar, water and cinnamon over a high heat for about 15 minutes until the sugar has dissolved and the syrup is thick. Remove from the heat, add the brandy or liqueur and strain the syrup. Remove the cake from the oven. Pour the hot syrup over the cake and allow it to cool completely, then cut into square or diamond pieces and serve with whipped cream.

Revani
SEMOLINA CAKE

This is an aromatic, sweet cake – at least sweet enough by Greek standards. The syrup used in this recipe is quite pleasant and not too overpowering. Revani *is a traditional cake which is very popular in northern Greece. It is served with the afternoon coffee.*

Prehear the oven to 180°C/350°F/gas mark 4.

Beat the sugar and eggs in a deep bowl using an electric mixer set at high speed for 10 minutes and adding the milk in small quantities until the mixture is fluffy and the sugar has completely dissolved.

In another bowl mix the semolina, flour, baking powder, vanilla essence and salt. Gradually fold the flour mixture into the egg mixture a spoonful at a time. The final mixture should be light and smooth. Pour into a 30 cm (12 in) round cake tin and bake in the oven for 40–45 minutes until the cake is golden brown.

Meanwhile, boil the sugar and water until the sugar has dissolved. Add the butter, lemon juice and rind, then set aside to cool. Take the cake out of the oven and spoon the syrup over the top. Do not pour the syrup as the cake may collapse. Allow the cake to cool for a couple of hours, then transfer it to a serving plate and cut it into triangular pieces. Decorate with whole almonds.

225 g (8 oz) caster sugar
6 eggs
5 tablespoons warm milk
225 g (8 oz) fine semolina
150 g (5 oz) self-raising flour
2 teaspoons baking powder
1 teaspoon vanilla essence
A pinch of salt

For the syrup
450 g (1 lb) sugar
400 ml (14 fl oz) water
75 g (3 oz) unsalted butter
2 tablespoons lemon juice
Grated rind of ½ lemon

For decoration
A few whole blanched almonds

Revani me Yiaourti
YOGHURT SEMOLINA CAKE

This is a variation of the revani *cake using coarse-ground semolina, almonds and yoghurt.*

Combine the semolina with half the sugar and mix in the yoghurt, cognac, bicarbonate of soda and orange rind. Set aside for about 1 hour until the semolina grains are softened. Then add the melted butter and mix well.

225 g (8 oz) course-ground semolina
225 g (8 oz) caster sugar
225 g (8 oz) strained Greek yoghurt
1 tablespoon cognac
½ teaspoon bicarbonate of soda
Grated rind of 1 orange
50 g (2 oz) unsalted butter, melted

3 eggs
75 g (3 oz) ground almonds

For the syrup
300 g (10 oz) caster sugar
250 ml (8 fl oz) water
1 tablespoon lemon juice

For decoration
A few whole blanched almonds

Preheat the oven to 200°C/400°F/gas mark 6.

Beat the eggs and the remaining sugar using an electric mixer until the mixture is fluffy and the sugar has dissolved, then add the ground almonds, avoiding beating the eggs further. Combine the egg mixture with the semolina and pour into a 30 cm (12 in) round cake tin. Bake for 30–35 minutes until the cake is golden brown. Remove it from the oven and allow it to cool for 15 minutes. Cut into triangular pieces.

Boil all the syrup ingredients for 10 minutes, then pour it hot over the cake. Decorate with whole almonds and allow it to rest for a couple of hours before serving.

Makedonikos Halvas
MACEDONIAN HALVA

MAKES
1 kg (2¼ lb) halva

2 egg whites
450 g (1 lb) sesame paste (*tahini*)
100 g (4 oz) unsalted pistachio nuts or sliced almonds

For the syrup
450 g (1 lb) caster sugar
250 ml (8 fl oz) water
2 teaspoons vanilla essence

*There are basically two types of halva in Greece, with many variations. One type is made from sesame paste (*tahini*), glucose, sugar and pistachio nuts (*fistikia*) grown in the island of Aegina. The best halva of this type is produced commercially in Macedonia and Thessaly and exported in tins or sealed blocks. It has a delicious taste of honey and nuts. You can eat it any time of the day as a sweet, dessert or snack, with coffee or tea. You can sprinkle it with a little ground cinnamon or fresh lemon juice, or serve it with a light white wine as an after-dinner dessert. It stays fresh with no refrigeration for up to six months. The other type of halva is home-made with fine or coarse semolina (*simigdali*), almonds and butter. This recipe is similar to the commercial halva.*

First make the syrup by boiling the water, sugar and vanilla essence for about 15 minutes until the mixture begins to form a semi-hard ball. Set aside to cool slightly.

Beat the egg whites with an electric mixer until they form stiff peaks. In another bowl beat the *tahini* until the sesame oil and paste are well integrated into a smooth mixture. Gently fold in the egg whites until the mixture becomes stiff and pulls away from the side of the bowl. Then fold in half the syrup and the nuts and mix gently. Finally stir in the remaining syrup a little at a time. Line a 900 g (2 lb) loaf tin with greaseproof paper, pour in the halva mixture, cover with another piece of greaseproof paper and chill for 2–3 days.

Pascalinos Halvas
EASTER HALVA CAKE

This halva uses a coarse type of semolina (semolina flour), which is also used for cakes and sweet breads. It is a traditional Easter cake, but is often made for Sunday guests or special occasions.

Preheat the oven to 220°C/425°F/gas mark 7.

Beat the butter until soft, then beat in the sugar until light and fluffy. Add the semolina, eggs, orange rind and juice, baking powder and ground almonds and beat until all the ingredients are well blended. Butter a 23 cm (9 in) ring mould well, turn the cake mixture into the mould and bake in the oven for 10 minutes. Reduce the oven temperature to 180°C/350°F/gas mark 4 and continue baking for a further 30 minutes until the cake is cooked and the top is golden.

Meanwhile, put all the syrup ingredients in a pan and boil for 5 minutes until the syrup thickens slightly. Remove the cinnamon stick and any scum formed.

Remove the cake from the oven and let it cool for a few minutes. Then ease it gently with a knife and turn it over on to a deep, warm plate. Reheat the syrup to boiling point and pour it gently over the cake. When the cake has soaked up the syrup and cooled, sprinkle on the ground cinnamon. The cake is light and moist and will keep for a few days if it is covered with clingfilm.

100 g (4 oz) unsalted butter
100 g (4 oz) caster sugar
175 g (6 oz) coarse semolina
3 eggs
Grated rind and juice of 1 orange
2 teaspoons baking powder
100 g (4 oz) ground almonds

For the syrup
250 g (9 oz) caster sugar
300 ml (½ pint) water
2 tablespoons lemon juice
2.5 cm (1 in) cinnamon stick
A little ground cinnamon

MAKES
1 kg (2¼ lb) cake

For the yeast
1 teaspoon sugar
120 ml (4 fl oz) lukewarm water
1 tablespoon dried yeast

For the dough
700 g (1½ lb) strong plain flour
175 g (6 oz) caster sugar
½ teaspoon salt
120 ml (4 fl oz) warm milk
4–5 eggs
100 g (4 oz) unsalted butter, melted
1 aniseed pod
1 teaspoon vanilla essence
Grated rind of ½ orange
Grated rind of ½ lemon

For the decoration
1 egg yolk
1 tablespoon milk
1 tablespoon sesame seeds or flaked almonds
4–5 hard-boiled eggs dyed deep red

Tsoureki
PLAITED EASTER BREAD

On Maundy Thursday, most Greek women will dye the Easter eggs red, polish them with olive oil and then start the preparations for the paschal lamb and the other special dishes for the Easter festivities. Part of this religious tradition is to bake a tsoureki *bread to be ready for the Easter Sunday breakfast. Many shapes and sizes of breads and buns will be baked, and most will be decorated with red eggs.*

In villages and religious communities in towns, the Easter spirit unites the people more than on any other occasion in the Greek calendar. Children love it and everyone walks to the church with a candle for the midnight service. The instant 'Christ is risen' is proclaimed by the priest, bonfires are lit and firecrackers shoot into the sky. The people embrace and wish each other 'Happy Easter' (Kalo Pasca). Then they crack each others' red eggs; if your egg is cracked, you must offer it to the other person. Children love this custom, because they go around cracking and winning as many eggs as possible!

The secret of a good Easter bread is to prepare it in a warm kitchen with no draughts. Dissolve the sugar in the water and sprinkle over the yeast. Whisk well, cover with a towel and stand in a warm place for 15 minutes until frothy. Whisk the liquid again before using it.

Simmer the aniseed pod in a little warm water for 10 minutes, strain and reserve 4 tablespoons of the aromatic liquid.

Place the eggs in a large bowl and beat for 4–5 minutes until creamy but not frothy. Add the sugar, a spoonful at a time, and whisk until dissolved. Add the melted butter and continue beating for 3–4 minutes. Add the warm milk, salt, grated rinds and vanilla essence and mix well. Add the yeast liquid and the aniseed liquid. Add the flour, a spoonful at a time, and mix well with your hands until the dough is spongy and no longer sticks to the bowl. Place the dough on a floured surface and knead it with your hands for 15 minutes. To prevent your hands sticking to the dough, oil them with a drop of light oil. After this exhausting work, place the dough in an oiled bowl, cover it with 2 towels or cloths and leave it in a warm place for about 2–3 hours to rise until doubled in size.

Turn the dough on to a board, punch it down and knead it for 3–5 minutes. Divide the dough into 3 equal portions and roll out each portion into a sausage shape about 30 cm (12 in) long. Pat the middle of each rope so that it becomes slightly flatter than the ends and tapers evenly. Plait the 3 braids, starting from the middle, twisting the ends together so that they form a long plait. Pinch the ends and tuck them under. Place on a well-buttered baking tray, cover with a towel and leave to rise again for about 2 hours until double its original size.

Preheat the oven to 200°C/400°F/gas mark 6.

Beat the egg yolk and milk and brush over the bread. Sprinkle with sesame seeds or almonds and press in the red eggs. Bake for 10 minutes, then reduce the oven temperature to 180°C/350°F/gas mark 4 and bake for a further 30 minutes until the top is golden brown. Allow the bread to cool for 2–3 hours before cutting.

Vasilopita
NEW YEAR'S CAKE

New Year's Eve is a family celebration. All members of the family and relatives gather at the head of the family's house to eat and to cut the vasilopita – *the cake dedicated to St Basil, the patron saint of the New Year and good fortune. The cake contains a silver coin, and whoever gets the piece of cake with the coin is supposed have luck for the rest of the year.*

The story of the cake dates back to the fourth century AD, when St Basil, the Archbishop of Cesarea, was responsible for collecting coins and jewels to hand over to the District Commander who was regularly plundering the province. Apparently, on one occasion, St Basil decided to welcome him so lavishly that the Commander felt acutely embarrassed and never plundered the city again. The problem then for St Basil was how to return the coins and jewels that had been collected, since they were all mixed up. St Basil's idea was to make small cakes, inserting a coin or a jewel in each, and hand over the cakes to everyone in the congregation on New Year's Eve. Those who found their coins or jewels were allowed to keep them.

MAKES
1 kg (2¼ lb) cake

25 g (1 oz) fresh yeast
150 ml (¼ pint) warm milk
700 g (1½ lb) strong plain flour
½ teaspoon salt
175 g (6 oz) sugar
4 eggs, lightly beaten
Grated rind of ½ orange
Grated rind of ½ lemon
½ teaspoon ground cinnamon
½ teaspoon grated nutmeg
3 tablespoons brandy
100 g (4 oz) unsalted butter, melted

For the decoration
1 egg yolk
1 tablespoon milk
A pinch of sugar
A few blanched almonds
1 tablespoon sesame seeds

The vasilopita *is cut by the head of the family at midnight, amid greetings (*hronia polla, 'many happy years'*), hugs and kisses for everyone and lots of noise and excitement. The first slice is offered to the Holy Mother, the next is for the house and the next to the head of the family; the last piece is set aside for the poor. Which of the members of my childhood family would be the one to find the hidden coin was always a bone of contention. My grandmother would always make sure, by some inexplicable trick, that my grandfather found the coin, otherwise he would be grumpy for the rest of the week!*

In a small bowl, combine the yeast with half the milk and 2–3 tablespoons of flour to make a batter. Cover with a towel and leave to stand in a warm place for 15 minutes until frothy.

In a large mixing bowl, sift the flour and salt and make a well in the centre. Add the yeast batter, sugar, eggs, orange and lemon rinds, cinnamon, nutmeg, brandy and the rest of the milk. Mix the ingredients together well, then pour in the melted butter a little at a time. Knead for 10–12 minutes until all the butter is fully integrated and the dough starts to leave the sides of the bowl. If the dough is sticky add a little more flour, if too stiff add more milk.

Brush the dough with a little oil or melted butter to prevent it from forming a crust while rising, cover it with a couple of kitchen towels, and place it in a warm, draught-free place for about 2 hours, or until it doubles its bulk.

Next, punch the dough down, place it on a lightly floured surface and knead it for 2–3 minutes. Shape it into a round loaf, insert a silver or gold coin inside it and place it on a well-buttered baking tray. Cover and let it rise again for about 30 minutes until doubled in size.

Preheat the oven to 180°C/350°F/gas mark 4.

Flatten the dough slightly. Mix the egg yolk, milk and sugar and brush over the cake. Write the number of the New Year on top using whole almonds and sprinkle with sesame seeds. Bake in the oven for 45–60 minutes until golden brown. Cool on a wire rack and then wrap it in clingfilm to keep it fresh.

Variations

There are many variations in making and decorating a *vasilopita*. In fact, many cooks use the same recipe for *vasilopita* and *tsoureki* (see page 186).

1. One version, which comes from Smyrna, uses bicarbonate of soda and baking powder instead of yeast and orange juice instead of milk. The final dough is kneaded to a thick long rope which is then coiled in a spiral and placed on a round baking dish.

2. Another popular version uses ground *mahlepi* instead of orange and lemon rinds. *Mahlepi* is an oriental spice similar to allspice; the nearest substitute is to boil 3 cloves, a bay leaf and ½ cinnamon stick in 150 ml (¼ pint) of water for 20 minutes. Use the liquid to flavour the cake. Alternatively, use a star-anise boiled in a little water for 10 minutes; this gives a pleasant liquorice flavour to the cake.

3. Yet another version, which comes from Macedonia, is to use self-raising flour and bicarbonate of soda instead of yeast, and yoghurt instead of milk.

Mastiha Glyko
SUGAR PASTE WITH MASTIC

This thick, white and sugary preserve is a favourite with children and adults alike. It is also known as vanilia, *because it often tastes of vanilla essence. A teaspoon of the sweet is always served on a saucer with a glass of iced water. In Greek cafés they call it* hipovrihio – *'submarine' – because instead of sipping the water with the sweet, one dips the sweet into the water, and then puts it in the mouth.*

300 ml (½ pint) water
450 g (1 lb) caster sugar
2 teaspoons lemon juice
A few drops of vanilla essence
3 teaspoons mastic, finely pounded
with a little sugar

Heat the water and sugar in a pan, stirring continuously until the sugar has completely dissolved. Add 1 teaspoon of lemon juice, bring to the boil and cook for about 20 minutes until the syrup begins to thicken. You can test this stage using a thermometer measuring 115°C–120°C (240°F–250°F), or by dipping a little syrup in cold water and then forming a little ball with your hand. Remove the pan from the heat and dip the base in cold water to stop the syrup from boiling further. Leave to cool.

When the syrup has cooled, add a teaspoon lemon juice, the vanilla essence and mastic and stir briskly with a wooden spoon. Stir around in one direction only until the paste is clear, shiny and white. Add a little water if the paste is too thick. Place it on a damp surface and knead it, as you would with bread, until the paste becomes plastic and gooey. Place it in an airtight jar; it will keep for ever. If it becomes dry, simply warm the jar in a bowl of warm water and adjust the consistency by mixing the paste with a little water.

You can use mastic paste to decorate cakes and biscuits. Instead of vanilla essence, you may also add other aromas and colours.

Rizogalo

RICE PUDDING

SERVES

6–8

100 g (4 oz) short-grain rice
1.2 litres (2 pints) full-fat milk
2 teaspoons cornflour
1 tablespoon cold milk
2 egg yolks
150 g (5 oz) caster sugar
Grated rind of ½ lemon
½ teaspoon vanilla essence
1 teaspoon ground cinnamon

Quite often, Greeks eat a plate of cold rice pudding as a snack when they are hungry, for breakfast or late at night. It is a creamy and sweet dessert, full of flavour, and a favourite pudding with the children.

Wash the rice well and strain. Bring the milk to the boil in a heavy-based pan and add the rice. Return to the boil, lower the heat to minimum and simmer for about 30 minutes, stirring occasionally, until the rice is very soft.

Dilute the cornflour in the cold milk, add the egg yolks and blend over a low heat until the mixture is thick. Add it to the rice with the sugar, lemon rind and vanilla essence, and simmer over a very low heat for a further 5–6 minutes, stirring continuously. Pour into individual bowls or dessert plates. When cold, dust with cinnamon. Keep it in the fridge covered with clingfilm.

Variations

1. Leave out the egg yolks if you find the pudding is too rich.
2. On the other hand, you can use evaporated milk instead of fresh milk to make the pudding more like a custard.
3. Instead of grated lemon rind, use a small piece of lemon rind in the milk, then remove it at the end of cooking.

Ellinikos Kafes
GREEK COFFEE

———

Coffee was unknown to the ancient and medieval world outside Ethiopia. It was introduced to the Arabs in the fifteenth century and to Europe in the sixteenth, and then to Martinique and the West Indies. It is said that the Turks were initiated to coffee in 1550. They liked it because it kept them awake during the long hours of prayer day and night. The French tasted it in 1611 and gave it the name *'café'*. So much for history. Nowadays, there is Greek coffee and Turkish coffee, but nobody can explain the difference!

Coffee is ordered by a name which signifies the quantity of coffee used, the amount of sugar and water, the method and the duration of brewing. The art of making and enjoying coffee is akin to making love. The difference is that there are only 46 ways of making coffee!

A person who is experienced and passionate about coffee (known as *meraklis*) knows how to order a coffee that is 'not too sweet, rather light medium', and will be sure to tell you the difference! The method of drinking coffee is purely a personal affair. A *meraklis* Greek would probably drink it as follows:

> *He would take the first short sip slowly, serenely . . .*
> *He would blow once or twice to savour the aroma, a*
> *maximum of five times.*
> *He would then sigh deeply . . . 'ah!'*
> *He would then light a cigarette.*

All these steps would be accompanied by a variety of facial expressions which are difficult to describe. After he has drunk the coffee, he would turn his cup over on his saucer and enter a new phase of concentration – that of reading his fortune. However, telling fortunes is beyond the scope of this brief introduction.

In Greece, the tourist knows only about three ways of ordering coffee:

Sketo - unsweetened;

Metrio - with some sugar;

Glyko - sweet.

How to Make *Metrio* Coffee for Four

You need a *briki* – a long-handled brass pot with a pouring lip. The pot comes in various sizes, depending on the number of coffees you wish to make. If you do not have a *briki*, use a small enamelled or stainless steel pan. Use well-roasted coffee beans, usually finely ground Brazilian beans. Measure 4 small coffee cups of water and bring to the boil. Remove from the heat, add 4 teaspoons of coffee and 3 teaspoons of sugar. Stir with a small wooden spoon.

Hold the *briki* over a very low heat and watch it until the coffee rises to the top. Immediately remove it from the heat, and never allow it to boil. Pour the froth equally into 4 cups, then pour the rest of the coffee to the brim. Serve at once. They say that whoever has more froth in the cup is the luckier, and every bubble on the froth represents a kiss. Always serve coffee with a glass of cold water.

Tyña ke Yiaourti

CHEESES AND YOGHURTS

It is very likely that in prehistoric Greece goats' and sheeps' milk cheeses were made and aged in caves. Today some of the best table cheeses in Crete are still aged in caves. Soft white cheeses (called *tyros* in Ancient and *tyri* in modern Greek), such as cream cheeses and cottage cheeses, were made in Homeric times by draining curdled milk through wicker baskets. The resulting cheeses were eaten either fresh or dipped in brine to harden; they were subsequently dried in a process that is similar to that of making modern feta cheese.

Firmer cheeses were made by compressing curds in a wooden box or mould called *phormos* (*forma* in Latin, *formage* in medieval French – whence *fromage* in modern French). These cheeses were further processed by drying, salting or ripening them by means of yeasts or natural enzymes contained in the stomach or bladder of slaughtered animals. The resulting mature cheeses, particularly those made with full-cream milk, were widely used with other ingredients in the making of all sorts of pastries and cheesecakes. They were also grated and seasoned with salt, spices, garlic and aromatic herbs to which wine and dried fruits were added. A famous cheese dish called *hypotrima,* with a sour and piquant taste, was made with various such ingredients grated and pounded up together.

Today Greeks eat cheese as a *meze*, before the main meal and during the meal – in fact they eat a lot of cheese. It may surprise the French and Italians to know that cheese consumption per capita in Greece is higher than in any other country in Europe. It is used in salads, pies, sauces, stuffings, garnishes, cakes and fruit dishes. There are several types of cheese available, with feta – the best–known of all Greek cheeses – being eaten daily by most Greeks.

There are half a dozen popular cheeses on the market, including feta, *kaseri* and *kefalotiri*, some of which are exported. There are a few dozen cheeses around the country and the islands, which are made according to local traditions by shepherds and small farmers. Such cheeses include the wonderful *anari* from Cyprus; the hard sheep's milk cheese, *ladotiri*, from Lesbos, which is cured in olive oil; the popular unsalted

Soft cheese, hard cheese, sausages and smoked meat – what else is missing in a humble home!

———

Cretan proverb

soft goats' cheese, *anthotiro*, from Crete; and the highly salted white cheese, *telemes*, from Macedonia and Thrace. There are some excellent cheeses named after the town or region in which they are made, for example, *agrafa* (a passable kind of Gruyère from Thessaly), *pindos* (a superior hard cheese from the Pindus mountains), *metsovone* (a rich, smoked cheese from the attractive town of Metsovo in Epirus) and *psiloriti* (a hard cheese with a strong flavour from Crete).

When you buy cheeses in Greece, you would be well advised to ask for a sample to taste, since the quality varies. Most of all, when you are in a village or farmhouse, ask to taste the local cheeses – you will be pleasantly surprised by their high quality and excellent flavour.

Below is a list of some of the cheeses you can find easily in Greek supermarkets; some of these, such as feta and *halloumi*, are available in supermarkets abroad, others may be found in specialist shops.

Anthotiro

Meaning 'blossom' in Greek, this Cretan whey cheese is made from goats' milk. It is a soft, buttery, slightly salted cheese with a hint of yellow colour. It is similar to *mizithra* and often baked into sweet pasties or eaten with honey or jam.

Nearest substitute: None to match its flavour, but 1 part grated feta and 4 parts strained cottage cheese is satisfactory for pies.

Feta

Feta was originally made exclusively with ewes' milk. It is now made from sheeps', goats' or cows' milk curdled with a starter and rennet. The curd is drained and cut into large blocks or slices, dry-salted, washed, then placed in wooden barrels or tins with a salt brine solution. The barrel-matured feta is tastier, as it gains its flavour from the wood of the barrel. Fresh feta ripens in about a month at 18–20°C, harder feta in three months. Feta is a protected Greek cheese under the European Union regulations – like Stilton in Britain and Roquefort in France.

Fresh feta is a white, salty and moist cheese; it has a flaky texture and crumbles easily. Because of high demand, feta is now widely produced by many milk-producing countries; most of this feta is made from cows' milk; some is fair, some bears no resemblance to real feta. In Greece, the best feta comes from Dodoni in Epirus, which the poet Lord Byron visited, Arahova, near the site of Delphi, and the island of Kefalonia.

Buy feta in jars or tins containing a salt-water solution. If feta is imported in the barrel (*varelisio*), buy a big cut and keep it chilled in jars in a solution of 1 tablespoon of salt to 600 ml (1 pint) of water. You would then be able to surprise your guests with a marvellous feta soufflé.

Nearest substitutes: None, but white Lancashire, white Cheshire, Wensleydale, white Stilton or Caerphilly may be used in pies.

Graviera

A poor imitation of the Swiss Gruyère made nowadays from sheeps' or cows' milk. On rare occasions, you would be pleasantly surprised to find *graviera* tasting better than the famous Swiss cheese: in Crete, for example, where they make a creamy and slightly salty version called *kefalograviera*, and in some mountainous parts of Greece where cows graze in pastures covered with aromatic grasses and sweet flowers. It is eaten fresh or left to mature and used grated.

Halloumi

A soft or semi-hard full-fat, white cheese from Cyprus made from goats' milk. The milk is curdled using powdered rennet and the curd is cut into tiny pieces and cooked in the whey, then rolled in salt and dried mint and kept in a whey-brine mixture in earthenware jars for a month. It has a rich, salty flavour and is often mixed with dried mint or coriander. It makes an ideal *meze*: cut *halloumi* into slices, fry in a little olive oil or grill it over a charcoal fire, and then sprinkle with lemon juice. *Saganaki* with *halloumi* (see page 11) is an excellent cheese dish.

Nearest substitutes: None, but for fried cheese dishes use *kefalotiri*, Gruyère, Cheshire or mature Cheddar.

Kaseri

A very popular, mild, pale golden, spun-curd cheese made from cows' or ewes' milk. It is a manufactured cheese that is often served as a cheap *meze*. Some find its taste delightful, some too plastic. The *kaseri* with holes should be avoided.

Nearest substitutes: *Kefalotiri* or Italian provolone.

Kaskavali

A hard, full-fat cheese produced mainly in the north of Greece and most Balkan countries. It is made from ewes' milk that is slightly heated after the curd is separated from the whey. It is then pressed, drained in the mould for three hours and salted before being cured for about 3–4 months. It has a thin rind, pale yellow colour and an aromatic salty flavour.
Nearest substitutes: Parmesan, Cheddar or *kefalotiri*.

Kefalotiri

A hard and salty cheese made from a mixture of goats' and ewes' milk. The curd is pressed for 10 hours, then dry-salted and ripened in three months. During ripening, it is kneaded every other day until a fungus forms. It is dry, pale yellow in colour and formed in the shape of a head (*kefali*). It is easily grated and used over pasta dishes.
Nearest substitutes: Parmesan, Italian pecorino or Roquefort.

Kopanisti

A fine blue feta cheese with a smooth texture made using the same process as feta, except that the curd is left to develop a blue-green veining which is kneaded into the cheese and then left to ripen for two months. It has a creamy and peppery flavour and is excellent served as a *meze* with Kalamata olives. The island of Mykonos is famous for its pink-coloured *kopanisti*.
Nearest substitutes: Blue Stilton or Danish Blue.

Lathotiri

Made exclusively in the islands of Lesvos and Zakinthos from sheeps' milk, it is shaped like a miniature barrel and then steeped in olive oil (hence its name 'oil-cheese') in which it ages for several months. The real *lathotiri* (for there are inferior products) is pungent and delicious.

Manuri

A sweet, creamy white and very pleasant cheese made from sheeps' or cows' milk. *Manuri* made by shepherds in the mountains has a pleasant smoky flavour; I remember as a child how much I loved to eat slices of *manuri* with dollops of local honey.
Nearest substitute: Unsalted curd cheese.

Mizithra

A soft, white cottage cheese made from any milk, although sheeps' milk makes a better *mizithra*. The curd is made with animal rennet or the milky sap of the fig tree. The cheese is sold salted or unsalted, firm or slightly hard. The fresh, unsalted version is eaten with fruit, honey, smoked meats or on its own; the harder version (about three months old) can be grated and eaten with pasta dishes. The best semi-hard *mizithra* comes from Crete. One of the best soft *mizithra* made from goats' milk comes from the island of Santorini; a hard version of this cheese called *xiromizithra*, is also produced there. Cyprus makes a creamed cheese similar to fresh *mizithra*, known as *anari*. Fresh *anari* is rolled in salt and left to dry for a few months, then used like any other hard cheese.

Nearest substitutes: Italian ricotta or any fresh cottage cheese.

Touloumotiri

This is the speciality of the islands of Samos, Lesbos and Crete. I believe this is one of the most delicious cheeses. It is a feta cheese made of sheeps' milk and packed into goatskins to mature for about three months – hence the name 'skin-cheese'. When it is opened the cheese is pure white and semi-soft, with a wonderful musty aroma, which some people like and some hate.

To Make Feta

Heat about 3 litres (5 pints) of full-fat milk until lukewarm. Dilute 2 teaspoons of sweet rennet in a little warm milk and stir into the rest of the milk. Cover and leave it undisturbed for 1–1½ hours. Insert your finger into the milk; if it feels sticky, the milk has congealed. Cut the curd finely and leave to stand for about 1 hour to allow the water (whey) to separate. Transfer the curd on to a large piece of fine muslin using a slotted spoon, tie the edges of the muslin to form a bag, and hang the bag over a bowl for about a day, so that the whey is completely drained.

Untie the muslin bag and cut the cheese into four pieces. Salt the cheese by distributing a handful of sea salt evenly among the pieces. Tie the bag again and place a small weight on the bag to allow all the whey contained in the cheese to drain. After about 20 days, the cheese is ready.

Yiaourti
YOGHURT

Yoghurt has aquired an excellent reputation for promoting health and prolonging life. Certainly low-fat natural yoghurt, which has around 60 calories per 100 g (4 oz) and a fat content of 2 per cent, makes a good substitute for single cream, which has 20 per cent fat and 200 calories, and double cream, with 50 per cent fat and 450 calories. It is also easily digestible.

Yoghurt is made by heating milk so that it becomes bacteria-free, then adding a live yoghurt culture with particular bacteria which multiply rapidly, turning the milk into yoghurt. With home-made yoghurt, the milk will set as an unbroken curd in containers and the whey (water) will be separated. With commercially produced yoghurt, the curd will be cut when it has soured in large vats and then transferred into cartons or pots. Taste, thickness, texture and acidity will be determined mainly by the starter culture.

Yoghurts are not suitable for freezing and can be kept at a temperature of 5°C/41°F for about a fortnight without deteriorating.

Greek yoghurts are exceptionally creamy. Those made from ewes' milk (*provio yiaourti*) have a fat content of about 5 per cent and those made from cows' milk contain about 9 per cent milk fat. The quality of Greek yoghurt which is manufactured on a large scale or by local producers in Greece is probably superior to any other obtainable in Europe. Greek yoghurt is sold as 'strained' because most of the whey has been drained. It has a better flavour than single cream or crème fraîche.

Yoghurts produced in Greek villages are nowadays made using the old methods, in large earthenware basins or wooden containers (*vidouria*), which impart a special texture and flavour that is difficult to forget. They are sold in village bakeries by weight or in attractive earthenware bowls.

Sweetened with honey or mixed with fruits and walnuts, natural Greek yoghurt makes an excellent breakfast or dessert. It can be added to salads and cooked dishes or used as a marinade. Drained for a couple of hours, the resulting yoghurt cheese, sprinkled with a few drops of olive oil, black pepper and chopped parsley, makes a delicious light lunch.

To make Yoghurt

Bring 1 litre (2¼ pints) of full-fat milk to just under boiling point and then pour the milk into a glass or earthenware dish. Let the milk cool to about 42°C/104°F. Mix 2–3 tablespoons of commercial plain yoghurt or from a previous home-made yoghurt (at room temperature) with a few tablespoons of milk, and pour into the milk carefully without disturbing the skin that may have formed on the surface of the milk. Cover with a cloth, place in a warm, draft-free place for 8–12 hours or overnight, and do not disturb it until the yoghurt thickens. Drain any excess liquid and store in the fridge for 4–5 days. To make a 'thick' yoghurt, remove the skin on the surface of the yoghurt just made and pour the yoghurt into a muslin bag. Hang the bag over a bowl and let drain for about 2 hours or until the desired thickness is obtained.

Votana ke Baharika

HERBS AND SPICES

Every country around the Mediterranean has its own favourite selection of herbs and spices: coriander and basil in Italy; cumin in Morocco and Turkey; saffron in Spain; chervil and tarragon in France; parsley, dill and oregano in Greece.

Herbs (*botana*) grow wild in profusion on the hillsides and mountains of Greece, with thyme predominating. Every household is well stocked with herbs, bought by the bunch in country markets and hung in the kitchen together with bunches of garlic and onions. Every housewife is an expert in the use of herbs: those herbs that are complementary, those that clash, those that enhance the natural flavours of food, these are all grist to her mill. It is a highly esoteric practice and tradition that can be learnt only by constant trial, adjustment and tasting.

Greece has a long history in the use of plants for culinary and medicinal purposes. Documented accounts of herbs and their usage in medicine, the art of magic and cooking, date back to 2000 BC. In Babylon, the various uses of thymes, mints, rosemary and coriander were tried, tested and their healing properties documented. In Ancient Egypt, a trade in aromatic oils, spices and herbs flourished in response to the rising demand for their use in food, medicines, cosmetics, perfumes, dyes and the art of embalming; such trade was probably the dominant link with the outside world for many centuries.

The Ancient Greeks built upon the knowledge gathered by older civilizations and added to it, specifically in medicine, in the easing of pain and curing of diseases. The medical writings of Hippocrates in 400 BC form the basis of modern medicine. Theophrastos (372–288 BC), who is considered to be the father of botany, examined and recorded over 550 plants and categorized them according to their characteristics in a massive work, *Inquiry into Plants*, consisting of nine volumes.

It was not until the first century AD that the Greek physician Dioscorides (40–90 AD) listed the medicinal properties of all known plants and herbs, including 600 herbal medicines. This became the standard reference for over 16 centuries. Antiphanes, who died in 306 BC, listed the spices and ingredients used for seasoning foods during the classical period: grape

Aroma – the smell of a ploughed field.

———

An ancient definition

juice, salt, cooked wine, silphium (asafoetida, an evil-smelling fennel), cheese, thyme, sesame, natron (soda), cumin, pomegranate, honey, marjoram, fine herbs, vinegar, olives, capers, eggs, salt fish, cress and garlic. Spices such as black and white pepper, cinnamon, mint and cardamom were not in dietary use in Greece; their exquisite aroma was more appreciated in other parts of Europe, where they were used in the preparation of foods. Most of the exotic spices we know today, such as ginger, cloves, nutmeg and mace, although well known in Greek and Roman times, were viewed with suspicion. They were first introduced into the kitchen with caution by the Byzantines in the sixth century AD, as their incorrect dosage was thought to act like a hallucinatory drug. It was not until the eighteenth century that these spices were well established in Europe, and particularly in the French and Dutch cuisine.

This section lists the most commonly used herbs and spices in the Greek kitchen today. When substituting dried herbs for fresh, remember that dried herbs are often twice as strong as fresh ones. Spices and herbs should always be bought in small quantities and replenished frequently.

Glykaniso
Anise

A delicate bush from the hemlock family, with seeds that are used to give a sweet aniseed flavour to ouzo and similar drinks, cakes and breads. Star anise is an oriental spice that is stronger than anise seeds and is used essentially for the same purpose.

Use: Buy anise seeds in small quantities as it quickly loses its flavour, and use to flavour biscuits and breads.

Vasilikos
Basil

A fragrant, sensitive and aromatic herb of the mint family that is used to flavour tomato sauces and some regional dishes. Almost every Greek home has a pot of growing basil on the balcony or close to a door in the house, as it is believed to keep flies away. Visitors and passers-by always pinch a leaf or two and rub it in their hands for its fresh and peppery fragrance.

Use: Use only fresh basil or keep basil leaves in jars filled with olive oil. Dried basil bears little relation to the flavour of fresh basil. Used rarely in Greek dishes, but if you wish to use it with tomatoes and salads, use it raw, either whole or lightly torn.

Dafni
Bay leaves

The Ancient Greeks bestowed wreaths of bay as crowns on winning athletes, warriors and poets. After a while, dark bay leaves turn a marvellous bronze colour. Bay leaves come from the sweet bay or laurel tree. Fresh leaves can be dried in a dark place and used after four or five days. Dark bay leaves are those left to dry in a cool, dry place for two to three weeks; they are then stored in airtight jars and can be used for up to a year. Very old bay leaves have little flavour and should be avoided.

Use: The flavour of bay leaves is strong and aromatic; break them up into pieces and use sparingly. Use in stews, boiled meats, tomato and fish soups, marinades and stocks, and in *souvlaki* kebabs – threaded on skewers with onions, tomatoes and peppers. Remember to remove them before serving. Infuse a small bay leaf with milk in sweet rice puddings and custards.

Kapari
Capers

Capers are the unopened flower buds of a bush native to Mediterranean and North Africa. They grow wild throughout Greece. The best are those hand–picked and salted. Others are usually pickled in brine or white wine vinegar. Greek capers are expensive and difficult to find, but are probably the best in the market. Tripoli in the Peloponnese is famous for pickling capers together with young and tender sprigs of the caper plant.

Use: Capers are used for garnishing soups, fish dishes, salads and mayonnaises. To make a delicious caper sauce for boiled lamb or meat dishes, add 1 tablespoon of capers to 250 ml (8 fl oz) of béchamel sauce. Use the same sauce mixed with chopped hard-boiled eggs for garnishing poached or steamed fish or vegetables.

Selino
Celery

The celery most commonly found in Greece is the wild, dark green variety with a bitter-sweet taste. The leaves look like overgrown Mediterranean parsley. It requires sandy soil and is often found in gardens along the coast. Because of its strong flavour, it is used in soups and stews.

Use: For a good substitute, use the darker part of English celery and blanch for 1 minute in boiling water. It gives pungency to soups, sauces and pork dishes. It is rarely used in salads. Use the root for making pickles.

Kanela
Cinnamon

Cinnamon and cloves (*gariphalla*) have a sweet and spicy scent that gives an exotic quality to many foods. The trade in cinnamon and other spices from the East and China dates back to Ancient Egypt and Greece; cinnamon, known as *cassia*, was sparingly used for bread-making.

Use: Cinnamon sticks are much used in Greek cookery and baking; they flavour syrups for various sweet cakes such as *baklava* and give a wonderful scent to biscuits and pies; ground cinnamon is always sprinkled on rice puddings. Use cinnamon to flavour *moussaka* dishes, stuffed peppers and aubergines, deep-fried mussels, baked pasta casseroles, pea and lentil dishes, *avgolemono* soups and lamb casseroles.

Koriandro
Coriander

Although coriander has been cultivated in Greece since ancient times, it is not as extensively used today as it is in Italy, England and Scandinavia, for example. Powdered coriander seeds are often used as preservatives or marinades for meats and sausages.

Use: Certain dishes known as 'à la grecque' use fresh coriander instead of flatleaf parsley; these are mainly vegetable (mushrooms, celery, cauliflower, carrots) dishes. Pork with coriander (*Afelia*, see page 100) is the only traditional Greek dish to use this herb. Although coriander blends well in certain pungent dishes, flatleaf parsley is generally a much more pleasant herb for summer dishes and salads.

Anithos
Dill

Dill is probably one of the most wonderful and versatile herbs. It is more aromatic than fennel and gives a delicate flavour to most Greek dishes, particularly to salads and fish dishes.

Use: Use fresh dill only; dried dill is a poor substitute. Ideal in *tzatziki*, *avgolemono* sauce and *dolmades*, it easily loses its flavour when cooked, so it should always be added at the end of the cooking time. It enhances all soups and vegetable salads.

Marantho
Fennel
With their sweet and aniseed taste which the Greeks particularly love, fresh fennel leaves are added to almost all dishes in the springtime. In the summer, dried fennel leaves are used in sweet breads and pork dishes. In Ancient Greece a wreath of fennel was a symbol of success.
Use: Known as the 'fish herb', chopped fennel leaves are added to fish sauces and to poached or boiled fish dishes. Powdered fennel is also added to flour in bread-making to produce a sweet bread that goes well with fish dishes.

Skordo
Garlic
Garlic is an essential ingredient in Greek cuisine and throughout the Mediterranean. As in ancient times, some people eat it raw for strength and endurance; it was given to the builders of the pyramids in Egypt. Homer tells us that Ulysses escaped the charms of the enchantress Circe by using garlic! In Greek cuisine, garlic is used lavishly in sauces, salads, meat stews and fish dishes; chopped garlic and oil are sprinkled in *meze* dishes and whole cloves of garlic are cooked with meat roasts.
Use: Use garlic sparingly – enough to flavour the dish, and not for its own sake. Fried garlic is less strong, while boiled or cooked garlic becomes mild and sweet. If you use raw garlic, always rub it with salt and serve it with virgin olive oil. With the exception of a few dishes, you can always halve the amount of garlic suggested in recipes with no drastic reduction to the flavour of the dish. This is particularly true of the famous garlic dish *skordalia*. Best buy the garlic whole, then separate a clove from the bulb as necessary. Crush the clove with the flat of a knife and remove the skin. Chop or mash it with the addition of a little salt; this will absorb its juice.

Mastiha
Mastic
Mastic is a resin from mastic trees grown mainly around the Mediterranean. The largest commercial producer in the world is the island of Chios. Mastic has a cedar-like taste and a pleasant texture. It looks like pea-sized globules. A drink called *mastiha*, closely related to ouzo, is flavoured with mastic in addition to aniseed. It is considered a lady's drink and

often referred to as the 'feminine' ouzo.

Use: Pulverize mastic before use, adding a little sugar or salt. Half a teaspoon is sufficient for a dish or cake. Use in baking breads, pastries and 'spoon sweets'. The recipe for the traditional speciality, *Mastiha Glyko*, is given on page 189.

Diosmos or *mentha*
Mint

There are many varieties of mint: water mint, spearmint, peppermint, lemon mint, corn mint and so on. It is an easy plant to grow in the garden. Dried mint is just as delicious as fresh mint.

Use: Greeks use mint sparingly in combination with oregano and parsley in meatballs, *dolmades*, stuffed courgettes, peppers and tomatoes. It does not go well in dishes with garlic or most other herbs. It gives a tangy flavour to *tzatziki*, yoghurt and cheese dishes, which are often an acquired taste. Use the young leaves of garden mint only.

Moustarda
Mustard

Like most other countries, Greece imports French, German and English mustards. Greek mustards are an emulation of these. Indigenous mustards are made by crushing seeds of the plant and mixing them with vinegar or grape must.

Use: Use a mild mustard with salad dressings, and a stronger one for meat *meze* such as *souvlaki* and *keftedes*. A vinaigrette mixed with mustard and honey makes an excellent salad dressing.

Moskokarido
Nutmeg and Mace

The nutmeg seed is encased in a bright red outer covering which, when dried in the sun, is known as mace. Mace has a warm, sweet, spicy flavour; nutmeg is more pungent.

Use: Buy a good-quality large nutmeg and grate it fresh into the dish, as it quickly loses its aroma. Use with cinnamon in rice puddings, nut cakes and sweets. Use mace to flavour the milk used for sauces, such as béchamel, and cheese sauces. Some dishes of foreign origin, such as *pastitsio*, improve with the addition of nutmeg.

Rigani
Oregano

Rigani is perhaps the most popular herb for flavouring meats, tomato salads and fried cheeses. It grows wild in most parts of Greece. The name *rigani* (*Origanum vulgare*) comes from the ancient words *oros*, 'mountain', and *ganos*, 'brightness'. It is said that Aphrodite took *rigani* from the bottom of the ocean to the top of Olympus where it was closest to the sun.

In Greece, you would find *rigani* in tied bunches with the flower buds hanging for drying. Greeks use the flower-heads of the plant rather than the leaves, which they find bitter. *Rigani* is stronger and sharper than the English wild or sweet marjoram (called *matzourana* in Greek), and is nearest in flavour to dried oregano.

Use: Use dried oregano in small quantities in dishes with garlic and lemon. Add to meat and game dishes, marinades, fresh vegetables, stuffed peppers and tomato dishes, roast potatoes, spaghetti dishes and kebabs.

Maidanos
Parsley

The flatleaf variety is used by the handful in most Greek dishes; it has a mild and delicate flavour. A very versatile herb: somebody once said that parsley is the Magnum 45 of the Greek food armoury. It is particularly rich in vitamins A and C, calcium, iron and manganese.

Uses: If you cannot find flatleaf parsley, use the curly-leaf variety in smaller quantities than called for in the recipes. Chop curly parsley finely and wring well with a cloth to remove excess moisture. Avoid chopping flatleaf parsley; instead, pull the leaves from the stalks by hand. It goes well with salads, meatballs, casseroled vegetables, boiled fish, and as a garnish for almost any dish.

Dendrolivano
Rosemary

A strong aromatic plant with pale blue flowers, it grows wild in mountains and by the coast. The Ancient Greeks would twine rosemary flowers in their hair in the hope that it would quicken the mind and improve the memory. It is used to rinse clothes in the belief that it has disinfectant qualities. Rosemary is basically an Italian herb; in Greece it is restricted to tomato soups and grilled lamb.

Use: Add fresh rosemary to meat dishes and fish such as halibut. It gives an unusual flavour to fruit salads, wines and biscuits. Avoid powdered rosemary.

Krokos
Saffron

The saffron stigma or powder is very expensive and, therefore, hardly used in Greek cooking. It is cultivated in Macedonia and Crete and mainly used in the distillation of certain spirits and liqueurs and in the spicing of wines.

Thymari
Thyme

Used infrequently because of its strong flavour, thyme begins to flower in May and grows widely in the mountains by June; its scent radiates everywhere. The wild thyme of the Hymetos mountain, near Athens, gave its fragrance to the wonderful *Hymetos* honey of ancient times, as it does today.

Use: It is ideal for pork dishes and games, especially stuffing chicken. It gives a stronger flavour to lamb dishes. It is used for pickling olives and in bouquets garni together with parsley, bay leaves and rosemary for flavouring stews.

Ellinika Krasia: Doro Dionysou Theou

GREEK WINES: THE GIFT
OF DIONYSUS

The origin of wine is firmly rooted in the civilization of Ancient Greece. Nowadays, Greek wine production, combining tradition with modern technology, continues to offer wines of the highest quality and exceptional value. Wine production today amounts to 5 million hectolitres per year, of which 60 per cent is white and 40 per cent is red. Agriculture contributes 17 per cent of the gross national product in the country and wine accounts for only 4 per cent of the agricultural income. Only a small percentage of production is currently exported, but Greek wines are steadily gaining recognition among most wine-producing nations throughout the world, as indicated by the international prizes, awards and medals awarded to Greek producers such as Achaia-Clauss, Kourtakis and others. Greece is blessed with many varieties of indigenous grapes, ideal climatic conditions and well-trained and talented wine-makers with the confidence to compete in the international market.

If you want to, come in for a drink, and if you have money, my friend, pay. If you have money, and don't wish to pay for your drink, don't come in.

———

Written outside a little taverna in Athens

Greek Wine Labels

Wine labels are like pedigrees: some indicate cheerful mongrels, others describe thoroughbreds. There is a lot to be learnt from Greek wine labels: most are written in Greek only and some in a mixture of Greek, French and English. Many have fanciful designs, others carry intriguing quotations from ancient texts or the Bible.

Since the fourth century BC, Greek wines have been distinguished by their appellation of the area of origin – a concept which is now used in all wine-producing countries of the world. In 1981, just after Greece joined the European Union, the Greek wine industry adopted the EU appellation system which is now administered by a department of the Ministry of Agriculture. Under the present legislation, wines fall into two broad categories: Table wines, which are outside the appellation system, and Quality wines, which are produced in particular regions and are further controlled by grading regulations.

Table wines include Country wines (*Topikos oinos*) and Table wines (*Epitrapezios oinos*). Both are made with indigenous grapes alone or are blended with foreign grapes. These wines represent excellent value for money. Wines with the label *Cava* are left to mature under appropriate temperature and humidity conditions in the cellar or casks for a minimum of two years for whites and three years for reds. Wines with the label *Vins de pays* indicate another category of everyday wines with slightly more character than Table wines. This label, in conjunction with the geographical area, indicates local wines from low-yield vineyards with appropriate soil structure and from a determined grape variety. In 1997 there were 37 regions producing Table wines.

Quality wines are those labelled Appellation of Origin of High Quality (*Onomasia Proelefseos Anoteras Piotitos* or *OPAP*). These are authenticated by the Ministry of Agriculture for grape variety, yield and production methods, and carry a pink paper seal affixed over the mouth of each bottle. OPAP wines are aged and bottled according to the appellation laws of each designated region. In 1997 there were 20 such regions producing wines of superior quality which are on a par with the French AOC (*Appellation Origine Contrôlée*) wines. The other wines in this category are Appellation of Controlled Origin (*Onomasia Proelefseos Elenhomeni* or *OPE*) wines, which are also authenticated and carry a blue paper seal. OPE wines are the sweet Muscat and Mavrodaphne wines from Patras, Cephalonia, Limnos and Samos. In 1997 there were seven regions producing such dessert wines which are on a par with the French VDQS (*Vins Délimités de Qualité Supérieure*) wines and, in many cases, superior in terms of aroma and taste, since they are usually bought near where they have been produced.

Grapes for Greek Wines

By recognizing grape varieties, you can learn what taste to expect when drinking wines made from those varieties. There are a dozen prominent grape varieties out of some 300 indigenous grapes grown in small plots and regions in Greece.

WHITE GRAPES

Assyrtiko. Taste the crisp, sweet and bone-dry grapes. Look for buttercup yellow colour. Enjoy it in the wines of Halkidiki and the island of Santorini.

Athiri. Taste its citrus flavour and creamy texture. Look for bright, light colour. Enjoy it in Halkidiki and the islands of Rhodes and Crete, and as part of the blend with other acidic varieties.

Debina. Taste its fresh acidity and delicate, apple aroma. Look for yellow/silver colour grapes. Enjoy it in the wines of Zitsa in Epirus.

Moschofilero. Taste the sweet, dry and aromatic grapes. Look for light pink to dark purple colour. Enjoy it in the best aperitif wines from southern Peloponnese.

Muscats. Taste the whole spectrum from dry to sweet grapes. Look for bright gold colours. Enjoy the dessert wines of Samos, Cephalonia and mainland Greece.

Robola. Taste this lemony, dry and smoky grape used for dry and sweet wines. Look for bright yellow, almost silver colour. Enjoy it in the wines from the Ionian islands and western Epirus.

Roditis. Taste the fresh fruits in both its pink and white variety. Look for small, reddish grapes usually grown at high altitude. Enjoy it in the most juicy wines including retsina, from Patras and central Greece.

Savatiano. Taste the orange blossom and peaches of this grape, which is often resinated to produce dry wines. Look for pale yellow grapes. Enjoy it in the branded table wines and retsina of Attica and central Greece.

RED GRAPES

Agiorgitiko. Taste one of the finest grapes, rich in colour and soft tannins. Look for ruby red, almost blue colour. Enjoy the dry, full-bodied wines from the Corinth region (Nemea).

Limnio. Taste this ancient variety with its unique character of sage and laurel flavour. Look for a colour of hot metal under the hammer of the god of the forge. Enjoy it in the wines from Domaine Carras and Ktima Lazaridi in Drama.

Mandelari. Taste this strong, acidic but smooth and aromatic grape variety. Look for red-black colour. Enjoy it in the wines of Rhodes and those from Crete and Paros made by Boutari.

Mavrodaphni. Taste this sweet, dry but smooth grape. Look for deep red colour. Enjoy the port-like dessert wines from Patras with their unmistakable character.

Negoska. Taste the plums and mulberries in this noble variety. Look for deep red colour. Enjoy the soft tannins and fruity wines from the vineyeards of Goumenissa in the north of Macedonia.

Xynomavro. Taste Greece's finest grapes. Look for blackcurrant, deep red colour. Enjoy the full-bodied wines of Naoussa and Goumenissa in Macedonia with their supple and rich bouquet. If you say that they are better than Burgundy reds, you wouldn't be far wrong.

A Selection of Greek Wines

Descriptions of wines by wine buffs, and those found on bottle labels, may often seem pretentious. The problem is that wine, though made of grapes, does not taste grapey (unless it is a muscat). As a guide to enjoyment alone or with food, wine is likened to something else you are familiar with, such as honey, melons, spices and so on. In fact, the wine might actually share some of the same chemical constituents.

There are very few Greek wines that can be kept with advantage for over ten years. These are mainly the red wines from the Domaine Carras in Macedonia and particularly those mixed with Cabernet Sauvignon grapes. Some light reds reach the peak of their maturity in three to five years, and the rosé and whites should normally be kept no longer than three years.

The standards of Greek wines are improving all the time, but selecting a quality wine is not easy. The following is a representative selection of Greek wines currently available in Greece; a small number of these are available in supermarkets abroad, others can be obtained directly from the suppliers' representative. The wines described below are rated, in the author's opinion, as very good or excellent and they represent good value for money.

WHITE WINES

Boutari Aidani-Assyrtiko. Named after the white varietals cultivated on the volcanic island of Santorini, this semi-aromatic but thin wine has a flowery bouquet.

Cambas Attikos. A local dry wine from the Athens region made from selected Savatiano grapes. It has a subtle, fruity aroma and a clear pale, gold colour.

Cambas Mantinia. An Appellation of Origin of High Quality dry white made from the aromatic Moshofilero grapes of Cambas's own estate on the slopes of the Arcadian mountains in the Peloponnese. It has been described as 'a modern clean, fresh white that has not been stripped of personality'. A crisp, grapey, fruity wine that is excellent with autumn and winter dishes.

Domaine Carras Melissanthi. The dry, acidic Assyrtiko grape is balanced by the Athiri variety to produce this delicate and flavoursome wine from the Sithonia peninsula (the middle finger) of Halkidiki in Macedonia.

Emery Villaré. A lovely amber-coloured wine from Mount Ataviros in Rhodes, with a bouqet of fruits and mixed flowers. A creamy wine that goes well with fish, poultry and feta or spinach puff pastry.

Gerovassiliou White 95. From the domain of Epanomi (east of Thessaloniki) based on the Assyrtiko grapes, this is a lively and spicy wine with a touch of lemon peel.

Gerovassiliou Fumé. Another impressive wine with a lingering combination of fruit, peppermint and oak flavours.

Kourtakis Kouros. An up-market, strong wine from Patras suitable for winter dishes. It is made from the Roditis grapes with a slight oaky flavour and acidity.

Ktima Lazaridi Amethistos. Greek for 'sober' and the jewel amethyst, this wine is based on the old belief that you never get drunk while holding an amethyst! It is a blend of Sauvignon Blanc, Semillon and Assyrtiko grapes from the plains of Drama in Macedonia. A delicate, well-balanced, light green wine with an aroma of blackcurrants, peaches and citrus fruit.

Château Lazaridi Magico Vouno. Greek for 'magic mountain', not to be confused with Ktima Lazaridi, this very dry, strong and smoky wine with a lemon and honey flavour is allowed to age for four years; a classic wine.

Papaioannou Slopes of Ai Lia. An aromatic, fruity wine with a honey finish. A very classy white based on the noble Assyrtico grapes of Nemea in the Peloponnese.

Semeli Aspro. A dry wine from the Savatiano grapes planted in northern Attica at an altitude of 400 metres. Very pleasant with fish dishes.

Tselepou Mantinia. Produced according to Appellation laws of the Mantinia region of the Peloponnese. It is a pleasant dry wine suitable for fish and cheese dishes.

ROSÉ WINES

Domaine Carras Rosé. An excellent blend of Limnio grapes (originally from the island of Limnos, now cultivated in Halkidiki), Cabernet Sauvignon and Cabernet Franc. Beautifully balanced and spicy.

Emery Grand Rosé. If you want a spicy aperitif with a touch of the aroma of quince, the Nouveau rosé is perfect. The Grand version is exclusively made from the rare Amorgiano grapes of Rhodes; a fruity wine full of character.

Kourtakis Vin de Crète Rosé. A Cretan country wine, dry with a taste of pomegranates and strawberries.

Oenoforos Esperitis. Greek for 'wine-bearer', 'dusk', a lovely dark (like the summer sunset) rosé made from the Agiogritiko grapes cultivated at 650-metre vineyards overlooking the gulf of Corinth.

Semeli Rosé. This pale and delicate rosé with hardly any tannin comes from the Agiorgitiko (Greek for 'St George') grapes of Nemea. One of the best rosés in Greece.

Tsantalis Agioritiko. Greek for the wine 'of Athos', produced by the Tsantalis vineyards, which are situated 300 metres above sea level in Mount Athos. This brilliant rose-coloured, dry rosé has a rich aroma of freshly cut flowers and strawberry taste. Drink chilled with barbecued fish, red meats or cheeses.

RED WINES

Antonopoulos Nea Dris. Greek for 'new oak', this red with its heavy aroma of ripe fruit, strong tannin and oak flavour, is a blend of Cabernet Sauvignon and Sauvignon Franc grapes. The vintage '95 is ideal for dishes with strong sauces.

Boutari Wineries. Founded in 1879, Boutari now have established wineries in Macedonia (Goumenissa and Naoussa), Crete (Arhanes), Peloponnese (Nemea) and the island of Santorini. The following reds are among their finest: **Naoussa Grande Réserve** is made from the Xynomavro grape cultivated on the slopes of Mount Vermion. Probably the best regional red wine, it is well-balanced, fruity and an excellent choice for red meat dishes and strong cheeses. **Cava Boutari** is a favourite red sold in most tavernas in Greece. Matured in oak, it is well-balanced and tastes of red berries and bitter almonds. **Naoussa** is a similar dry red wine, the '93 vintage being the best. **Goumenissa** is a splendid ruby-red wine, powerful, well balanced, with a bouquet of spicy cloves. The Xynomavro grape is blended with the local Negoska grape to give this wine a softer acidity.

Domaine Carras Limnio. Probably the best value-for-money red in Greece, full of fruits, body and sufficient acidity; ideal for spicy meat and game dishes.

Domaine Carras Château Carras. One of the leading wines made with Greek and French grapes, 40 per cent of which is exported. It has been described as 'very expressive, with ripe, tarry fruit, fully oaked but with the fruit weight and structure to carry the day'.

Gerovassiliou Red. From the domain of Epanomi (east of Thessaloniki) based on French grape varieties, this is a bold, gutsy and rich wine.

Ktima Mercuri '93. Not far from the ancient site of Olympia in the Peloponnese, the Mercuri estate produces one of the most pleasant reds: a combination of 85 per cent acidic Refosco wine (from northern Italy) enriched with 15 per cent sweet Mavrodaphne. The result is a firm, well-balanced and enjoyable wine.

Semeli Chateau '92. This rich red/black wine from around Athens is aged for two years in the cask and one in the bottle. It combines Cabernet Sauvignon and Merlot grapes for a complex bouquet and a taste of lots of ripe fruit. **Semeli Red** is another popular and less expensive superior table wine.

Skouras Megas Oinos. From the area of Nafplio in the Peloponnese, a charming town founded by the Venetians and the first capital of modern Greece, this red is made with 80 per cent Agiorgitiko and 20 per cent Cabernet Sauvignon grapes. It is a lively, fruity, deep red wine with a hint of tannin and spicy oak.

Tsantalis Rapsani '93. From the dark grape varieties grown near the foot of Mount Olympus, this light and very dry wine goes well with well-herbed foods such as *souvlaki*, spinach and cheese pies, and salty *mezedes*.

DESSERT WINES

Above all other wines, the sweet wines of Ancient Greece were held in high esteem, for they were drunk equally by the heroes of Ancient Greek history and the Gods on Mount Olympus. Such wines were always reserved for special occasions. The sweet wine was described by the expression 'idys oenos', or wine that is pleasant and causes no pain. Homer tells us that pale honey was added to the famous Pramnian wine of Ikaria that was basically dry, hard and of extraordinary strength.

Today, the town of Patras in the Peloponnese is renowned for its dark red Mavrodaphne (Greek for 'black laurel') grape variety which produces a dessert wine with a very individual bouquet. This full-bodied, aromatic liqueur wine requires age-ing in order to be at its best: it is aged in wooden vats and oak barrels which are periodically drawn off and topped up. The resulting wine has the strength of 15 per cent alcohol.

Mavrodaphne of Patras. This wine is made up of a mixture of 51 per cent Mavrodaphne grape and 49 per cent black Korinthiaki grape. Because of its low yield, Mavrodaphne is an expensive grape to grow and, consequently, there are only two major producers in the region (and a greater number of small ones): the Achaia-Clauss firm established in 1861 and Patraiki – the Union of Agricultural Co-operatives of Patras. The following is a selection of Mavrodaphne of Patras wines:

Achaia-Clauss. Six years in barrel, warm and mellow and not too sweet.

Boutari. Ripe fruit, sweet.

Cambas. Refined, rich and smooth.

Kourtakis. Strong in fruit, smooth.

Patraiki. 14 per cent; matured for 2–4 years in oak, orange peel taste.

Tsantalis. Medium deep red, not very rich, sweetish.

MUSCAT WINES

Two other dessert wines of Patras deserve to be mentioned: the Muscat of Patras and the Muscat of Rion of Patras Appellation wines. These lovely, topaz-coloured liqueurs are produced from the white Moschato grapes, which gives them their characteristic aroma and individual taste. They are natural aperitifs and dessert wines. Other equally famous sweet wines, which have been known for 3000 years, come from the island of Samos. These muscat wines have enjoyed some privileges granted by the Turkish Sultan in 1562 and have been traded to all European countries since 1700. Most of the following wines should be served chilled as aperitifs with dry fruits, nuts or strong cheeses.

Achaia-Clauss Patras Muscat. A dry wine with a grapey, honey and toffee taste.

Boutari Visanto. From the volcanic island of Santorini, this is like a fresh and dry sherry with a taste of dates and quince.

Koutrakis Samos Muscat. Golden, moderately aromatic with a rich, fruity flavour, it has a Controlled Appellation of Origin.

Montofoli Vin de Liqueur. Comes from the island of Evia. One of the finest Greek aperitifs with a pleasant amount of acidity and 16.5 per cent alcohol.

Samos Nectar. From the Samos Co-operative, a remarkable sweet aperitif with an amber colour and ripe apricot taste that is aged in oak casks for two or three years. It was used as an aperitif by middle-class women in the nineteenth century.

Samos Anthemis. Greek for 'flowery', this is aged for five years. A superior, well-balanced wine with a dry, creamy and spicy taste.

Samos. Another excellent wine from the Samos Co-operative, this is popular and inexpensive.

Tsantalis Samos Muscat. Golden yellow, aromatic, fruity and crisp.

CYPRIOT WINES

Cyprus has been making wines for 4000 years and is proud to claim one the oldest wines in the world: Commanderie St John, produced back in 1191 when the island was acquired by Richard the Lionheart, who subsequently sold it to the *Commanderies* – the Knights of the Order of St John.

The turbulent times in recent years have greatly affected the wine industry in the island. Furthermore, in 1986, when Spain joined the European Union, the EU banned the use of the name 'sherry' in Cyprus fortified wines for export. In 1990 Cyprus lost its wine and spirit market in Russia as a result of Russia's policy against alcohol abuse. In spite of these setbacks, Cyprus has quickly recovered by modernizing its industry and by exploiting further its neglected native varieties, such as the Ofthalmo, Maratheftiko (red) and Promara (white) grapes, in addition to the existing Mavro (red) and Xinisteri (white) varieties, which cover 85 per cent of the total vineyard area.

Cyprus has been a well-established exporter of strong wines, notably the superb **Commandaria**, a good quality brown dessert wine made in the hills of Limassol with sun-dried Mavron and Xinisteri grapes, and kept in oak barrels for at least two years. It has a honey-sweet, burnt aroma with tones of mature grapes, cacao and vanilla with a beautiful tannin taste. Today, Commandaria is protected by legislation as a traditional wine. Other native wines are produced in the south of the Troodos mountains and include **Keo's Othello**, which is a good standard dry red, **Keo's Aphrodite**, a full-bodied medium dry white, **Keo's Thisbe**, a light, fruity white, and **Etko's Semeli**, a traditional red. Cyprus also produces a range of fine and dry sherry-style wines with a characteristic chestnut aroma, which accompany perfectly Cypriot *mezedes*.

RETSINA

Whether by accident or intention, the application of resinous material from the trees in Thessaly and the island of Evia to the wine of the region had a preservative and improving effect in ancient times. Today, a small amount of resin of the Aleppo pine is added to the must during fermentation to give the characteristic taste to the white wine – **retsina** – and to rosé wine – **kokinelli**. Consumers find that the Savatiano grapes flavoured with resin (which is subsequently removed) result in a retsina with a delicate smell, which, served chilled, is the ideal wine for grilled or fried fish, especially sardines.

Retsina is made in exactly the same way as any dry white table wine and is subject to the regulations that apply to all Greek wines. It is now recognised by the EU, and ratified by international agreement, as an exclusively Greek product in the category of Traditional Appellation.

There are a great number of local grape varieties and many producers of retsina. The white Savatiano and the pink Roditis grapes are particularly suitable and used for 85 per cent of the retsina produced. Within Greece, it is sold either in bottles or in bulk by the weight taken from the barrel (*khyma* or *varelisio*) in any local taverna or shop. All large producers export their retsinas widely. On top of the list is **Kourtakis's Retsina of Attica**, which is the most popular and holds 65 per cent of the domestic market; it is dry, piquant and lacks the taste of resin. Next comes **Retsina Malamatina** from Macedonia, which is remarkable for its light acidity. Very flavourful and fruity retsinas are **Boutaris Retsina** from Attica, **Cambas's Retsina of Messogia**, **Achaia-Clauss's Retsina** from Patras and **Tsantalis's Retsina** from Halkidiki.

Retsina and other wine should not be drunk together at a single meal. It is a gastronomic error to serve retsina with rich food which might require a full-bodied or even a soft, velvety wine. Most Greeks drink retsina occasionally, especially in the hot summer months. Some are moderate drinkers and prefer to drink it with fish, lamb dishes with garlic or substantial snacks. Some aficionados would go out of their way to find the best retsina in town. Surprisingly enough, visitors to Greece drink a lot of retsina either while in Greece or back home. Despite what is said about retsina, it is a distinctive and refreshing wine, and some even claim that it helps prevent hangovers. As Lawrence Durrell said in his book on the Greek islands, 'If you drink retsina you will live for ever, and never be a trial to your friends or to waiters.'

OUZO

No other drink is more closely associated with Greece than ouzo – the clear spirit that is distilled from pressed grapes and then flavoured with anise seeds and, occasionally, with a touch of fennel, mastic and aromatic herbs. It contains 38–48 per cent alcohol. It can be consumed neat or with water or ice (turning milky white), and is deceptively gentle until it goes to your head. It can be taken as an aperitif and has the advantage that it does not overwhelm your palate for the hors d'oeuvres, *meze* or food to follow.

A great deal of ouzo is produced and distilled both by co-operatives and the main wine producers. The ouzo of the island of Mytilini (Lesbos) has a considerable reputation: the highly perfumed and aromatic **Ouzo Athenee** is probably one of the best although not very well known; there is also the **Ouzo Mini** which is very popular. From the Attica area come **Mastikha Sans Rival**, with its strong taste of mastic, and the popular **Ouzo 12**. Macedonia is the home of numerous ouzo producers from which **Babatzim's Ouzo 1** and **Ouzo Classic** from Kavala and **Tsantalis's Ouzo Olympic** from Halkidiki excel.

A number of highly alcoholic spirits such as schnapps are also produced. These are *Raki* (46 per cent), *Tsipouro* (42 per cent) and the Cretan *Tsikoudia* (60 per cent). Some of these are highly perfected grape distillates but the majority are rough and fiery.

Matching Greek Wines and Food

Matching wine to food to achieve a harmony of taste so that one complements the other, rather than overpowering it, is a highly personal art. If you like red wine with fish or white with meat, ignore the supercilious looks of your friends and enjoy your choice. On the other hand, if you have no idea what you want to drink and are confronted with a choice of unfamiliar Greek wines, there are a few simple rules to follow, based on some experience and logic.

1. Consider the menu as a whole: dominating strong flavours should follow delicate or distinctive favours, and simple flavours should precede more complex flavours. For example, red wines should follow whites, dry should precede sweet wines and fresh or new wines the more mature ones.

2. The aroma of a dish should more or less match the aroma of the wine. For example, a dish containing cinnamon or spices goes well with a spicy red wine, while smoked fish or meat should be matched with an aromatic, fuller wine that has aged in the barrel.

3. Fish often needs a touch of something acidic, for example, a squeeze of lemon, a sharp sauce or a white wine to match – since white wines are usually more acid than reds. Grilled fish (except oily fish such as tuna) served with lemon is quite a light dish and an Assyrtiko white wine from the island of Santorini or a white Robola from Cephalonia are an ideal match. Some dry rosé or lighter, fruity reds can also be served with fish: those from Limnio grapes (such as the Carras rosé) or the Tsantalis Agioritiko rosé are superb when cool.

4. Fuller-flavoured dishes, particularly those cooked in a wine-based sauce, could well be served with a wine to match the colour of the cooking wine. In fact, it is simple to serve the wine that went into the pot. Dishes such as a beef stew (*Vodino Stifado*, see page 101), a meat ragout (*Kreas Kokinisto*, see page 95), meat casseroles (*Kapamas*, see pages 98-9) and pork with quinces (*Hirino Kidonato*, see page 102) should be served with a sturdy red wine: Boutari Goumenissa, Domaine Carras Limnio or the Gerovassiliou Red. Light red wines should be avoided since these dishes contain a much reduced, and hence stronger, sauce. On the other hand, medium dry white wines should be matched with fish, chicken or lamb dishes cooked in an egg and lemon (*avgolemono*) sauce. The Koutrakis Kouros white with its slight acidic flavour based on the Roditis grapes is an excellent wine for these dishes and would please most palates.

5. It is customary to serve game dishes with a fruity red wine. Plain roasted young birds deserve a good red such

as Boutari Naoussa or a Semeli. With game meat cooked in casseroles, both red or white wines, particularly the concentrated aromatic and often alcoholic wines, are suitable; the Cambas Mantinia, for example, is an excellent match for the richness of partridge, woodcock and duck dishes cooked in wine. Very often, game from a certain district goes well with wines of the same district, as in the case of wines from Naoussa, which are a perfect match for the game dishes of Macedonia.

6. In the case of pasta dishes, the choice of wine will depend on the sauce used. For butter or creamy sauces, an aromatic Tsantali white with sufficient acidity will be perfect. For spinach sauces a dry, crisp wine based on the Assyrtiko grapes is ideal. For tomato sauces with or without meat, a Boutari Naoussa red has the right flavour to match the sauce. Richer pasta dishes such as *Pastitsio*, (see page 93), which contain a meat and cream sauce, are difficult to match: Kourtakis Retsina or Kouros white based on the Roditis grapes are, however, ideal.

7. The numerous traditional starters (*mezedes*) and typically Greek dishes (moussaka, fried cheeses, meat balls, kebabs, garlic sauces, fried fish, mussels) present a problem to wine selection in Greece more than in any other country. One often tends to select a single wine which can harmonize and even enhance all the flavours of these dishes. Such wines are rare, and so the casual drinker usually resorts to a cool glass of retsina, kokkineli, ouzo or some popular wine such as Tsantalis Rapsani. Quite often, a wine that totally clashes with the flavour of every dish on the table can offer the maximum of pleasure; classic examples are the strong, salty cheeses or hot, peppery vegetable dishes that require a sweet fortified Samos Nectar or a Muscat wine from Patras. To select a single wine is difficult, yet a wine par excellence that has an uncanny ability to match the variety of flavours of most *mezedes* is the Emery Villaré white from Rhodes. This dry wine is full of intense yet pleasant, aromatic fruit flavours which are exclusively produced from the ancient Athiri grapes.

GLOSSARY

Amýgdala Almonds
Angináres Artichokes
Ánitho Dill
Arakás Peas
Arní Lamb
Astakós Lobster
Avgó Egg
Avgolémono Egg and lemon

Bakaliáros Cod
Baklavá Layered filo and nut dessert
Bámies Okra or ladies' fingers
Barboúnia Red mullet
Bizélia Peas

Calamarákia Small squid
Calamária Squid
Christópsaro John Dory

Dolmádes Stuffed vine or cabbage leaves
Domátes Tomatoes

Eliés Olives

Fakés Lentils
Fasólia Beans
Fasouláda Dried bean soup
Fasoulákia Fresh beans
Fáva Split peas
Féta Salted white cheese
Fílo Thin pastry
Foúrnos Oven

Garídes Prawns
Gála Milk
Glykó Sweet

Héli Eel

Hirinó Pork
Hórta Greens
Htapódi Octopus

Kafés Coffee
Kakaviá Fish soup
Kanéla Cinnamon
Karídia Walnuts
Kéfalos Grey mullet
Keftédes Little meatballs
Kóliandro Coriander
Kolokithákia Courgettes
Koríandro Coriander
Kóta Chicken
Kounéli Rabbit
Kourabiédes Sugared shortbreads
Krasí Wine
Kréas Meat
Kremídia Onions

Laderá Cooked in oil
Lagós Hare
Lahaniká Vegetables
Lavráki Sea bass
Lemóni Lemon

Maïdanós Flatleaf parsley
Manitária Mushrooms
Marídes Whitebait or any small fish
Marináto Marinated
Maroúli Cos lettuce
Méli Honey
Melitzánes Aubergines
Métrio Coffe with some sugar
Mezé Appetizers (plural *Mezédes*)
Mídia Mussels
Moshári Beef

Moussaká Aubergine, minced meat and white
  sauce pie
Neró Water

Orektikó Appetizer
Oúzo Anise-flavoured spirit

Païdákia Cutlets
Pápia Duck
Pastítsio Pasta and meat pie
Patátes Potatoes
Piláfi Rice pilaf
Piperiés Peppers
Píta Pie
Prása Leeks
Psária Fish
Psomí Bread

Retsína Wine flavoured with resin
Revíthia Chickpeas
Rígani Oregano
Rízi Rice

Saláta Salad
Sáltsa Sauce
Sardéles Sardines
Sikotákia Lambs' liver
Skordaliá Garlic sauce
Skéto Skéto unsweetened coffee, neat

Skórdo Garlic
Soúpa Soup
Soupiá Cuttlefish
Soúvla Spit roast
Spanáki Spinach

Tiganités Fried
Tiganítes Fritters
Thalasiná Seafood
Thymári Thyme
Tyriá Cheeses
Tzatzíki Yoghurt and cucumber dip

Yemistá Stuffed
Yiahní Braised or stewed
Yiaoúrti Yoghurt
Youvarlákia Meatballs in sauce

Xídi Vinegar
Xifías Swordfish

BIBLIOGRAPHY

Athenaeus.
The Deipnosophists
Trans. Burton Gulik, Charles.
(Cambridge, Mass, & London, 1927).

Barron, Rosemary.
Flavours of Greece
(Penguin, London, 1991).

Chatto, J. & Martin, W. L.
A Kitchen in Corfu
(Weidenfeld & Nicolson, London, 1987).

Dalby, Andrew.
Siren Feasts
(Routledge, London, 1996).

Dalby, Andrew, & Grainger, Sally.
The Classical Cookbook
(British Museum Press, London, 1996).

Duncan, M.
Cooking the Greek Way
(Hamlyn, London, 1964).

Durrell, Lawrence.
The Greek Islands
(Faber & Faber, London, 1978).

Lambert-Gócs, M.
The Wines of Greece
(Faber & Faber, London, 1990).

Lawson, John Cuthbert.
Modern Greek Folklore and Ancient Greek Religion
(Cambridge UP, Cambridge, 1910).

Manessis, Nico.
The Greek Wine Guide
(Olive Press, 30 Chemin des Chèvres,
CH-1292 Chambésy, Geneva, 1996).

Psilakis, M. & N.
Cretan Traditional Cuisine (in Greek)
(Heraklion, 1995).

Stubbs, J. M.
The Home Book of Greek Cookery
(Faber & Faber, London, 1967).

Toussant-Samat, Maguelonne.
History of Food
Trans. Anthea Bell.
(Blackwell, Oxford, 1992).

Tselemendes, Nicolas.
Greek Cooking
(DC Divry, New York, 1956).

INDEX